THE CAMBRIDGE COMPANION TO
THE PROBLEM OF EVIL

For many centuries philosophers have been discussing the problem of evil – one of the greatest problems of intellectual history. There are many facets to the problem, and for students and scholars unfamiliar with the vast literature on the subject, grasping the main issues can be a daunting task. This Companion provides a stimulating introduction to the problem of evil. More than an introduction to the subject, it is a state-of-the-art contribution to the field which provides critical analyses of and creative insights on this long-standing problem. Fresh themes in the book include evil and the meaning of life, beauty and evil, evil and cosmic evolution, and anti-theodicy. Evil is discussed from the perspectives of the major monotheistic religions, agnosticism, and atheism. Written by leading scholars in clear and accessible prose, this book is an ideal companion for undergraduate and graduate students, teachers, and scholars across the disciplines.

Chad Meister has published extensively on the subject of evil, including *Evil: A Guide for the Perplexed* (2012), *God and the Problem of Evil: Five Views* (2017), and *The History of Evil* in six volumes (2017). He has done research on the topic at the University of Oxford and as the William Patton Fellow at the John Hick Centre for Global Philosophy of Religion. His book, coedited with William Lane Craig and entitled *God Is Great, God Is Good* (2009), won the Christianity Today Book award. At Bethel College he received the Professor of the Year award for teaching excellence.

Paul K. Moser is Professor of Philosophy at Loyola University Chicago. He is the author of *The God Relationship* (Cambridge University Press, 2017); *The Elusive God* (Cambridge University Press, 2010), winner of national book award from the Jesuit Honor Society; *The Evidence for God* (Cambridge University Press, 2010); *The Severity of God* (Cambridge University Press, 2013); *Knowledge and Evidence* (Cambridge University Press, 1991); and *Philosophy after Objectivity* (1993); coauthor of *Theory of Knowledge* (1997); editor of *Jesus and Philosophy* (Cambridge University Press, 2008) and *The Oxford Handbook of Epistemology* (2005); coeditor of *The Wisdom of the Christian Faith* (Cambridge University Press, 2012). He is the coeditor with Chad Meister of Cambridge Studies in Religion, Philosophy, and Society.

CAMBRIDGE COMPANIONS TO RELIGION

This is a series of companions to major topics and key figures in theology and religious studies. Each volume contains specially commissioned chapters by international scholars, which provide an accessible and stimulating introduction to the subject for new readers and nonspecialists.

(*continued after index*)

THE CAMBRIDGE COMPANION TO

THE PROBLEM OF EVIL

Edited by

Chad Meister
Bethel College, Indiana

Paul K. Moser
Loyola University, Chicago

CAMBRIDGE
UNIVERSITY PRESS

CAMBRIDGE
UNIVERSITY PRESS

University Printing House, Cambridge CB2 8BS, United Kingdom

One Liberty Plaza, 20th Floor, New York, NY 10006, USA

477 Williamstown Road, Port Melbourne, VIC 3207, Australia

314-321, 3rd Floor, Plot 3, Splendor Forum, Jasola District Centre, New Delhi - 110025, India

79 Anson Road, #06-04/06, Singapore 079906

Cambridge University Press is part of the University of Cambridge.

It furthers the University's mission by disseminating knowledge in the pursuit of education, learning and research at the highest international levels of excellence.

www.cambridge.org
Information on this title: www.cambridge.org/9781107636026
DOI : 10.1017/9781107295278

© Cambridge University Press 2017

First published 2017

A catalogue record for this publication is available from the British Library

Library of Congress Cataloging in Publication data
Names: Meister, Chad, 1965– editor. | Moser, Paul K. 1957– editor.
Title: The Cambridge companion to the problem of evil / [edited by] Chad Meister, Bethel College, Indiana Paul K. Moser, Loyola University, Chicago.
Description: New York: Cambridge University Press, 2017. | Series: Cambridge companions to religion | Includes bibliographical references and index.
Identifiers: LCCN 2017004141 | ISBN 9781107055384 (hardback) | ISBN 9781107636026 (paperback)
Subjects: LCSH: Good and evil. | Good and evil – Religious aspects.
Classification: LCC BJ1401 .C27 2017 | DDC 170–dc23
LC record available at https://lccn.loc.gov/2017004141

ISBN 978-1-107-05538-4 Hardback
ISBN 978-1-107-63602-6 Paperback

Contents

Contributors

John Cottingham is Professor Emeritus of Philosophy, University of Reading, and Visiting Professor of Philosophy, Kings College, University of London.

Paul Draper is Professor of Philosophy at Purdue University.

Paul S. Fiddes is Professor of Systematic Theology in the University of Oxford and Director of Research, Regent's Park College, Oxford.

Lenn E. Goodman is Professor of Philosophy and Andrew W. Mellon Professor in the Humanities, Vanderbilt University.

Margo Kitts is Professor of Humanities and Coordinator of East-West Classical Studies and Religious Studies at Hawai'i Pacific University in Honolulu.

Chad Meister is Professor of Philosophy and Theology at Bethel College.

Paul K. Moser is Professor of Philosophy at Loyola University Chicago.

Graham Oppy is Professor of Philosophy at Monash University.

Timothy Perrine is a Ph.D. candidate at Indiana University, Bloomington.

Michael Ruse is Lucyle T. Werkmeister Professor of Philosophy and Director of the Program in the History and Philosophy of Science at Florida State University.

J. L. Schellenberg is Professor of Philosophy at Mount Saint Vincent University in Halifax, Nova Scotia.

Christopher Southgate is Associate Professor in Interdisciplinary Theology at the University of Exeter, UK.

Charles Taliaferro is Professor of Philosophy and Chair of the Department of Philosophy, St. Olaf College.

N. N. Trakakis is Senior Lecturer in Philosophy, Australian Catholic University.

Timothy Winter is Shaikh Zayed Lecturer in Islamic Studies, Faculty of Divinity, University of Cambridge.

Stephen J. Wykstra is Professor of Philosophy at Calvin College.

Acknowledgments

We thank the contributors of this volume for writing their chapters and for their enthusiasm and collegiality. Their first-rate scholarship, creative insights, and care for detail have made our editorial task gratifying.

We also thank the referees for Cambridge University Press for helpful suggestions and the editorial staff at the Press for their support for our project. In particular, we thank Beatrice Rehl, Publisher, for seeing this into production.

Introduction

CHAD MEISTER AND PAUL K. MOSER

EVIL AND GOD

"The problem of evil" arises from an apparent conflict between two claims: the claim that God exists and the claim that the evil in the world is real. Calling it "the problem of evil," however, can be misleading, because various problems for theism arise from the reality of evil. One problem occurs among theists who seek to answer a question about God's purposes. In ancient and medieval times, for example, Jewish, Christian, and Islamic theologians generally assumed that God exists and is fully good, merciful, and all-powerful. A central question they sought to answer about God was: Why has God permitted evil in a world that God created? More recently, a different but related question has arisen: Is it reasonable to believe that God exists when there is so much evil in the world and, if it is reasonable, on what ground?

The general concept of evil covers a wide domain and can include everything that is harmful and destructive in the world. It thus connotes all bad or nefarious actions, states of affairs, and character traits. For instance, a theft, a drought, or an individual who routinely lies can be evil. Even so, the concept of evil has a deeper dimension. The moral deficiency of such actions as the beheadings of innocent civilians by ISIS, the serial killings of John Wayne Gacy, or the murders of the Holocaust does not qualify as simply wrong or immoral. Similarly, the harm of such events as the Bangladesh cyclone in 1991 (when more than 140,000 people lost their lives), the tsunami in Indonesia in 2004 (more than 250,000 victims), or the Tangshan China earthquake in 1976 (more than 700,000 people killed) is not simply bad or even dreadful. Such events encompass a deeper dimension of evil – one that generates a philosophical problem for theists.

The evil challenging theism does not reduce to human suffering. It can include what we may call "the fragility of human life," that is, its vulnerability to its destruction or demise. Even if human life includes a test of human character, some humans are not given the opportunity to undergo the test. For instance, some humans die in infancy, in advance of any test of their character. This seems to be a missed opportunity for them, and it is arguably not good, even if they die without suffering. Human fragility, with or without suffering, seems to be part of the world's evil, and it prompts the question of why a morally perfect God would allow it. Credible answers do not come easily here.

In philosophical discussions, a common classification divides evil into two broad categories: *moral* evil and *natural* evil. Moral evils are brought about by the intentions or negligence of moral agents. Some moral evils are horrible, such as the previous examples from ISIS, Gacy, and the Holocaust. The evils of human trafficking, economic exploitation, and animal and human torture are further examples of horrible moral evils. Other cases of moral evil are less severe, such as speaking ill of another person or neglecting to recycle one's plastic garbage. In addition, certain character defects also can be moral evils, such as selfishness, excess vanity, and dishonesty.

Natural evils are not brought about by moral agents but result from such naturally occurring events as the devastating cyclone, tsunami, and earthquake mentioned earlier. Similarly, other natural events that cause harm to human beings and other living creatures would be cases of natural evils. Disabilities and diseases that have deleterious effects on humans and other animals, such as AIDS, Zika, deafness, and blindness, are also natural evils.

Attention to evil extends beyond the Abrahamic theistic faiths of Judaism, Christianity, and Islam. It occurs in the Vedas, Upanishads, and Puranas – the sacred scriptures and central religious texts of Hinduism. In traditional Buddhism, evil is the perpetuation of illusion by factors that foster constant becoming – a becoming that leads to suffering. This suffering, or *dukkha*, is the focus of the Four Noble Truths. In Daoism, evil is the result of a lack of balance between the two opposing and fundamental principles of Yin and Yang.

All of the major world religions attempt to address problems raised by evil, but evil is not problematic only for the religions of the world: it raises difficulties for atheism too. For a typical theist, evil is an aberration, something repugnant about the world. It is unwanted, unwilled by God, and contrary to the purpose of creation and the way things ought to be. On a typical atheistic account, in contrast, evil is a natural part of the world, simply part of the way the world is. Typical atheists thus make a philosophical concession to the reality of evil that does not occur within various religious traditions, including the Abrahamic faiths that view evil as contrary to the way the world was meant to be.

Traditional theism faces profound problems raised by evil. It portrays God as the ultimate locus of being, meaning, and value; as omnipotent, omniscient, and omnibenevolent; as a person or at least not less than a person (possessing consciousness, will, and intentions); and as worthy of human worship and hence morally perfect. The problem of evil demands some accounting for the evil in a world allegedly created by this maximally exalted God.

Typical discussions of the problem of evil bear directly on divine omnipotence and omnibenevolence (and sometimes omniscience). It seems, at least at first glance, that if a God with such attributes exists, then a world created by God would not include evil. As omnibenevolent, God would not want evil to exist. As omnipotent, God would have the power to make the world exist without evil. As omniscient, God would have the knowledge to accomplish the task. Since there is evil – widespread, horrific evil – there is some reason to believe that such a God does not exist. While there are theoretical problems for the non-Abrahamic faiths and nontheists raised by the reality of evil, they pale in comparison to the problem of evil for traditional theism. This book focuses on the problem of evil for theism.

The problem of evil has two major theoretical versions: the logical problem and the evidential problem. The logical problem concerns whether the basic claims of theism about God are inconsistent with the reality of evil. In the latter half of the twentieth century, some significant philosophers argued for an inconsistency here. A prominent atheist, J. L. Mackie, stated the following in an influential article: "Here it can be shown, not that religious beliefs lack rational support, but that they are positively irrational, that several parts of the essential theological doctrine are inconsistent with one another" ("Evil and Omnipotence," *Mind* 64 (1955), 200). Mackie holds that evil is a problem for theists in that there is a contradiction between the fact that evil exists and the claim that the God of traditional theism exists. In particular, he alleges an inconsistency in affirming the following propositions:

(1) God is omnipotent.
(2) God is omnibenevolent.
(3) Evil exists.

While one or two of these propositions may be true, Mackie argued, taken as a group, the three form a logically inconsistent set. Almost everyone agrees that (3) is true; Mackie thus inferred that an omnipotent or omnibenevolent God does not exist. Various theists have argued that if God (possibly) has a morally acceptable reason for allowing evil to occur, the logical problem of evil fails to show the nonexistence of God. In any case, whether the nonexistence of God can be demonstrated remains a matter of philosophical debate.

The evidential problem of evil suggests that, given the reality of evil, theism is probably not true, even if it is logically consistent. While there are various types of evidential arguments, the kind of reasoning employed is usually inductive. Such arguments also generally rely on actual cases of evil and suffering, sometimes described in graphic detail. A typical claim is that the existence of evil in its vast amounts and horrible forms provides reasonable evidence that the God of traditional theism (probably) does not exist.

A philosophical response to the problem of evil may attempt to show that arguments from evil against theism are unsuccessful. Such a response is often called a "defense" against evil, the most common being a "free will defense" that assigns responsibility for (some) evil to human freedom. A defense aims to support the view that God could have morally sufficient reasons for permitting the evils in question. Another approach aims to vindicate God by offering a plausible *explanation* for evil. An attempt to identify God's morally sufficient reasons or purposes for allowing evil is sometimes called a "theodicy." No single theodicy has convinced all inquirers about the problem of evil, and the book of Job suggests that humans, given their cognitive limitations relative to God's purposes, are not in a good position to have a theodicy, at least so long as God does not supply one. Many inquirers, including many theists, doubt that God has supplied a theodicy. Even so, it is an open question whether one could have evidence of God's reality even in the absence of a theodicy.

CHAPTER SUMMARIES

This book is divided into two parts. Part I, including Chapters 1 through 7, takes up some prominent conceptual issues and controversies regarding the problem of evil. Part II, including Chapters 8 through 13, examines some significant interdisciplinary issues related to the problem of evil, including those from Near Eastern religious studies, philosophy, science, and the history of science and religion.

In Chapter 1, "Evil and the Meaning of Life," John Cottingham notes that in the Judeo-Christian tradition, suffering is redemptive and that this redemptive component is understood in a unique way. This tradition differs from a secularist approach to evil that either simply accepts that the world has evil or attempts to find temporary meaning in the midst of the contingencies of life. The redemptive component in question does not entail that the purpose for evil emerges solely from something achieved in an afterlife. Scriptural and religious teachings promote the idea that the moral quality of human life and experience is central to the meaning and value of that life and that redemption aims to enhance that moral quality. According to Cottingham, the Judeo-Christian view that meaning is to be found within a moral framework – which includes such fundamental values as love, justice, and compassion – fits with common human intuitions.

In Chapter 2, "Beauty and the Problem of Evil," Charles Taliaferro presents an approach to the problem of evil within a version of Anselmian theism – the view that God is that than which none greater can be conceived. The essay is structured as a reply to those (such as Galen Strawson) who maintain that to suppose that the Christian God exists is morally repugnant and ugly. Taliaferro advances four reasons why responses to the problem of evil are incomplete if they do not include the aesthetics of beauty and ugliness. He also argues that the ugliness and beauty of the cosmos are compatible with a beautiful God, and he emphasizes that this God can be experienced, as represented in the works of Julian of Norwich and W. H. Auden. In confronting evil, according to Taliaferro, our sense of ugliness and beauty needs to be underscored.

Various philosophers have claimed that logical arguments from evil have been rebutted by one or more versions of the free will defense. In Chapter 3, "Logical Arguments from Evil and Free Will Defences," Graham Oppy argues that this is not the case. He grants that there is currently no successful logical argument from evil against God's existence, but he argues that the logical arguments from evil are no worse off than any other logical arguments for or against the existence of God. It may well be, according to Oppy, that there are yet-to-be-discovered versions of the logical argument from evil that are successful. He finds no reason to rule out such a claim.

In Chapter 4, "God, Evil, and the Nature of Light," Paul Draper discusses scientific debates about the nature of light as he evaluates the evidential problem of evil. By focusing on the structure of the reasoning in those debates, he notes a similarity in the debates between theism and what he calls "source physicalism." Comparison of certain theories of light with other incompatible ones, he argues, has shown some of them to be improbable – at least with other evidence held equal. Similarly, in his story, a popular version of theism can be shown to be improbable in comparison with an incompatible theory of physicalism entailing that physical reality is the source of the mental. Given various data about good and evil, Draper argues that this version of physicalism is much more probable than theism and that, with other evidence held equal, theism is likely false.

We do well to recognize the cognitive limitations of human beings when thinking about the problem of evil. A position called "skeptical theism" takes this consideration seriously. Skeptical theists are typically skeptical about whether evil can disconfirm theism and not about whether God exists. They are skeptical of our ability to have adequate knowledge of the moral matters crucial to the success of the evidential argument from evil. In Chapter 5, "Skeptical Theism," Timothy Perrine and Stephen Wykstra point out that skeptical theistic responses to evidential arguments from evil are typically grounded on two claims. The first is that if the God of theism exists, we should not be surprised that we are not privy to God's reasons for permitting evil. The second is that many of the evidential arguments for atheism are weaker than one might think. They examine the approaches of various leading skeptical theists and evaluate some of the central issues raised by critics of skeptical theism. They conclude the essay by sketching a next step for skeptical theism given emerging versions of evidential arguments.

The problem of evil suggests reasons for the claim that God does not exist. A related problem, "the problem of divine hiddenness," does the same. Some inquirers have asked whether the latter problem is a version of the problem of evil. In Chapter 6, "Evil, Hiddenness, and Atheism," J. L. Schellenberg argues that it is not. He contends that there are different motives that might be attributed to God (anti-bad, pro-good, and pro-relationship) and that the divine hiddenness argument is more fundamental than the argument from evil. He proposes, however, that it may be beneficial for the two types of arguments to work together.

In Chapter 7, "Anti-Theodicy," Nick Trakakis describes how anti-theodicy presents an oppositional stance toward the project of theodicy. He discusses some of the morally objectionable and historically conditioned aspects of theodicy. He also engages with some recent criticisms of anti-theodicy, in particular one arguing that various approaches to anti-theodicy are committed to Schopenhauerian pessimism, the view that it would have been better if the world had never come into being. In addition, using the pastoral response to the problem of evil developed by John Swinton, Trakakis responds to another criticism of anti-theodicy. He argues that anti-theodicy can avoid the dangers of both Schopenhauerian pessimism and Leibnizian optimism while also providing the means to resist the destruction of faith, meaning, and hope in the face of the world's evil.

Part II of the book addresses interdisciplinary issues related to the problem of evil. The systematic study of the natural world and the scientific knowledge thereby obtained have been remarkably informative for our species. In Chapter 8, "Cosmic Evolution and Evil," Christopher Southgate examines some implications of the sciences for the problem of evil. He focuses on cosmic theodicy, understood as the theological problem of suffering caused by the natural processes of the cosmos, including natural disasters, disease, and evolutionary development. This focus includes consideration of various theodicies and what may be needed for an account that preserves the loving character of God given the pain and suffering found in the natural world. Southgate argues that such an account may include claims about eschatological redemption and the cosuffering of God with God's creatures.

In Chapter 9, "Ancient Near Eastern Perspectives on Evil and Terror," Margo Kitts examines the use of literary and artistic illustrations and religious idioms in the Ancient Near East to justify killings and mass-casualty violence. She notes that many idioms unearthed since cuneiform and hieroglyphic writings were deciphered reflect both an understanding of evil as cognate with death and terror and a captivation with displays of might and the terror of its victims. Using hermeneutics, Kitts aims to show that reading certain ancient texts may allow us to peer into our own intuitions about evil.

The last four chapters of the book are written from the perspective of either a particular religious tradition or, in the case of the final chapter, atheism. In Chapter 10, "Judaism and the Problem of Evil," Lenn Goodman approaches evil from a Jewish perspective focusing on "the suffering of innocents." Drawing from Maimonides, Goodman notes that unlike what is presented in some rabbinical teachings, the Torah's affirmations of the justice of God disallow the tormenting of the innocent for the purpose of enhancing eternal reward. Death and suffering, in this account, are consequences of human finitude and the cycles of the natural world, but life remains meaningful nonetheless. Finite embodiment, in this perspective, also underlies the individuality that allows us to imitate the divine perfection through getting to know God's wisdom, grace, and compassion and to conform to them in our own lives.

In Chapter 11, "Christianity, Atonement and Evil," Paul Fiddes considers the problem of evil from a Christian viewpoint implying that God overcomes evil and sin through the atonement of Jesus Christ. He focuses on the interconnection between atonement and theodicy, arguing that a free will theodicy requires the suffering of God, while the *Christus Victor* view of atonement, which affirms an objective conquering of evil, requires a subjective shift in the ability of humans to deal with pain and suffering. These two theodicies need to intersect, according to Fiddes, in order to yield a satisfactory account of the reality of evil. The result will expand the concept of atonement to include the enablement of response to God by all of creation.

In Chapter 12, "Islam and the Problem of Evil," Timothy Winter notes that while the various traditions within Islam include a range of approaches to the problem of evil, they share an adherence to the Qur'an. Using this sacred text, Islamic thinkers conclude that the suffering of the guilty was just punishment for their sin, but the suffering of the nonguilty can be directed toward the purification of the soul. In addition, many Islamic thinkers hold that the guiltless, including animals and infants, will receive compensation in the afterlife for the sufferings experienced in this life. Going further, a perspective common among Sunni thinkers includes the doctrine of "theistic subjectivism" entailing that the "evil" experienced by guiltless humans is not intrinsically evil, because God's ways are always wise even though human minds may be unable to grasp them as such.

In Chapter 13, "Naturalism, Evil, and God," Michael Ruse takes it as a given that the problem of evil is a challenge to belief that an all-powerful and all-loving God exists. He considers whether methodological naturalism, entailing that scientific explanations must not include divine interventions, exacerbates the problem of evil. He denies that it does so while acknowledging that to affirm methodological naturalism now is to affirm a Darwinian theory of evolution through natural selection. Ruse argues that a Darwinian understanding of humans (a) suggests that they are a combination of selfishness and altruism, (b) supports that humans can choose between right and wrong, and (c) acknowledges the existence of much pain and suffering in the world.

CONCLUSION

The intellectual challenges raised by the reality of evil, suffering, and terror continue to be vexing for theists of all stripes. Although scholarly research has advanced in the areas of philosophy, theology, history, religious studies, and science, final solutions to the problem of evil remain elusive. Even so, many insights have arisen from various areas in relation to inquiry about the problem of evil. Some of these insights emerge in this book's chapters.

Part I

Conceptual Issues and Controversies

1 · Evil and the Meaning of Life

JOHN COTTINGHAM

EVIL AND THE THREAT TO MEANING

In that masterpiece of early twenty-first-century fiction, W. G. Sebald's *Austerlitz*, one of the themes is the erosion of meaning in life. The eponymous protagonist of the book, Jacques Austerlitz, vividly describes his loss of any sense of meaningfulness in his actions:

> Like a tightrope walker who has forgotten how to put one foot in front of the other, all I felt was the swaying of the precarious structure on which I stood, stricken with terror at the realization that the ends of the balancing pole gleaming far out on the edges of my field of vision were no longer my guiding lights, as before, but malignant enticements to me to cast myself into the depths ... I sensed that in truth I had neither memory, nor the power of thought nor even any existence, that all my life had been a constant process of obliteration ...[1]

This is strong stuff, but it turns out to be far more than the sometimes rather self-indulgent existentialist *Angst* that has become a commonplace of modern literature. For as the narrative unfolds, it emerges that the haunting horror and emptiness that Austerlitz experiences on his odyssey round post-war Europe is bound up with the half-forgotten story of his own early life, which he is desperately trying to recover. Raised by Welsh foster parents and ignorant of his true name, he eventually discovers that he was sent away to Britain from Czechoslovakia on a *Kindertransport* in 1939, at the age of five, and that his mother and father died in the Holocaust.

The suffering that countless human beings undergo is indeed horrifying, and that of children perhaps especially so, but what gives Austerlitz's

---

[1] W. G. Sebald, *Austerlitz* [first published in German, 2001], trans. A. Bell (London: Penguin, 2002), 173–4.

narrative its particular horror is a growing awareness that his suffering was the direct result of human evil – an awareness that crystallizes as the protagonist gradually reconstructs the story of the systematic brutality and callousness which his family, and so many like them, endured. Philosophers have traditionally distinguished between 'natural' evil (suffering caused by disease, earthquakes, hurricanes etc.) and 'moral' evil (such as that perpetrated by the Nazis). No doubt both kinds can leave people so shaken as to question whether their lives make any sense, but the latter kind seems especially corrosive of meaningfulness. People may perhaps recover a sense of meaning and purpose after a natural disaster or a serious illness, but the kind of vertigo that Sebald describes, as he confronts the cruelty and malevolence of those who robbed him of his family and his childhood, seems to be specially destructive as far as meaningfulness is concerned. We are, to be sure, helpless both in the face of natural shocks and in the face of deliberate human cruelty, but the latter, especially when it is unchecked and triumphant, as it was in Germany and occupied Europe in the early 1940s, seems to shake our confidence in humanity itself. It makes us wonder whether the highest achievements of human culture and civilization may not be a thin and fragile efflorescence on an ugly flood of savagery and barbarism that flows on blindly, with no ultimate purpose or meaning.

From a philosophical point of view, there are, I think, several possible responses to these sombre features of the human predicament. One might be called the *resignation strategy*. The line of thought here, often combined with a radically naturalist or secularist outlook, is that we should give up the idea that human life ought to have a meaning in the first place. On this way of thinking, science has shown that the emergence of humanity is part of an inexorable process of random mutation and competition for survival on a planet itself shaped over billions of years by a purposeless nexus of contingent causes and conditions. The results of this process will include both the 'natural evils' that can wreak such havoc on our lives and recurring instances of human cruelty, which are just as inevitable a part of our genetic inheritance as a species as the more altruistic behaviour we like to praise as 'moral'. But to expect any overall meaningfulness in the inexorable process is, according to this line of thought, simply a confusion, since there is no reason why human life should be 'meaningful' in any ultimate sense. In reality, there are simply conditions that arise and pass away, and we ought to expend our energies trying to maximize the resulting benefits and minimize the resulting harms during the short time we are here and forget about the vain attempt to discern any meaning or pattern in the whole.

A second possible strategy might be called that of *piecemeal salvage.* Given that humans have a strong desire for meaning in their lives, but meaningfulness is threatened by natural and moral evil, the right response, on this view, is not to resign ourselves to a life without meaning, but rather to salvage what meaning we can in the individual projects we pursue, which can at least bring a sense of localized value and purpose into our lives. It will be admitted by those who follow the strategy now being considered that such meaning is ephemeral and that our chosen plans and projects can never endure long and are often cut short by natural misfortune or destroyed by the malice of others, but what we can do, on this line of thought, is to make the best of them we can, since this is the only kind of meaningfulness that human life can offer. As the voice of the speaker in T. S. Eliot's *The Waste Land* puts it, surveying the ultimate fragility and futility of all human endeavour, yet identifying a few remnants of literature and culture that have given him some fleeting sense of meaning: 'these fragments have I shored against my ruins'.[2]

The two strategies just canvassed are not, of course, entirely distinct but merely bring to the fore different elements in a characteristically modern package of responses to the problem of living a meaningful life in the face of the gloomy facts of our vulnerability to misfortune and to evil. The underlying tone in these responses is conditioned by a loss of faith in the viability of the traditional theistic outlook – the abandonment of any sense of a benign teleology at work in the cosmos, any sense that we were 'put here' for any end or purpose. One of the most eloquent philosophical spokesmen for this bleak but for many people realistic way of thinking was Bernard Williams, whose view of the human condition was an ultimately pessimistic one. As he put it in his much-admired *Shame and Necessity*, the view is one that 'refuses to present human beings [as] ideally in harmony with their world' and which 'has no room for a world that, if it were understood well enough, could instruct us how to be in harmony with it'.[3] It is perhaps worth adding here that although this kind of picture typifies the framework within which much modern philosophizing operates, its origins go well back beyond the birth of modernity, as indeed Williams's own work showed, when (in the book just mentioned) he traced some of its roots back to the recurring themes of ancient Greek drama.

2   T. S. Eliot, *The Waste Land* [1922], final section.
3   Bernard Williams, *Shame and Necessity* (Berkeley: University of California Press, 1993), 164.

The explorations of evil found in the great Greek tragedians cannot be called non-religious, since they often make reference to the gods of the Greek pantheon. But their underlying outlook is not a theistic one, as that term is now normally understood; for the divine denizens of Mount Olympus are not unequivocal sources of goodness, nor are they particularly on the side of a loving or just outcome of our human tribulations but are simply more powerful than humans, often preoccupied with their own selfish rivalries, and typically inclined to view our sufferings from an aloof position of coldness or indifference (*agnōmosunē*), as Sophocles puts it in his play *The Women of Trachis*. If we compare this with the kind of picture found in the theistic worldview of the great Abrahamic religions, we find a striking contrast. In the Hebrew Bible, natural evil is often interpreted as itself having a moral dimension, being a punishment imposed by God on human wrongdoing. And as for moral evil, this is never presented in the Judaeo-Christian and Islamic traditions as something to which God could be indifferent; but on the contrary it is seen as something running deeply counter to the purposes which a compassionate and just God has intended for humankind. Notwithstanding these points, however, the exact status of evil in the theistic world picture and the extent to which it affects the question of the meaning of human life are complex and difficult questions, and to these we will now turn.

THEISTIC INTERPRETATIONS OF EVIL AND THE MEANING OF LIFE

One of the difficulties in assessing the significance of evil in a theistic worldview is the prevalence of certain crude sketches which presume to capture the theistic outlook – caricatures that often bear little relation to what the thoughtful theist actually holds or what a reflective reading of the relevant scriptural writings actually discloses. Thus Martha Nussbaum, a philosopher noted for her nuanced and sensitive readings of Classical pagan texts on evil and suffering, is sometimes content to offer a most cursory account of the presumed Judaeo-Christian stance. Discussing the case mentioned earlier, the tragic events in *The Women of Trachis* and the apparently callous indifference of the gods, she comments that the message of Sophocles' play is one of burning anger and outrage at these events, whereas 'a Judaeo-Christian text probably would have said ... that everything that has happened is just and good'.[4]

---

[4] Martha Nussbaum, 'Tragedy and Justice: Bernard Williams remembered', *Boston Review*, October/November 2003.

Nussbaum no doubt has in mind a Leibnizian style theodicy, where 'all's for the best in the best of all possible worlds;' and in fairness there is no doubt that several Christian theists have indeed taken such a glib line, not least Leibniz himself, for example in his notorious gloss on the rape of Lucretia: 'the crime of Sextus Tarquinius serves for great things: it renders Rome free; thence will arise a great empire, which will show noble examples to mankind'.[5] But the Judaeo-Christian scriptures themselves are for the most part strikingly free of this kind of consequentialist or instrumentalist construal of the significance of evil.

What one tends to find instead in the long catalogue of human anguish recorded in the Hebrew Bible and the Christian New Testament is that evil is presented in all its stark reality, with not one iota of the suffering omitted or rationalised. One can scarcely imagine a more terrible fate than that of King Zedekiah, who is forced to watch as his two sons are slaughtered in front of him and is then blinded, bound in bronze chains and led away to captivity in Babylon (2 Kings 25:7). And the central Christian narrative, in which Jesus of Nazareth is subjected to the utmost humiliation, brutally flogged by the Roman occupying forces and then put to death in one of the most prolonged and agonizing forms of execution ever devised by human cruelty – this is described without any attempt to disguise or explain away the savagery. But the main question for present purposes is about the extent to which the theistic framework within which these events are narrated allows the meaningfulness of human life to be preserved despite its vulnerability to the evil depicted in such narratives.

One answer that will inevitably come to mind here is that the theistic worldview is able to maintain that when human life is marred or truncated by evil it can still be meaningful because of the future existence that awaits us after death. The afterlife is actually not a pervasive feature of Judaism, certainly not in all its forms, but it has an important place in Islam, and in Christianity it has great prominence because of the doctrine of the Resurrection of Christ, who, moreover, is regarded as the 'first fruits' (1 Corinthians 15:20), prefiguring the possibility of eternal life for redeemed mankind in general. But it would probably be rash to conclude (as many critics of religion appear apt to) that on the theistic picture it is the afterlife that bears all or even most of the weight when it comes to allowing a life to be meaningful in spite of the ravages of evil. For it seems highly implausible to suppose that the prolongation of life after death could, *in itself*, bestow meaning on a life that was otherwise

⁵ Gottfried Wilhelm Leibniz, *Theodicy* [*Essais de théodicée*, 1714], Part II, §416.

a meaningless horror. To put the point somewhat crudely, if a child is subjected to protracted torture (or allowed to be so subjected by someone who could stop it) and then is *subsequently* cossetted and given toys and sweets, that does not seem to do anything to make the horror it has endured meaningful. As Mark Johnston has put it, discussing the problem of extreme and arbitrary suffering, 'nothing that subsequently happens can diminish the tragedy or the horror ... the attempt to put an otherworldly frame around such things, so they seem not to be the tragedies or the horrors that they manifestly are, borders on ... the obscene'.[6]

It is, however, far from clear, despite the prevalence of caricatures to the contrary, that all or most theists do in fact maintain that the role of the afterlife is to 'make everything okay' or that the 'otherworldly frame' of the afterlife is supposed to restore the meaningfulness of our human existence simply by positing its continuation in a blessed post-mortem state. Let us take a specific instance to make this point clearer. Suppose that someone finds meaning in life in virtue of some particular project or endeavour to which he devotes his energies. Let us take a close personal relationship as an example (surely a paradigm case of something generally regarded as worthwhile and meaningful) and imagine the case of someone for whom a major part of his 'reason for living' is the love and companionship afforded by his marriage. And now imagine that this marriage is cut short as a result of some horrendous evil – perhaps his partner is gunned down at random in a shopping mall by a psychopathic killer bent on destroying those who belong to a particular community or race or religion. Our bereaved victim loses all sense of purpose and meaning in life. The question now arises for standard forms of theism that invoke the afterlife: is meaning supposed to be restored, for this individual, by a future existence in which he is eternally reunited with his slain partner?

There seem to be reasons for doubting that things can be as simple as this. For the Christian, for instance, it will be highly relevant to recall that Christ is on record in the Gospels as saying that 'in the Resurrection people will neither marry nor be given in marriage' (Matthew 22:20; Mark 12:25). Whatever the promise of eternal life can mean, then, it appears it does *not* mean the continuation, *ad infinitum*, of the earthly projects, however worthy, which give people a sense of meaning during the course of their mortal life. On the contrary, the afterlife, as conceived of in mainstream theism, does not seem to be a 'continuation' at all, in

---

[6] Mark Johnston, *Saving God: Religion after Idolatry* (Princeton, NJ: Princeton University Press, 2009), 15.

this sense, but rather a radical change (1 Corinthians 15:35–52), which will allow a progressively closer union with God, or the good.

Such union is what is meant by 'heaven', which is traditionally described as a state rather than a place. So (if we rule out construing the afterlife as the mere post-mortem continuation of earthly pursuits) our question now shifts to whether, for those believers who hope to 'go to heaven', it is this possibility of eventual union with God that is the key to the meaningfulness of human life. In one sense, this seems correct, since union with God represents, on the theistic view, the final goal for which we were created, but even here one should beware of crude caricatures. Traditional Christian doctrine does not take heaven to be, as it were, an extraneous destination that externally and retrospectively confers meaning on the journey of human life; it has always been seen as a kind of culmination or seal set on a life well and meaningfully lived. In other words, the meaningfulness of a life is by no means wholly derivative from this supposed final culmination, on the theistic view, but is importantly determined by what is done here on earth (cf. 1 Timothy 4:8). As it is expressed in that once widely circulated summary of the Catholic faith, the 'Penny Catechism', humans are created 'to love and serve God in this world and to be happy with him in the next'. And the doctrine of the Last Judgement found in the Christian gospels (e.g. Matthew 7) and elsewhere implies that the two parts of this conjunction are intimately interconnected: happiness in the next world depends on what is done now (though theologians differ on the precise respective roles here of divine grace and of our own voluntary actions). The upshot of all this is that on the theistic view it is the moral quality of a lived human life that is vital to its value and meaning, and the question about evil then becomes whether evil has the power to erode that quality.

The authentic theistic answer to this complex question would appear to be that evil can destroy a meaningful human life only by its corrupting effects on the *perpetrator* of evil but not in virtue of what it does to the victims of evil. This may appear a paradoxical result, but it is by no means confined to adherents of traditional theism, since it accords with the Socratic intuition, widely shared by those of many faiths and of none, that it is better to suffer evil than to do it.[7] So it will follow, for example, that Abel had a more meaningful life than Cain, because the former, though his life was cruelly cut short by the murderous attack of his brother, lived a life that was good and worthwhile, whereas Cain, by indulging his envy and murderous anger, ended up as a 'wanderer on the

---

[7] Plato, *Gorgias* [c. 380 BC], 469–479.

face of the earth', living the futile existence of one who had wasted his life by giving way to evil (Genesis 4:14). And similarly, Judas's betrayal of Christ ended up, when he finally understood its import, robbing his life of all meaning and value and leaving him no option but suicide, whereas the victim of that betrayal, despite his agonies, overcame that evil and died forgiving his enemies (Matthew 27:5; Luke 23:34).

At this point, however, we are inevitably brought back to the issue raised by W. G. Sebald's *Austerlitz*, with which this chapter opened. For though some heroic figures may be able to overcome evil with good, it appears from the Austerlitz case and many similar ones that being the victim of serious evil can bring about an irreparable disorientation and loss of meaning in life. To address this issue, we need to explore a concept that has hitherto not surfaced in our discussion: the concept of redemption and the idea that meaning may somehow be recoverable through the redemptive power of suffering.

EVIL AND SUFFERING

In one of his letters, St Paul provides a graphic list of the sufferings he has undergone: 'in afflictions, in necessities, in distress, in floggings, in imprisonments, in riots, in hard labour, in sleepless nights, in going without food … as dying and yet we live, as beaten and yet not killed, as sorrowful yet always rejoicing, as having nothing, and yet possessing all things…' (2 Corinthians 6:4–10). This is far from being a self-pitying or resigned attitude to the evils he has endured but is rather a kind of glorying in the suffering; as Paul says in another letter, in all such tribulations we are 'more than conquerors through him who loved us' (Romans 9:37). Some hostile critics of theism may perhaps be inclined to construe this in a crudely mechanical way, as if the believer supposes he can count on supernatural invention to make everything right. But Paul's point seems to be *not* that he has a magical shortcut to rescue him from his sufferings but rather than *through and in the midst* of his sufferings he is aware of the redemptive power of love.

Paul's story, as it is unfolded in the Acts of the Apostles and in the letters, seems a paradigm of a meaningful life, certainly in the subjective sense that the subject takes himself to be engaged on a mission of the utmost importance and value, giving a sense of purpose to everything he does, and this is part of what enables him to retain his sense of meaning in life. However, there is a difference between subjective and objective meaningfulness: people can be mistaken in supposing that their activities, or even their life's work, are meaningful. If we take, for example, the case of a devoted Nazi who gives his all to serving the cause of fascism and Aryan superiority, we may be inclined to say that for all his subjective sense of meaningfulness, he is in fact devoting himself to a cruel and pointless enterprise based on false and confused ideas about race and that his life is, unbeknownst to him, a meaningless waste of all his efforts. Indeed, one could imagine a deathbed scene in which his wounds are dressed by one of those he had persecuted and the humanity of the hitherto despised group is brought home to him so that he comes to see that all his past endeavours, previously regarded as so meaningful, were in fact revolting and tragic mistakes. Paul himself, of course, had undergone just such a shift of perception early on in his career, in his conversion experience, but was given the chance to make it good in the extraordinary life that remained to him. But how is it to be decided whether the resulting life, beset by all the evil and suffering that Paul so graphically describes, was indeed objectively meaningful?

The question of whether the subsequent life of the (converted) Paul was objectively meaningful will depend in part on whether the Christian vision to which he subscribed is true, and here the secularist may be inclined to say Paul's belief in the (objective) meaningfulness of what he was doing was false, because his vision was founded on ideas for which there is inadequate evidence (for example, the idea that Christ rose from the dead or that the God Paul took himself to be serving really exists). But it would be a mistake to suppose that the objective meaningfulness of a way of life requires all the elements of the worldview that supports it to be definitively validated – that would surely be to place the bar of objective meaningfulness of a life impossibly high. It seems enough for a life to count as objectively meaningful if it is lived in a way that genuinely succeeds in furthering goals and bearing fruits that our careful reflections and intuitions judge to be important and significant. Paul in fact mentions many 'fruits of the spirit' that he takes to be signs or seals set on a meaningful and valuable life of the kind he strove for: 'the fruits of the spirit are love, joy, peace, forbearance, kindness, goodness, faithfulness, gentleness and self-control' (Galatians 5:22–3). The upshot is that there seems a strong case for claiming that the evils that Paul endured do not in the end erode or undermine the objective meaningfulness of his life or the lives of those like him in so far as such lives succeed in instantiating these shining ideals. Just as the harvest gives meaning to the farmer's toil, so the 'fruits of the spirit' give meaning to the trials and persecutions that are endured in the face of evil.

To be sure, Paul and many of the saints and martyrs are recognized as people of truly heroic stature, and one may reasonably be concerned that the fact that such heroes are able to preserve meaningful lives despite terrible suffering does not help the vast numbers of more ordinary people, such as the Austerlitz character, for whom the role of evil seems altogether more destructive and overwhelming of meaning. As with all questions about suffering and theodicy, it seems crass, if not worse, to try to deny that there may be those for whom the ravages of evil disrupt their lives beyond healing, and the best recent work on the subject is notable for not attempting to gloss over this.[8] But in spite of that, it may be argued that there is a valid lesson to be gleaned from the analysis we have offered in the Pauline case and in the examples (of Cain and Abel, Jesus and Judas) discussed in the previous section and that it is a lesson that holds good for the heroic and the ordinary alike. The lesson, expressed in summary form, is that what makes a life meaningful is above all the striving to hold fast to the good, and what ineluctably erodes meaningfulness is not the evil to which people are subjected but their turning away from the good. So even in the Austerlitz case, heartbreaking though it is, there is perhaps a kind of redemptive courage in the agonizing journey the narrator undertakes as he strives to recover his identity amid the wreckage of post-war Europe. The whole novel is, in a way, a testimony to the truth that it is the perpetrators of evil, not its victims, who are excluded from the true humanity which alone must be the framework for any genuinely meaningful life to take shape. No one has perhaps put the underlying point better than George Eliot, in her novel *Adam Bede*:

> Let us ... be thankful that our sorrow lives in us as an indestructible force, only changing its form, as forces do, and passing from pain into sympathy – the one poor word which includes all our best insight and our best love ... For it is at such periods that the sense of our lives having visible and invisible relations beyond any of which either our present or prospective self is the centre, grows like a muscle that we are obliged to lean on and exert.[9]

The redemptive power of suffering is here seen precisely in its power to connect us to the rest of humanity and to the love which is the key to what is best in our nature. And meaning flows from that, taking us outwards beyond self-preoccupation towards those 'visible and invisible

---

8   See Eleonore Stump, *Wandering in Darkness* (Oxford: Oxford University Press, 2010), 480.

9   George Eliot, *Adam Bede* [1859], Ch. 50. For further discussion of this passage see J. Cottingham, *On the Meaning of Life* (London: Routledge, 2003), Ch. 3.

relations' that give shape and purpose to our lives. Eliot's reflections are phrased in secular terms, but they are unmistakably shaped by the Judaeo-Christian culture she inherited, with its deeply moralistic core and its central emphasis on love and compassion as the keys to a meaningful human life.

The lesson about the intimate link between morality and meaning might perhaps even be pushed further and applied to what is widely regarded as the ultimate evil, the evil of death itself. For when St Paul says 'the sting of death is sin' (1 Corinthians 15:56), this could be understood in part as saying that the erosion of meaning comes not from the ending of life in itself but from the misuse of the gifts of life in wrongdoing. This is part and parcel of the uncompromising message of the Judaeo-Christian tradition, which gives absolute primacy to the moral over all other possible dimensions of meaning. Any philosophical inquiry into how evil affects the meaning of life will therefore have to tackle the question of whether this notion of the absolute primacy of the moral is defensible, and this will be the starting point of the next section.

ALTERNATIVE SOURCES OF MEANING

The 'moralistic' tone of our conclusions so far may seem to strike the wrong note for those philosophers who take a pluralist view of the sources of meaning in human life and regard morality as but one among many incommensurable values, any one of which can be the basis for a meaningful human existence. The ideas of Friedrich Nietzsche have been highly influential here, since he is famous for extolling the *Übermensch*, who rises above the constraints of 'herd' morality, with its 'almost feminine inability to remain spectators, to *let* someone suffer', and instead finds meaning through creativity and self-expression, which, as he put it in *Beyond Good and Evil*, may require 'the conscience to be steeled and the heart turned to bronze'.[10] Following on from this, in our own time, Bernard Williams has mounted a comprehensive critique of what he called the 'morality system' – that 'peculiar institution', with its associated idea of a special class of inescapable obligations. Williams felt that this institution exerted a kind of tyranny over our thinking about ethics and that we would be better off without it.[11] One of his examples was

---

[10]   Friedrich Nietzsche, *Beyond Good and Evil* [*Jenseits von Gut und Böse*, 1886], §§202–3.

[11]   Bernard Williams, *Ethics and the Limits of Philosophy* (London: Collins/Fontana, 1985), Ch. 10.

the 'Gauguin case' (loosely based on the painter Paul Gauguin's flight to Polynesia), in which it is suggested that achieving a meaningful life as a successful creative artist vindicated the painter's abandonment of his wife and family.[12] There is, of course, a conflict of values here, but Williams saw no reason to cede universal precedence to the 'morality system' and pointed out that there are many varieties of human excellence, which it is simply a mistake to try to fit into a hierarchical order or a 'harmonious whole'.[13]

For the purposes of our present inquiry what is significant here is the severance of the link between morality and meaning and, as a result, the rejection of the idea of moral evil as necessarily eroding meaning in life. Indeed, the very title of Nietzsche's treatise, *Beyond Good and Evil*, implicitly suggests that a life of the kind he favoured, the life of power and creativity, may require the agent to abandon normal moral rules in the search for self-expression and meaning. The avoidance of evil, on this picture, ceases to be an absolute requirement that constrains our choices and sets limits on the possible meaning and value our lives can achieve. Instead, the idea is that it is up to us to set our own standards of meaning and value, subject only to the need to fulfil ourselves. In the words of Alexander Nehamas (another supporter of the Nietzschean position), the goal for the individual agent is to 'dislodge what was in place as the good and the true in order to find a place for himself, for his *own* truth and goodness'.[14]

These positions, whether one finds them attractive or repulsive, clearly contain an element of plausibility. It is patently true that there are various forms of human endeavour, including for example musical, artistic, athletic, scientific and many others, which require determination and effort in order to achieve excellence and which, for those who pursue them, contribute very significantly to their sense that their lives are meaningful and worthwhile. But to concede this is certainly not to concede that any of these activities require the practitioners to go 'beyond good and evil' or justify them in so doing. If we return to the Gauguin case, there seems to be no evidence that artistic excellence somehow requires the sacrifice of moral values (as if Gauguin could not have been a great painter had he done his duty to his family). If anything, the evidence seems to point the other way: for in so far as

---

[12]   See Bernard Williams, *Moral Luck* (Cambridge: Cambridge University Press, 1981), Ch. 2.

[13]   Williams, *Ethics and the Limits*, Ch. 8, 153.

[14]   Alexander Nehamas, *The Art of Living: Socratic Reflections from Plato to Foucault* (Berkeley: University of California Press, 1998), 183.

great art involves the full engagement of our human sensibilities and responsiveness to others, there is every reason to suppose that the cultivation of artistic and of moral sensibility are intricately interlinked. This is not to deny that many great artists have led very selfish lives, but it does call into question the self-exculpatory fantasy that addressing such failings might have threatened their artistic achievement.[15]

In the light of this we can see that the idea of the absolute primacy of the moral, which in the previous section we argued has its roots in the religious perspective found in Judaism and Christianity, does not necessarily crowd out all other values. It is no doubt true that in aiming to live a meaningful and worthwhile life we may have to make hard choices; indeed, even in the overwhelmingly moralistic framework of the gospels, it is allowed that there may, for example, be a choice between doing something 'fine' or 'noble' (*kalon*) and maximizing welfare (by selling an asset and giving the proceeds to the poor) and that the maximizing answer may not always be the correct one (Matthew 26:8). But none of this implies that human life can remain meaningful for the agent if there is a deliberate turning away from the good, a deliberate violation of what is right. To hold, *pace* the Nietzschean position, that evil is fundamentally corrosive of meaning in the life of the perpetrator, is something that is not just a matter of religious dogma but is supported by a wide spectrum of human experience. It is this that enables us to recognize something profoundly true in the way that Shakespeare portrays Macbeth, for example, or Iago: by allowing ambition and envy respectively to turn them towards murder and treachery, these two protagonists end up at the close of the drama as completely cut off from any source of meaning in their lives. For Macbeth, life becomes 'a tale told by an idiot, signifying nothing'; for Iago, there is nothing but grim empty silence 'from henceforth I never will speak word'.[16] Nietzsche himself of course ended up going mad; and although it would no doubt be grossly unfair to treat this as an argument against the tenability of his position on evil, there does seem to be something fundamentally incoherent or at least wilfully myopic in his extolling of the *Übermensch* as the model for a truly great and meaningful human life. As Philippa Foot put it (in very simple and low-key but highly effective terms), in looking down on 'inferiors', as Nietzsche did, he lacked that deep sense that 'one is always, fundamentally, in the same boat as everyone else, and that therefore it is quite unsuitable for anyone to see himself as "grand"'.[17]

15 See further Cottingham, *On the Meaning of Life*, Ch. 1.
16 William Shakespeare, *Macbeth* [1606], Act V, scene 5; *Othello* [1603], Act V, scene 2.
17 Philippa Foot, "Nietzsche's Immoralism." In *Nietzsche, Genealogy, Morality.* Ed. R. Schacht (Berkeley: University of California Press, 1994), 3–14, at p. 9.

CODA: EVIL AND REDEMPTION

The main focus of our discussion has been on the power of moral evil to corrode the meaning of life for its perpetrators and the extent to which its victims may at least sometimes be able to preserve meaning in their lives despite the ravages of evil. In this latter context we have spoken of the redemptive power of suffering. Redemption is a topic that, in many of its dimensions, takes us beyond human philosophizing into matters of theology and faith. But it is worth noting as we bring our discussion to a close that the concept of redemption is not one that applies only or even chiefly to the victims of evil but which is traditionally taken to be something that is specially applicable to sinners, to those who commit evil. Although the so-called problem of evil is invariably taken by philosophers to be concerned with undeserved suffering, there is also another kind of 'problem of evil' that impinges on us all as agents rather than patients: the problem that we all to a greater or lesser extent blight our lives by harming others or failing them in compassion and love. This is the 'wretchedness' of humankind of which Pascal spoke and which he saw as redeemable only by the grace of God.[18]

It would take us far beyond the confines of this chapter to explore the idea of divine redemption, but this much can perhaps be said that is relevant to our special focus on evil and the meaning of life. If we share that characteristically human impulse to make sense of our lives as a whole, then we need to come to terms not just with the fact that our projects may be arbitrarily damaged by natural accident or the malice of others but with the in some ways much more worrying fact that we ourselves may damage our lives by our own selfishness and wrongdoing. The path of redemption here may be a very hard one, but some have suggested that suffering can play a very significant part, by shaking us out of our former complacency, bringing us in touch with our own finitude and dependency, and thereby making us vividly aware of how we have failed others who were dependent on us. This connects with the 'vale of soul-making' idea that is familiar from the theodicy literature: the idea that suffering and stress may have the function of enabling moral growth.[19]

Whether such strategies are successful as theodicies (that is, whether they 'exonerate' God for permitting the kind and extent of suffering in the world) is very much open to question, but the issue for present

---

[18]   Blaise Pascal, *Pensées* [1670], ed. L. Lafuma (Paris: Seuil, 1962), no. 6.

[19]   See J. Hick, 'Soul Making Theodicy' [1981], repr. in *Philosophy of Religion: Selected Readings*. Ed. M. Peterson et al., (Oxford: Oxford University Press, 1996, 2nd edn

purposes is not that but whether suffering can play a role in shaping the meaning and significance of a human life. The answer to this seems clearly to be an affirmative one: as we saw in the third section, it is possible to think of conversion cases where it takes a traumatic event to shake someone out of an ingrained pattern of wrongdoing and make them start to see for the first time the full significance of the harm they have done to others. In such cases, they may come to look back on their trauma, whether caused by natural mishap such as illness or even by the morally evil actions of someone else, as the turning point that allowed their life to take a truly meaningful direction for the first time.

This in turn suggests a final point: that the evil that we perpetrate and that which we suffer at the hands of others do not fall into such discrete compartments as we sometimes like to think. The famous dictum from one of the meditations of John Donne, 'no man is an island',[20] reminds us that all human lives are interconnected and that however we may like to see ourselves as victims (sometimes with good reason), there will always be others who are to a greater or lesser extent victims of what we do or allow. Understanding this at a deep level may perhaps move us a small way towards seeing the overall meaning of our existence; for if the implicit argument of this chapter has been on the right lines, such meaning can only validly be sought within a moral framework which has at its centre the overriding imperatives of justice, compassion and love. In Charles Dickens's novel *Barnaby Rudge* there is a passage which, though no doubt tinged with a Victorian sentimentality that is not to modern taste, nevertheless captures well this strange interconnectedness of doing and suffering evil, tribulation and comfort, suffering and redemption:

> In the exhaustless catalogue of Heaven's mercies to mankind, the power we have of finding some germs of comfort in the hardest trials must ever occupy the foremost place; not only because it supports and upholds us when we most require to be sustained, but because in this source of consolation there is something, we have reason to believe, of the divine spirit; something of that goodness which detects amidst our own evil doings, a redeeming quality; something which, even in our fallen nature, we possess in common with the angels; which had its being in the old time when they trod the earth, and lingers on it yet, in pity.[21]

2001), part v, and Richard Swinburne, 'The Problem of Evil', in *Reason and Religion.* Ed. S. Brown (Cornell: Cornell University Press, 1977).

[20]   John Donne, *Devotions upon Emergent Occasions* [1624], Meditation XVII.

[21]   Charles Dickens, *Barnaby Rudge* [1841], Ch. 47.

Despite the references to heaven and to angels, which some readers may find off-putting, the underlying insights here do not have to be expressed in religious terms. The search for meaning in life is arguably an ineradicable part of what it is to be human, and that search cannot be satisfied merely by security, comfort and convenience. We can try to satisfy it by self-aggrandisement or by the single-minded pursuit of our personal goals, but that again can never be quite enough. Given the kind of creatures we are, a life that is meaningful, subjectively and objectively, in the end requires some attempt to understand our human predicament, and that in turn requires us, whether we like it or not, to come to terms with our own 'evil doings', as Dickens puts it, and to realise how these impact the lives of others. The struggle is not just to endure the evil that may impinge on us through the actions of others but also to rise above the evil in our own flawed nature, and to understand that both kinds belong to our common humanity. Whether this struggle is one that can be undertaken from our own resources alone may be a subject for dispute between believers and non-believers, but what seems hard to dispute is that a life that turns its back on that struggle will be hard put to it to be a truly meaningful life.

FURTHER READING

Adams, Marilyn McCord. *Horrendous Evils and the Goodness of God*. Ithaca, NY: Cornell University Press, 1999.

Cottingham, John. *Philosophy of Religion: Towards a More Humane Approach*. Cambridge: Cambridge University Press, 2014, Chapters 5 and 6.

Moser, Paul K. *The Severity of God*. Cambridge: Cambridge University Press, 2013.

Seachris, Joshua W. (ed.). *Exploring the Meaning of Life*. Oxford: Wiley-Blackwell, 2013.

Stump, Eleonore. *Wandering in Darkness*. Oxford: Oxford University Press, 2010.

2 Beauty and the Problem of Evil

CHARLES TALIAFERRO

There are at least four reasons for thinking that philosophically addressing the problem of evil for theism is incomplete without taking seriously
the role of beauty and its correlate, ugliness.

First, the problem of evil for theism inextricably involves concern
for whether it is beautiful that there is a God, especially as this concerns
the God of Anselmian theism. In that tradition, the concept God is the
concept of an unsurpassably excellent, perfect being who merits worship
and love. Worship and love have affective dimensions in accord with the
awesome delight that is a part of some experiences of what we find beautiful. In fact, in the Anselmian theistic tradition, beauty itself is often
recognized as a divine attribute. Divine beauty is a matter of God's merit-
ing adoration, pleasure, and delight; it is often traditionally linked with
God's holiness, majesty, glory, and splendor. As such, the problem of evil
for theism may be seen as a problem of beauty and ugliness: If God is the
highest in beauty, love, power, and knowledge, deserving awesome reverence, why is there so much ugliness? From petty vices like snide expressions of narcissism to grotesque, abominable cases of mass killings, why
is there so much ugliness in the cosmos? If God is essentially good, why
isn't the cosmos an overwhelmingly beautiful site of unimpeded flourishing? Putting the problem of evil in terms of the aesthetics of beauty and
ugliness brings to the fore an affective dimension that would otherwise
be missing if the problem of evil is advanced in terms of only abstract,
analytic principles and reasons.

Second, in addition to beauty and ugliness having a role in the
general concern with the problem of evil, there is reason to think that
in debating the problem of evil, there is considerable attention to *the
beauty or ugliness of believing or denying the existence of God*, even
if such aesthetic terms are not used explicitly. While those defending
the idea that God is supremely good explicitly affirm or imply that it
is beautiful to believe that such a divine reality exists, those who reject

the belief that there is an all-good, all-powerful God sometimes imply or reveal that they are disgusted by, and find ugly even, the supposition that such a God might exist. Galen Strawson is representative of this second position:

> It is an insult to God to believe in God. For on the one hand it is to suppose that he has perpetrated acts of incalculable cruelty. On the other hand, it is to suppose that he has perversely given his human creatures an instrument – their intellect – which must inevitably lead them, if they are dispassionate and honest, to deny his existence. It is tempting to conclude that if he exists, it is the atheists and agnostics that he loves best, among those with any pretensions to education. For they are the ones who have taken him most seriously.[1]

Strawson proposes that it is even immoral to believe Christian theistic claims about God's goodness and power. In the following passage, he accuses those who claim to rely on an experiential awareness of God's goodness through a sense of the divine (*sensus divinitatis*) of being both deluded and immoral.

> We can, for example, know with certainty that the Christian God does not exist as standardly defined: a being who is omniscient, omnipotent, and wholly benevolent. The proof lies in the world, which is full of extraordinary suffering. If someone claims to have a *sensus divinitatis* that picks up a Christian God, they are deluded. It may be added that genuine belief in such a God, however rare, is profoundly immoral: it shows contempt for the reality of human suffering, or indeed any intense suffering.[2]

I propose that given such an outlook, it is important to address the problem of evil not only in intellectual terms but also in terms of the affective motivation behind the different positions. It seems apparent that Strawson implies that Christian theistic belief is far from beautiful but something ugly.

Third, outside of philosophy of religion, many of us recognize that the pursuit of something beautiful – be it a work of art or a romantic relationship – involves a great good that can justify some suffering. To what extent might beauty have a fitting role in our understanding of why a God of perfection and beauty created and sustains a cosmos in which there is beauty as well as profound suffering and ugliness?

[1]   Galen Strawson, "What Can Be Proved About God?" Letter to the Editor, *New York Review of Books*, December 6, 2012.
[2]   Ibid.

Fourth, one reason to engage in philosophical reflection on the nature of evil is to form a deeper understanding of why persons are drawn to do evil. Sadly, one of the motivations to do what turns out to be evil is a striving for what is (wrongly) believed to be beautiful. One virtue of philosophical reflection on evil in relation to beauty is to uncover when it is that misleading concepts of beauty lead us to commit evil acts or to tolerate those we should prevent. The Russian novelist Fyodor Dostoevsky wrote about how beauty can play a role in our struggle with the sacred and the profane: "Beauty is mysterious as well as terrible. God and the devil are fighting there, and the battlefield is the heart of man."[3]

There are four sections that follow. In the first short section, I offer some general observations about beauty and ugliness that are employed in this chapter. The second short section sketches what, according to theism, is the beauty of God. A third section examines and seeks to reply to Strawson's bold, aggressive claim about Christian theism. In that section, I consider the reasons for thinking that believing in Christian theism is ugly or beautiful. In a final section, I consider how a theistic approach to the problem of evil in light of beauty and ugliness can provide some insight in terms of our seeking to confront and prevent evils. While Strawson ironically refers to what may be called *a God's-eye point of view* – noting that from God's perspective (if there were a God), the atheists and agnostics are more fitting than "the believers" – I shall make nonironic usage of appealing to a God's-eye point of view in thinking about beauty and goodness, ugliness and evil.

BRIEF NOTES ON BEAUTY AND UGLINESS

For the sake of argument, I shall assume a realist, what I believe to be a commonsense view of both beauty and ugliness, good and evil. In filling out this realist picture, I use a very broad brush and rely on the receptivity of readers to such a list without requiring refined, nuanced details. All of what follows should be read as having *ceteris paribus* conditions (which assumes that conditions are standard, e.g., in noting that torture is evil and ugly, I am referring to clear cases of when there is no extraordinary reason lurking in the background that might justify torture, such as that an instance of torture is the only alternative to avoiding an even more evil, more ugly act).

I shall assume, without argument, that murder, rape, torture, economic oppression, slavery are wrong and ugly. Birth defects, prolonged

3 Fyodor Dostoevsky, *The Brothers Karamazov* (Penguin Classics: London, 1982), 312.

suffering that seems to serve no purpose, warfare, deaths – especially the deaths of the innocent – due to drought, floods, diseases, and other natural or human-made disasters are also evil and ugly. I shall further assume to be evil and ugly the vices of vanity, unmotivated and irrational irascibility, willful infidelity and betrayal, the manipulation and subtle control of innocent persons for the sake of personal gain, malicious contempt for others, especially for the vulnerable, stealing, especially from the innocent, kidnapping, hypocrisy and moral weakness, sexism, racism, speciesism, ageism, human rights violations, causing there to be massive refugees. Suffering involving or caused by non–self-induced mental disorders are also ugly and evil. This is obviously a very woefully incomplete list. Among events and things that are beautiful, I assume that there are beautiful human and nonhuman animals, plants, and minerals. In human life, I assume that the powers to act, to sense and feel, to have emotions, to have ideals and exercise memory and reason, the ability to form good relationships with other humans and animals and the overall environment is (or can be) good and beautiful. I assume that friendship, love between persons, respectful sexual intimacy and romance, the well-being of families and just communities are good and beautiful, that acting with courage, compassion, and respect and the pursuit of justice and human flourishing are good and beautiful. I shall further assume that the capacities to work and share the benefits of one's work with others are good and beautiful. I believe that while it is evil and ugly when we misuse our moral and aesthetic judgments and freedom, our powers to have moral and aesthetic judgments and to act freely are also (at least when used rightly) good and beautiful. I comment later on the extent to which dying and death are ever good or beautiful or always ugly. Contra Strawson, I shall also indicate why and how it is that there can be good and beautiful religious experiences.

THE BEAUTY OF GOD

The terms translated as "beauty" and "beautiful" appear in the Bible 125 times. While God is not ascribed with beauty in the creeds of the Church, Psalm 27 explicitly refers to "the beauty of the Lord" (verse 4; see also Psalms 71:8; 90:17; 145:5). I propose that to claim that God is beautiful or to claim that it is beautiful that God exists is to claim that God or the fact of God's existence merits aesthetic delight or pleasure or awe. As an Anselmian theist in the social Trinitarian tradition, I propose that God's reality can and should be thought of as involving a threefold inner beauty. This outlook has been variously developed by Richard of St. Victor in the twelfth century and in our own time by Richard Swinburne and Stephen T. Davis.[4] On this model, the Godhead consists of three persons who have their own distinct reality; each person has self-love (the Father loves the Father; the Son loves the Son; the Holy Spirit loves the Holy Spirit), each person loves another (the Father loves the Son; the Father loves the Holy Spirit, and so on), and each person with a second person loves a third person (the Father and the Son love the Holy Spirit; the Son and the Holy Spirit love the Father, and so on). In this tradition, the triangular relationship within the Godhead is of such supremely co-equal abundance that it naturally leads (without necessitating) the Triune God to create and sustain a good creation. The tradition invokes a dictum attributed to the late fifth-/early-sixth-century philosophical theologian Dionysius the Areopagite to the effect that goodness is by nature diffusive (*bonum est diffusivum sui*). In *The Divine Names*, Dionysius (sometimes also referred to as Pseudo-Dionysius) refers to God as "the all beautiful and the beautiful beyond all. It is forever so, unvaryingly, unchangeably so... in itself [the Divine nature] is the uniquely and eternally beautiful."[5]

If there is such a divine reality of superabundant, overflowing goodness, then it seems that having an experiential relationship with such a reality would itself be good and beautiful insofar as it leads to a magnification of what is good and beautiful. As representative instances of when an experience of the divine might be life enhancing, consider two accounts. The first is by Julian of Norwich, the fourteenth- to fifteenth-century Christian mystic, as recorded in *Revelations of Divine Love* in which God reveals to her how the creation is loved by God; creation is pictured here as something small and fragile:

> And in this he showed me a little thing, the quantity of a hazel nut, lying in the palm of my hand, as it seemed. And it was as round as any ball. I looked upon it with the eye of my understanding, and thought, "What may this be?" And it was answered generally thus, "It is all that is made." I marveled how it might last, for I thought it might suddenly have fallen to nothing for littleness. And I was answered in my understanding: It lasts and ever shall, for God loves it. And so have all things their beginning by the love of God. In this

---

4   See Stephen T. Davis, *Christian Philosophical Theology* (Oxford: Oxford University Press, 2006) and Richard Swinburne, *The Christian God* (Oxford: Clarendon Press, 1994).

5   Pseudo-Dionysius, "The Divine Names." In *The Complete Works*, tr. Colm Luibheid (London: SPCK, 1987), 47–131. See also Augustine's *On the Trinity*, VI.10.11.

little thing I saw three properties. The first is that God made it. The second that God loves it. And the third, that God keeps it.[6]

Her vision of God's omnipresence adds an affective dimension to traditional, philosophical treatments of divine omnipresence. Traditionally, divine omnipresence is defined in terms of power and knowledge. For example, to claim that God is omnipresent is to claim that God causally has created and sustains everything at every place (no contingent thing has or is or will exist without such divine creativity and conservation), God has perfect, unsurpassable knowledge of every place, and God can exercise power at every place (that is compatible with divine omnipotence). Through her mystical experience, we may add that divine omnipresence also involves God's love for creation at any place; that is, there is no place where God's love is not exercised.

In the course of her mystical experience of God, Julian comes to affectively apprehend how the experience purges her (and can, in turn, purge us) of vice and makes us more receptive to the good.

> For this is what was shown: that our life is all grounded and rooted in love, and without love we cannot live; and therefore to the soul which through God's special grace sees so much of his great and marvelous goodness, and sees that we are joined to him in love for ever, it is the greatest impossibility conceivable that God should be angry, for anger and friendship are two contraries. It must needs be that he who wears away and extinguishes our anger and makes us gentle and kind, which is the contrary of anger; for I saw quite clearly where our Lord appears, everything is peaceful and there is no place for anger; for I saw no kind of anger in God, neither for a short time nor for a long one; indeed, it seems to me that if God could be even slightly angry we could never have any life or place or being ...[7]

To discourage our thinking that such mystical states are only medieval, consider a second account from the twentieth century in which the experience of a transcendent loving power seems to become manifest. The British poet W. H. Auden reports:

One fine summer night in June 1933 I was sitting on a lawn after dinner with three colleagues, two women and one man. We liked each other but we were certainly not intimate friends, nor had any

6   Julian of Norwich, *Revelations of Divine Love* (London: Penguin Books, 1998), 114.
7   Ibid.

of us a sexual interest in another. Incidentally, we had not drunk any alcohol. We were talking casually about everyday matters when, quite suddenly and unexpectedly, something happened. I felt myself invaded by a power which, though I consented to it, was irresistible and certainly not mine. For the first time in my life I knew exactly – because, thanks to the power, I was doing it – what it means to love one's neighbor as oneself.[8]

I have elsewhere argued for the cognitive, evidential significance of these experiences.[9] Here, my concern is largely with taking note of the aesthetic nature of such experiences, involving cases of when the ostensible experience of a loving divine reality gives rise to further love, which I take to be an ostensible (apparent) case of experiencing the divine as beautiful and one's having a beautiful experience.

Let us now consider the aesthetic dimension of Anselmian theism in terms of overall beauty and ugliness, especially in light of Galen Strawson's account of the ugliness of Christian theism.

JUSTIFICATION AND REDEMPTION

Does Christian theism eclipse or diminish or cause us to have contempt for those who suffer? It is surprising that Strawson thinks it does. Perhaps he has in mind a philosophy of values that has been defended by some Christian philosophers that depicts evil as a privation (the *privati boni* theory). But to the best of my knowledge, this philosophy has never denied the reality (or magnitude) of suffering. It holds, instead, that when persons do undergo evils, this consists in a kind of privation or (to use a better expression) a dysfunction. On this view, a person's having bone cancer or seeking to murder an innocent person is experiencing and pursuing something that is in violation of the *telos* or nature or purpose or good of being a person. In such cases, the person is deprived or depraved in terms of what makes up or constitutes being a good person. In any case, the privation theory does not deny the reality and horror of suffering, nor am I acquainted with any mainline philosopher or theologian who denies this. In fact, the virtually universal Christian testimony to the reality and horror of suffering is so central that if we have reason to believe that there is no suffering or to believe that suffering is in

---

8   W. H. Auden, *The Protestant Mystic* (New York: Mentor Books, 1965), 75.
9   See Charles Taliaferro and Chad Meister, *Contemporary Philosophical Theology* (London: Routledge, 2016) and Charles Taliaferro and Jil Evans, *The Image in Mind* (London: Continuum, 2011).

fact good, we would have good reason to think that Christianity is false or (perhaps worse) absurd. If the reality and evil of suffering (and other forms of evil and ugliness) did not exist, why would God seek to redeem created persons from evil through the costly incarnation that involves the torture, suffering, and death of the Second Person of the Trinity in the life of Jesus of Nazareth? In fact, one can find almost limitless condemnations of those who are contemptuous of those who suffer that go far beyond Strawson's venomous language in prophetic Biblical texts (see, for example, the ethical monotheism of Isaiah, Amos, and so on, the Sermon of the Mount) and in the teachings and actions of seminal Christian figures who have sought to confront injustice such as Martin Luther King Jr. While King did not (to the best of my knowledge) use the expression *sensus divinitatis*, he did testify to having an experience of God as a loving, just, and merciful reality, which invites this question: Is he a likely figure whom we should judge to be deluded and profoundly immoral? I revisit this question in what follows.

In the meantime, let us consider the bigger picture of what Christian theists claim about God, good and beauty, evil and ugliness. Richard Swinburne offers this general position on theism, beauty, and ugliness:

> God has reason to make a basically beautiful world, although also reason to leave some of the beauty or ugliness of the world within the power of creatures to determine; but he would seem to have overriding reason not to make a basically ugly world beyond the powers of creatures to improve. Hence, if there is a God there is more reason to expect a basically beautiful world than a basically ugly one.[10]

This passage is part of Swinburne's case for theism and against secular naturalism. Swinburne argues that the existence of our cosmos is more likely or reasonable given theism than naturalism. In this chapter, our concern is not this more general undertaking but a defense of the idea that the cosmos (as we experience and believe it to be) is worthy of being the creation of an unsurpassably excellent God. In any case, Swinburne's statement invites a fuller description of the distribution of beauty and ugliness in the cosmos from the standpoint of Anselmian theism. In considering the following account, an important point needs to be made about the nature of freedom. For many Christian philosophers (and what I shall be assuming in what follows), for a person to freely do some act is

---

[10]   Richard Swinburne, *The Existence of God*, 2nd edition (Oxford: Oxford University Press, 2004).

for the person to do the act and to have the power to do otherwise. This is sometimes referred to as *libertarian freedom*. For many of us, this power is a vital precondition for persons to be morally (and religiously) responsible for our action. On the basis of what he refers to as the basic argument, Strawson denies that any person is morally responsible, and thus worthy of praise or blame, for any of his or her acts. Strawson contends that to have morally relevant responsibility, a subject would have to be able to engage in self-creation (being *causa-sui*), an evident absurdity. I have argued against his line of reasoning elsewhere.[11] Here, however, I note the importance from the standpoint of Christian theism, the reality of libertarian agency and thus the reality of moral responsibility. Back to the passage from Strawson cited earlier, perhaps it is because he thinks that no one has moral responsibility that he thinks that the "perpetual acts of incalculable cruelty" we observe are all attributable to God and not to the human (and possibly other) agents we observe. But Strawson's position actually rules out that God, if there is a God, could be morally responsible for God's acts or state of being. (On this front, given his denial that any of us are blameworthy, Strawson's apparent blaming of both theists and God seems odd; possibly he can be better interpreted not in terms of blaming anyone or anything but just lamenting what he deems ugly).

Consider now the following overall portrait of the creation from the standpoint of Anselmian theism. I refer to this as the *Anselmian vision*.

There is an omnipotent, unsurpassably excellent, beautiful, all good, omniscient, necessarily existing being who is the Triune God of perfect love and inner beauty who has created and sustains a cosmos of at least one hundred billion galaxies in which there are (perhaps uncountably) many planets, at least one of which sustains life (there may or may not be many billions of others). All the elements of the cosmos, with their causal powers and liabilities, are dependent upon divine creation and conservation such that none of them would endure over time without God's causal powers. The cosmos appears to be marked by uniform, stable laws that we currently are discovering through physics, chemistry, and biology. The vastness and grandeur of this cosmos merits our awe and delight as something sublime and of extraordinary beauty. On earth, chemical bonding led to the emergence of life and through a long, complex evolutionary history, the emergence of plant and animal life, the biota and abiota. Amid the multitude of nonhuman animal life, some developed

11   Taliaferro and Evans, *The Image in Mind*.

and are developing powers of movement and sentience, and with some mammals including humans, there emerges persons (selves or subjects) who have powers of movement, a range of senses and feelings, memory, reason, the power to love or hate, fear and desire, and (eventually) powers to make moral judgments and to act in light of what seem to be right or wrong choices, virtues and vices. Some use these powers for the good and welfare of persons and other forms of life, and are beautiful, but some are profoundly ugly and wrong. In this cosmos, there are good and beautiful friends, families, adventures, creativity, and there are evil and ugly enemies, hateful rulers, and soul-destroying acts such as rape, torture, murder, enslavement. These evils are contrary to the will and nature of God, abhorrent to God's purpose in creation. God acts through prophets and created agents to fight and prevent some evils, but not always. Thus while God commands persons not to murder, and judges each murderer guilty of a heinous crime and sacrilege, God does not miraculously intervene to prevent every murder. God seeks to be revealed and in relationship with created persons through experiences and events, through prophets and, ultimately, in an incarnation in which, as Jesus of Nazareth, God calls persons from evil toward a good and fulfilling life. This Jesus teaches that the way of love and compassion is to be sought and creatures should shun violence and military conquests. Through Jesus's teaching, healings, passion, dying, death, and resurrection, there is a divine teaching that persons may be redeemed from evil through repentance, moral and religious rebirth, and through the power of being in relationship with the resurrected Christ in whom one finds a dynamic, renewing relationship with God. The physical death of persons is not their annihilation, for at biological death, God preserves persons in being and seeks to restore and renew persons in a life after life in relationship with each other and God and possibly uncountably many creatures of all conceivable, good types.

Note that the Anselmian vision fully preserves the repugnance of evil. There is no attempt to minimize the existence of suffering, nor is there any justification offered for evil itself, making unethical acts such as murder justified or not evil. Murder and rape do not become good nor is their reality to be deemed itself good. On this point, the Anselmian vision may be seen more as offering a vision of redemption rather than justification. To be sure, the Anselmian vision offers a perspective from which one can (if it is successful) understand world evils and ugliness as compatible with there being an all-good, beautiful, unsurpassably excellent God. But in this vision, *evil persons* are the object of redemption (in which God calls persons from evil to the good), though *evil itself* is not redeemed (or shown to be good).

The Anselmian vision may be amplified in any number of directions. One might focus on nonhuman animals suffering, for example, or highlight major atrocities or focus on or vividly describe individual heinous acts (such as the torture, rape, and murder of a young girl), or one might highlight the converse beauties of animal symbiosis or focus on mass movements that seem courageously wonderful or focus on particular, specific acts of courage and love. I propose, however, that when considering beauty and ugliness in the problem of evil, we need to think of *God as Creator of a whole cosmos* and not as a finite bystander in the cosmos. In the above framework, God does act in a finite form in the cosmos, but as an active agent with limited powers (omnipotence has been limited or subject to kenotic conditions – "Kenosis" being the Greek term for limitation), but the problem of evil should (in my view) be set on a cosmic scale.

Also of importance: I propose that those arguing that God should be blamed for creating and conserving the cosmos must (on some level) argue that they believe not only that *the cosmos as they believe it to be* is not worthy of being created and conserved by an all-good being but that *the Anselmian vision of the cosmos* (or one like it) *which includes more than they recognize (few secular naturalists allow for there being an individual, dynamic life after life) is contrary to the goodness of God* (or incompatible with the work of a good God). Of course, the first phase of a critique of Anselmian theism may be limited to contending that there are strong reasons to think that the cosmos as we observe it is not Anselmian, but in arguing that Anselmian theism is ugly and evidentially bankrupt, I suggest a more extensive taking on of possible evidence and reasons that Anselmians introduce is in order. A. C. Ewing counsels such a capacious approach to assessing the good or ill nature of the cosmos. According to Ewing, a critic of religious conceptions of the cosmos should, in principle, entertain and assess the possibility of expanded concepts of the cosmos that may be suggested by religious experience.

> We must follow truth wherever it leads, since the mind, once awakened, cannot rest in what it has no justification for thinking may not be a falsehood. At the same time we must study with respect and not

dismiss unheard the claims of those who think they have attained inspiring and comforting truths about Reality by means that cannot be brought under the ordinary categories of common sense. We must not take for granted that the claims to a genuine cognition in religious and mystical experience of a different aspect of reality are necessarily to be dismissed as unjustified just because they do not fit in with a materialism suggested but by no means proved or now even really supported by modern science.[12]

An analogy might be useful: when assessing someone's moral character, it is important (*ceteris paribus*) not to use only what one knows in a firsthand matter but to take into account the testimony of others and to weigh the possibility of there being either good or sinister states of affairs of which one is unaware in a firsthand fashion. Consider another analogy: imagine evaluating a work of art but only from the standpoint of a firmly held theory of art that is hostile to the very nature and purpose of the work of art. I suggest that a fair-minded or at least a more comprehensive evaluation of the work of art should take into account its own alternative models of art. This is not to claim that critics need to abandon their privileged, preferred theories. It is just to claim that their task as critics should (at some point) be expansive rather than contractive. So, to return to assessing the Anselmian vision, I propose that a critic who does not think persons survive biological death has some reason to consider whether the Anselmian vision is more sensible if the critic allows (if only for the sake of argument) that there might be life after life. This is a position long held by John Hick, who has firmly defended the coherence of life after life and maintained that if there is no such life after life, there is good reason to think that God (or ultimate reality) is not good. Interestingly, Hick also argues that if naturalism is true, it is highly likely that the cosmos itself is horrific.

Can honest, morally sensitive, non–self-deceived persons believe that the Anselmian vision of the cosmos is not just a remote possible world but our actual world? And if they can, might it be the case that their belief and the overall cosmos (as described) is overall beautiful? I believe that the answer to both is "yes" with some qualifications.

To fully secure the first point would involve more work than can fit into a chapter. I have elsewhere highlighted reasons why I think Anselmian

---

[12]   A. C. Ewing, *The Fundamental Questions of Philosophy* (London: Routledge & Kegan Paul, 1985), 25.

theism is plausible.[13] Here I simply note that some of the matters that Strawson seems to acknowledge (the existence of evil and good, suffering and thus the existence of consciousness, virtues of honesty, the existence of love, our capacity to reason) can function as part of theistic arguments that press forward the comparative explanatory advantages of theism over against naturalism (theistic arguments from consciousness, moral and teleological arguments). I suggest two perhaps combined arguments (the ontological and an argument from religious experience) may be seen as providing good reasons for someone to accept Anselmian theism.[14]

Given that there can (in principle), be sound, nonfallacious evidence for someone to believe the Anselmian vision, what about *the beauty or ugliness of believing* the earlier vision? Let us grant that someone might accept the Anselmian vision for selfish reasons (they believe in life after life based on their sense of their own self-importance and the conviction that life without them would be impossible); even so, there is no reason to think this is likely or common. There is a long-standing moral argument for belief in an afterlife that does not appeal to vain self-interest but out of a longing for cosmic justice. This is at the heart of Kantian practical faith. The beauty of the Anselmian vision might be enhanced when one also integrates the testimony of persons such as Julian, Auden, and Martin Luther King to have experientially apprehended the divine and sought to enhance the role of love and compassion with others.

Before moving to the fourth section and considering what our exploration of beauty and ugliness might offer us in confronting evil, let us consider three objections.

> Objection one: *A fantastic objection.* Some of the elements in the Anselmian vision may seem fantastic in the sense that it promotes a fantasy. What of philosophers who have argued that the very idea of God is incoherent or that the very idea of an individual personal life after life is incoherent?
>
> Reply: If there are compelling reasons to believe the ideas of God and an afterlife are incoherent, then game over. I have argued (as have many others) for not just the coherence but the plausibility of both theism and the life after life of persons.[15] If successful, neither supposition is a fantasy.

---

[13] See Taliaferro and Evans, *The Image in Mind.*

[14] See Charles Taliaferro, *The Golden Cord* (Notre Dame: University of Notre Dame Press, 2012) and Charles Taliaferro, *Dialogues About God* (New York: Rowan and Littlefield, 2008).

[15] Charles Taliaferro, *Consciousness and the Mind of God* (Cambridge: Cambridge University Press, 1994).

Objection two: *The devil-is-in-the-details objection.* The focus on the standpoint of the creator obscures the criminal nature of the supposedly all-great God of Anselmian theism. A bystander's tolerance or nonprevention of rape is not materially different from a being that creates a world in which rapes are tolerated and not prevented by the creator. Once we focus on the details of the evils at hand, the objection to a God of beauty becomes just as strong as ever.

Reply: If it is plausible to believe that there are evident, *absolute evils that should be prevented by any and all beings that have the power to interfere on every occasion that absolute evils occur* (no matter what the cause or history or possible future), then that is good reason to believe that, if there is a God, then God does not do what a good moral agent should do. There are, however, four points that should be taken into consideration.

First, it may be that the ability for creatures to do horrendous things to each other is an essential corollary for creatures to have deep responsibility for each other and the accompanying ability for us to do great and beautiful things to each other. It may be that for parents to truly have deep responsibility for their children, they have the powers to love, nurture, and raise the children and (tragically) the powers to do not this but the exact opposite, visiting on their children profound abuse.

Second, if it is good that there is a creation that is importantly independent of the divine (in which created persons can act freely), it is important that the creator not consistently and evidently interfere in the cosmos itself. If it is indeed good that persons have a deep responsibility to each other, they have to have an independence or some autonomy in their actions. If God's character and acts were regularly manifest, prudence would seem to undermine persons' abilities to act freely.

Third, it is open to the Anselmian theist to allow that some things occur that God should (that is, God has either a morally relevant duty or God should as a matter of justice) annihilate some part of the cosmos (annihilating all murderers and rapists), and yet out of mercy, God instead preserves them in being for the purpose of their being redeemed: murderers and rapists being transformed to not only become nonmurderous and nonrapacious but to become repentant, compassionate, morally regenerated beautiful beings who perhaps go on to seek the redemption of those who remain mired in evil. This position takes the controversial but, I believe, plausible view that justice and mercy are in tension with each other, such that (for example) a good magistrate may elect to act mercifully rather than follow the strict demands of justice. In certain circumstances, a good magistrate might even be deemed unjust (or at least not a follower of strict justice) without compromising her goodness. (This position is hinted at in Portia's plea for mercy in Shakespeare's *The Merchant of Venice*, Act IV, Scene 1: "in the course of justice, none of us should see salvation: we do pray for mercy").

Fourth, compare the Anselmian vision with secular naturalism, especially of the kind envisaged by Galen Strawson. In a form of secular naturalism in which there is no libertarian freedom, every act of rape, murder, and torture is necessary given the prior states of the cosmos and the laws of nature. Given Strawson's basic argument, he does not believe that any rapist or murderer is morally responsible for their acts. The Anselmian theist, instead, construes evil as an abomination, alien to the very nature of the cosmos and its purpose. This is not to propose that naturalists personally are accommodating evil or are more likely than theists to tolerate evil. But it is to point out that theism is able to capture what many of us find to be the unnatural, alien nature of evil.

> Objection three: The cosmos is more beautiful given naturalism than theism. Richard Dawkins complains about those who seek to defend the goodness of God by appealing to objects of beauty. His comments invite our considering whether the cosmos might be more beautiful without God. Dawkins observes:
>
> Another character in the Aldous Huxley novel just mentioned proved the existence of God by playing Beethoven's string quartet no. 15 in A minor ("Heiliger Dankgesang") on a gramophone. Unconvincing as that sounds, it does represent a popular strand of argument. I have given up counting the number of times I receive the more or less truculent challenge: "How do you account for Shakespeare, then?" (Substitute Schubert, Michelangelo, etc. to taste.) The argument will be so familiar, I needn't document it further. But the logic behind it is never spelled out, and the more you think about it the more vacuous you realize it to be. Obviously Beethoven's late quartets are sublime. So are Shakespeare's sonnets. They are sublime if God is there and they are sublime if he isn't. They do not prove the existence of God; they prove the existence of Beethoven and of Shakespeare. A great conductor is credited with saying: "If you have Mozart to listen to, why would you need God?"[16]

---

[16]   Richard Dawkins, *The God Delusion* (Boston, MA: Mariner Books, 2008).

One reason why you might want God and Mozart is that God can create and sustain uncountably many creatures with greater and greater powers of creativity and ever more awesome works everlastingly. The alternative in secular naturalism is, ultimately, the annihilation of persons. However great Beethoven, Shakespeare, and Mozart have been, they have ceased to be, as we shall cease to be ourselves, given secular naturalism. The greatness of such figures is enhanced in Anselmian theism. And perhaps your and my prospects in creativity may be enhanced in which we might come to be (as it were) our own version of Shakespeare *et al.*

WHAT CAN WE LEARN ABOUT EVIL AND GOODNESS THROUGH OUR REFLECTION ON BEAUTY AND UGLINESS?

This topic goes way beyond what may be adequately addressed at the end of this chapter, but I raise this question to stimulate further reflection. Part of what we can learn is how persons are led to do great, wrongful harms due to false, perverse concepts of the beautiful. Among the many figures who might be cited in support of this view, consider the Polish poet, dramatist, and member of the resistance movement during World War II Zbigniew Herbert. In such poems as "The Power of Taste," he conveys that an important source of resistance to totalitarianism is to find it ugly. For Herbert, a proper sense of beauty can aid us with exposing the seductive false "beauties" of power and domination. Perhaps this was behind Alexander Solzhenitsyn's observation that a true sense of beauty can assist us in promoting the good and the true.

> And so perhaps that old trinity of Truth and Good and Beauty is not just the formal outworn formula it used to seem to us during our heady, materialistic youth. If the crests of these three trees join together, as the investigators and explorers used to affirm, and if the too-obvious, too-straight branches of Truth and Good are crushed or amputated and cannot reach the light – yet perhaps the whimsical, unpredictable, unexpected branches of Beauty will make their way through and soar up to that very place and in this way perform the work of all three. And in that case, it was not a slip of the tongue for Dostoyevsky to say that "Beauty will save the world" but a prophecy. After all, he was given the gift of seeing much; he was extraordinarily illumined. And consequently perhaps art, literature, can in actual fact help the world of today.[17]

---

[17]   Aleksandr Solzhenitsyn, "Beauty Will Save the World." The Nobel Lecture on Literature, 1970.

I have elsewhere defended ideal-observer accounts of both goodness and beauty.[18] In such parallel accounts, there are at least three ideal conditions for proper or ideal ethical and aesthetic evaluations. One needs to strive for a maximal awareness of the nonethical and nonaesthetic facts in virtue of which we attain ethical and aesthetic judgment. One needs to be impartial. And one needs to have an affective awareness of the points of view of all persons involved. The latter involves a serious commitment to the exercise of our imagination in which, as Solzhenitsyn suggests, the arts and literature may be of great importance.

Due to limits of space, it will have to suffice for me to address just one problem involving justice or injustice, good and evil, beauty and ugliness. As I write this, the world is enduring the terrible plight of refugees. The numbers of persons who are forcibly displaced from their homeland are almost unimaginable. The United Nations Refugee Agency estimates that there are currently 59.5 million refugees; this figure is dramatically increased from the end of 2014, when it was estimated there were 19.5 million refugees. The ideal-observer theory of ethics and aesthetics enjoin us to affectively identify with (or seek to know what it is like to be in) such a plight. If we can strive to do so – thus, in a sense, imagining ourselves, who are comfortable, sharing their plight, it would be very hard indeed to remain indifferent to refugees and to steadfastly seek to protect our privileges. This broader point of view would address an issue that is of momentous importance as I am writing this chapter: European but especially United States lack of receptivity to Syrian refugees. Someone in the United States who sought to fulfill the ideals specified in the ideal-observer theories would be likely to contemplate a reversal of roles that took place in 1860 in Damascus when it was the Christians who were threatened, and yet as many as 100,000 were rescued through the brave intervention and protection of the devout Muslim warrior Abd al-Qadir. During a dangerous riot, he gave protection to European and United States diplomats, merchants and their families, priests, and nuns. Complacent, comfortable fellow United States citizens need to be cajoled into considering whether it is ugly to shun the needs of others the way we are doing and whether reaching out to aid refugees is indeed, rather, good and beautiful. The ideal-observer account of ethics and aesthetics beckons us to uphold such good and beautiful exemplars as Abd al-Qadir.

---

[18]   See my *Aesthetics* (Oxford: One World, 2011); *Contemporary Philosophy of Religion* (Oxford: Blackwell, 1998); and "The Ideal Aesthetic Observer," *British Journal of Aesthetics* 30:1 (1990) 1–13.

How might this, in turn, relate to theism? Arguably, I believe that the ideal ethical and aesthetic point of view is, essentially, what may be called a God's-eye point of view.[19] God is understood in Christian theism to be omniscient of all the relevant facts, including God's possessing perfect affective awareness of all states of the cosmos, and impartial. A secularist might accept this account while not believing there is any God to actually have such a point of view. But I note that how we go about tracking what is beautiful and good do match up with a theistic point of view. The same process is involved in our struggle over the problem of evil, beauty, and ugliness. As we assess whether theism and theists are contemptuous or disregarding of the suffering of others, we need to seek to know all the relevant facts, to be affectively aware of all involved persons, and to be impartial. Ironically, this broader God's-eye point of view was even hinted at in Strawson's antitheistic charges cited earlier.

In ending this chapter, I ask which worldview would be (or is) highly motivating to seek to bring goodness and beauty out of ugliness: the Anselmian vision or a deterministic view of secular naturalism? It could be that we should be agnostic and adhere to neither. As I have indicated at various places, I ask you to consult my other work, for example, *The Golden Cord*, to see why I think the Anselmian vision is not only beautiful and good but true.

FURTHER READING

Balthasar, H. U. von. *The Glory of the Lord: A Theological Aesthetics*, tr. J. Riches et al., 7 vols. Edinburgh: T & T. Clark, 1982–1991.

Brown, David. *God and Grace of Body*. Oxford: Oxford University Press, 2007.

Graham, Gordan. *The Re-enchantment of the World: Art versus Religion*. Oxford: Oxford University Press, 2010.

Hedley, Douglas. *Living Forms of the Imagination*. London: Continuum, 2005.

Sherry, Patrick. *Spirit and Beauty: An Introduction to Theological Aesthetics*. Oxford: Clarendon Press, 1992.

Taliaferro, Charles, and Jil Evans (eds.). *Turning Images in Philosophy, Science, and Religion*. Oxford: Oxford University Press, 2011.

Wynn, Mark. *Faith and Place*. Oxford: Oxford University Press, 2011.

[19]   See Charles Taliaferro, *Contemporary Philosophy of Religion* (Oxford: Blackwell, 1998), 206.

3 Logical Arguments from Evil and Free-Will Defences

GRAHAM OPPY

Brian Leftow writes:

> If you think that evil currently provides any very strong argument against the existence of God, you have not been paying attention. Purely deductive ('logical') versions of the problem of evil are widely conceded to be 'dead', killed off by Plantinga's free-will defence.... Once one sees the sort of thing a defence has to be to work, it seems pretty clear that some kind of free-will defence has to be available and adequate. The debate has shifted to 'evidential' versions of the problem of evil, and my own view, which is not uncommon, is that these are pretty thoroughly on the ropes – what's called sceptical theism provides an effective counter.[1]

Leftow's view is widespread amongst 'perfect being' theists. Nonetheless, it seems to me to be evidently mistaken. In particular, while it is plausible that the official logical argument from evil of Mackie[2] is 'dead' – and while it might reasonably be contended that considerations about free will are amongst several sets of considerations that suffice to 'kill' it – it is obvious that there are other logical arguments from evil that are not 'killed' by considerations about free will. Moreover, it is equally obvious that we have not examined all logical arguments from evil and that we have no neutral – 'non–question-begging' – grounds for claiming that those logical arguments from evil that we have not yet examined can be 'killed'.

LOGICAL ARGUMENTS FROM EVIL

A logical argument from evil contains three distinctive kinds of premises. The exemplars of the first kind of premise collectively make up

---

[1]   Brian Leftow, *God and Necessity* (Oxford University Press, 2012), 547.
[2]   J. L. Mackie, "Evil and Omnipotence," *Mind* 64 (1955): 200–12.

the characterisation: a claim about properties that God possesses if God exists. The sole member of the second kind of premise is **the datum**: a claim about the existence of suffering in our universe. The exemplars of the third kind of premise collectively make up **the link**: a claim that, in concert with the characterisation and the datum, entails – or is alleged to entail – that God does not exist.

The Characterisation: There are different claims that can serve as the characterisation in a logical argument from evil. A typical characterisation might be something like this:

> C1: If God exists, God is the omnipotent, omniscient, perfectly good, perfectly free creator *ex nihilo* of our universe.

Of course, this characterisation can be broken down into a collection of independent – or apparently independent or putatively independent – claims:

> C1a: If God exists, God is omnipotent.
> C1b: If God exists, God is omniscient.
> C1c: If God exists, God is perfectly good.
> C1d: If God exists, God is perfectly free.
> C1e: If God exists, God is sole creator *ex nihilo* of our universe.

Many logical arguments from evil do not include all of C1a–C1e in their characterisation. (Some logical arguments from evil make do with just C1a and C1c.) There is no reason why logical arguments from evil should not include independent claims other than C1a–C1e. The standard target of logical arguments from evil is perfect-being theism: and there are many other perfections that are standardly attributed to God by perfect-being theists. Of course, we require that the datum is a *non-redundant* premise in a logical argument from evil: if the characterisation and the link *alone* jointly entail that God does not exist, then we do not have a logical argument *from evil*.

The Datum: There are many different claims that can serve as the datum in a logical argument from evil. Here are some candidates:

> D1: There is suffering in our universe.
> D2: There is suffering in our universe that is due to human agency.
> D3: There is suffering in our universe that is not due to human agency.
> D4: There is *this* particular instance of suffering in our universe that is due to human agency.
> D5. There is *this* particular instance of suffering in our universe that is not due to human agency.

D6. There is a massive amount of suffering in our universe that is due to human agency.

D7. There is a massive amount of suffering in our universe that is not due to human agency.

D8: There is horrendous suffering in our universe.

D9: There is horrendous suffering in our universe that is due to human agency.

D10: There is horrendous suffering in our universe that is not due to human agency.

D11: There is *this* particular instance of horrendous suffering in our universe that is due to human agency.

D12: There is *this* particular instance of horrendous suffering in our universe that is not due to human agency.

D13: There is a massive amount of horrendous suffering in our universe that is due to human agency.

D14: There is a massive amount of horrendous suffering in our universe that is not due to human agency.

D15: There is *all of this* horrendous suffering in our universe that is due to human agency.

D16: There is *all of this* horrendous suffering in our universe that is not due to human agency.

None of these claims is controversial; none is denied by perfect-being theists. Since D15 and D16 are the strongest claims on the list, one might think that it would make most sense always to work with them (or with claims that are even stronger than D15 and D16, so long as those stronger claims are also uncontroversial). But many discussions of logical arguments from evil take the datum to be a weaker claim than D15 or D16: indeed, in many cases, the datum is taken to be D1.

I have formulated D1 through D16 in terms of 'suffering'; in many logical arguments from evil, the datum is instead formulated in terms of 'evil'. I shall write '$D_i(E)$' for the adjusted versions of the D_i framed in terms of 'evil'. So, for example, D1(E) is the claim that there is evil in our universe. There are other terms – for example, 'imperfection' – that could also figure as the key term in arguments of this kind.

The Link: There are many different claims that can serve as the link in logical arguments from evil. Obviously enough, variation in the characterisation may need to be accompanied by variation in the link. Perhaps slightly less obviously, variation in the *interpretation* of the characterisation may need to be accompanied by variation in the link.

Mackie,[3] working with a characterisation that included only C1a and C1c, took the link to consist of the following two claims:

Lm1: Good is opposed to evil in such a way that a good thing always eliminates evil as far as it can.

Lm2: There are no limits to what an omnipotent thing can do.

As Mackie says:

> From these it follows that a good omnipotent thing eliminates evil completely, and then the propositions that a good omnipotent thing exists, and that evil exists, are incompatible.

In Mackie's official logical argument from evil, the datum is D1(E).

Rowe, working with a characterisation that included C1a, C1b and C1c, can be interpreted as taking the link to consist of the following two claims:[4]

Lr1: An omnipotent, omniscient being could have prevented the truth of the datum without thereby losing some greater good or permitting some evil equally bad or worse.

Lr2: An omniscient, wholly good being would prevent the truth of the datum unless it could not do so without thereby losing some greater good or permitting some evil equally bad or worse.

In Rowe,[5] the datum is plausibly D7(E) (though some of the discussion makes it appear that the datum is D5(E)). If the datum is D7(E), then the link would be better framed in terms of non-arbitrarily reducing the amount of suffering or evil that there is rather than in terms of preventing the truth of the datum without thereby losing some greater good or permitting some evil equally bad or worse.

An argument working with all of C1a through C1e might take the link to consist of something like the following pair of claims:

Lo1: If a being that is omnipotent, omniscient and perfectly good makes a universe, then, up to arbitrary choice, that being makes a best universe.

Lo2: If datum is true in all of the best universes from amongst which an omnipotent, omniscient and perfectly good being could otherwise make an arbitrary selection, then that being does not make any universe.

---

[3] Ibid.

[4] William Rowe, "The Problem of Evil and some Varieties of Atheism," *American Philosophical Quarterly* 16 (1979): 335–41.

[5] Ibid.

To construct the strongest form of this argument, the datum should be taken to be D15 or D16, or the conjunction of D15 and D16 or some even stronger claim if there are stronger claims that entail D15 and D16 and that are no less evidently true. (Oppy[6] discusses an argument of this kind in which the datum is taken to be D2(E).)

LOGICAL PROBLEMS OF EVIL

Many philosophers talk about logical *problems* of evil rather than about logical *arguments* from evil. However, when philosophers talk about a logical problem of evil, the 'problem' that they have in mind is closely related to a logical argument from evil.

Suppose that we have a logical argument from evil involving a particular characterisation, datum and link. The characterisation is conditional; the consequent of the conditional is a set of claims about God. For example, the consequent of C1 is the claim that God is the omnipotent, omniscient, perfectly good, perfectly free creator *ex nihilo* of our universe. Call the consequent of the characterisation 'the characterising claim'. Then the problem of evil that arises from the logical argument with which we began is that the characterising claim, the datum and the link are – or are alleged to be – jointly inconsistent. (Here, I take it for granted that, for example, 'God is omnipotent' entails 'God exists'. If – for whatever reason – this is denied, then the further claim that God exists is also needed in order to generate inconsistency.)

Plantinga says,

> [P]resumably the atheologian ... never meant to hold that there was a formal contradiction here; he meant instead that the conjunction of [the characterising claim and the datum] is necessarily false. ... To show that he is right, therefore, he must produce a proposition that is at least plausibly thought to be necessary and whose conjunction with [the characterising claim and the datum] formally yields a contradiction.[7]

I don't think that this is *exactly* right. What the atheologian ought to have been saying is that there *is* a formal contradiction between claims to all of which the theist is committed. It is irrelevant whether the link is plausibly thought to be necessary, even if it is also true that any plausible candidates for the link are necessary if true: what matters is whether

6   Graham Oppy, *Arguing about Gods* (Cambridge: Cambridge University Press, 2006).
7   Alvin Plantinga, *The Nature of Necessity* (Oxford: Clarendon, 1974), 165.

the theist is committed to the link. If the link can be reasonably rejected by the theist – if there is a formulation of theism in which the link is denied that, all else being equal, could be reasonably believed – then, at least by my lights, the logical argument that goes by way of the link is unsuccessful.

THE LINK IN MACKIE (1955)

The link in the argument of Mackie[8] is obviously controversial. I expect that most theists will reject both Lm1 and Lm2.

I think that it is pretty clearly not true that good is opposed to evil in such a way that a good thing always eliminates evil as far as it can. It seems reasonable to accept that a good thing will have two aims: it will aim to promote that which is good, and it will aim to defeat that which is evil. Given these twin aims, it does not follow that a good thing will eliminate evil as far as it can. Rather, what is true is that a good thing will do what it can to advance both of its aims: insofar as those aims must be considered together, a good thing will do what it can to promote the best balance of good over evil.

Whether a good thing would endorse the goal of eliminating evil completely depends on how good and evil are related. If there are goods that a good thing might promote that can only obtain if there are evils, then whether a good thing would endorse the goal of eliminating evil completely depends on whether the best realisable balance of good over evil is one in which there are goods that can only obtain if there are evils. If there are goods that a good thing might promote but only at the cost of not ensuring that there is no evil, then whether a good thing would endorse the promotion of those goods – at the cost of leaving it open that the goal of eliminating evil completely is not fulfilled – depends on the judgment that the good thing makes about the balance of good over evil that is most likely to ensue (or some other judgment in that neighbourhood).

Depending on other parts of their worldview, theists will typically suppose that there are certain goods whose realisation is such that either God could have knowingly permitted the existence of *some evil* in order for those goods to be realised, or God could have knowingly risked the existence of *some evil* in order to have those goods realised. On the one hand, God might have knowingly permitted the existence of some evil in order to allow for freedom, moral responsibility, empathy, sympathy,

8   Ibid.

benevolence, love and so forth. On the other hand, God might have knowingly risked the existence of some evil in order to allow for freedom and moral responsibility (and, perhaps, for various other goods as well).

I think that it is even more obviously true that there are limits on what an omnipotent being can do. Moreover, there are limits on what an omnipotent being can do that are relevant to Mackie's logical argument from evil. An omnipotent being cannot do the impossible: it cannot do what is logically impossible, and it cannot do what is metaphysically impossible. An omnipotent being cannot act in ways that contravene logic or mathematics or at least some parts of metaphysics. An omnipotent being cannot change the past or make it that case that $4 + 5 = 17$ or make it that case both that Vin is strictly taller than Fred and that Fred is strictly taller than Vin. If the instantiation of certain goods requires the instantiation of certain evils, then an omnipotent being cannot bring about the instantiation of those goods in the absence of instantiation of those evils. If the instantiation of certain goods requires leaving it open that certain kinds of evils are instantiated, then an omnipotent being cannot bring it about that those goods are instantiated without leaving it open that the evils are also instantiated.

Theists will typically suppose that there are certain evils that God could not have eliminated without eliminating some greater goods whose realisation depends on the realisation of the evils in question. Perhaps, for example, God could not have eliminated certain kinds of evil from our universe without thereby also eliminating freedom or moral responsibility or empathy or sympathy or benevolence or love from our universe.

Putting together the preceding threads: theists might reasonably suppose that (a) God could not have eliminated certain kinds of evil from our universe without thereby also eliminating freedom or moral responsibility or empathy or sympathy or benevolence or love from our universe; and (b) either God might have knowingly permitted the existence of some evil in order to allow for freedom, moral responsibility, empathy, sympathy, benevolence, love and so forth, or else God might have knowingly risked the existence of some evil in order to allow for freedom and moral responsibility (and, perhaps, for various other goods as well). Hence, theists have a satisfactory response to the logical argument from evil involving C1a, C1c, D1(E), Lm1 and Lm2.

Given the foregoing response, it is pretty clear that the 'official' argument of Mackie[9] is 'dead'. Theists typically do not accept Lm1

---

[9]   Ibid.

and Lm2, and reasonably so. Moreover, while the discussion in Mackie suggests – or hints at – alternative versions of datum and link, it must be observed that Mackie does not provide an *explicit* presentation of any other logical argument from evil.[10]

PLANTINGA'S FREE-WILL DEFENCE

Plantinga explicitly formulates his free-will defence as a response to logical arguments from evil in which the datum is taken to be L1(E) and the characterisation is taken to be the conjunction of C1a, C1b and C1c.[11] However, he goes on to say that 'what is really characteristic and central to the free-will defence is the claim that God, though omnipotent, could not have created just any possible world he pleased',[12] which suggests that we should also take something like C1e to be part of the characterisation. Moreover, while the initial datum that he considers is really D2E, he goes on to consider extensions of this argument in which the datum is taken to be D6E, D7E, and the conjunction of D6E and D7E.

According to Plantinga,[13] the aim of the free-will defence is to find a proposition which satisfies the following two conditions: (1) the conjunction of the proposition with the characterising claim is logically consistent and (2) the conjunction of the proposition with the characterising claim entails the datum. By Plantinga's lights, the proposition need not be known to be true or true or even plausible: all that matters is that the proposition is logically consistent with the characterising claim.[14]

I think that Plantinga's aim is misguided. As noted, any logical argument from evil contains three premises: the characterisation, the link and the datum. Moreover, corresponding to any logical argument from evil, there is a logical problem of evil generated by the (alleged) inconsistency of the characterising claim, the link and the datum. Given that the characterising claim and the datum are non-negotiable for theists, the challenge that is posed to theists is that, if there really is inconsistency, they are obliged to reject the link. If the link is something that they

---

[10]   It should be noted that the considerations rehearsed – and the conclusions reached – in this section are entirely familiar: see, for example, Alvin Plantinga, *God, Freedom and Evil* (London: Allen & Unwin, 1974).

[11]   Plantinga, *The Nature of Necessity*. He cites Mackie, Mackie, "Evil and Omnipotence"; H. Aiken, "God and Evil," *Ethics* 68 (1957–8): 77–97; J. McCloskey, "God and Evil," *Philosophical Quarterly* 10 (1960): 97–114; as well as Epicurus, Hume, some of the French Encyclopaedists, Mill, Bradley, McTaggart, 'and many others' on page 164.

[12]   Plantinga, *The Nature of Necessity*, 168.

[13]   Ibid.

[14]   Ibid., 165.

are independently inclined to accept, then it is *obviously* of no avail to note that there are other *implausible* claims that are consistent with the characterising claim and jointly entail the datum.

Think about it this way. We are supposing that {the characterising claim, the datum, the link} is logically inconsistent. That is, we are supposing that the characterising claim and the datum entail the negation of the link. Moreover, we are supposing – if only for the sake of argument – that {the characterising claim, the datum} is logically consistent: we need the link in order to have logical inconsistency. So on our assumptions, {the characterising claim, the datum, the negation of the link} is logically consistent. But then, whatever the link might be, the conditional whose antecedent is the characterising claim and whose consequent is the conjunction of the datum and the negation of the link will always be a proposition that qualifies for the role that Plantinga identifies. However, that conditional is obviously of no use to theists who suppose that it is less plausible than the link. And any theists who judge that the link is more plausible than the negation of the link will judge that this conditional is less plausible than the link (at least given that they accept that the datum is more or less certain).

Plantinga[15] claims that {C1a, C1b, C1c, D1(E)} and {C1a, C1b, C1c, D2(E)} are consistent with the further claim:

(TD) God actualises a world containing moral good, and every essence suffers from transworld depravity;

and that {C1a, C1b, C1c, D6(E)} is consistent with the further claim:

(UE) God actualises a world containing moral good, and it was not within God's power to actualise a morally better world;

and that {C1a, C1b, C1c, D7(E)} is consistent with the further claim:

(FA) God actualises a world containing moral good; all natural evil is due to the free activity of non-human persons; there is a balance of good over evil with respect to the actions of these non-human persons; and there is no world God could have created that contains a more favourable balance of good over evil with respect to the free activity of the non-human persons that it contains.

But whether these are good and effective responses to logical arguments from evil involving the characterisation and datum in question depends on whether theists can reasonably prefer (TD), (UE) and (FA) to the links that feature in those logical arguments from evil. And that's not a matter that can be assessed in the absence of serious comparison of (TD), (UE) and (FA) with those links.

The point just made has significant implications for the distinction that Plantinga[16] draws between 'defences' and 'theodicies'. In the face of a (valid) logical argument from evil, in which the characterisation and the datum are held to be non-negotiable, the theist is required to reject the link. For the theist to note that some other claim that the theist takes to be implausible is consistent with the characterising claim and jointly entails the datum – which is all that Plantinga requires of a 'defence' – is manifestly insufficient to justify the theist's rejection of the link. Of course – at least by my lights – it would be sufficient for the theist to believe that the link is false, at least given that the theist is reasonable in so believing. That the theist must be reasonable in rejecting the link need not require that the theist has a fully developed theodicy; it could be that the theist reasonably rejects the link on 'sceptical theist' grounds or the like.

To probe the weakness of Plantinga's free-will defence, it may be helpful to consider a logical argument from evil with the following premises:

C2: If God exists, God is the perfect *ex nihilo* creator of our universe.
Dp: Our universe is imperfect.
Lp1: The actions of a perfect being cannot decrease the degree of perfection of the world.
Lp2: If God exists, then, prior to all creation, the world is perfect.

In this argument, the datum is weaker than – because entailed by – D1(E). Moreover, Lp1 seems obvious: how could it be consistent with the possession of perfection that a being acts to make the world less perfect than it was previously? And Lp2 is justified by the observation that, prior to creation, the world consists of nothing but God, and God is perfect. But given C2, Dp and Lp2, we infer that, if God exists, then, post creation, the degree of perfection of the world is less than it was prior to creation. And from this claim, together with Lp1, we infer that God does not exist.

This argument has perhaps the weakest datum that can be used in a logical argument from evil, and yet it is obvious that reasons for rejecting the link in this argument cannot turn on considerations about freedom. I take it that these considerations serve to show that there is much more to be said even about logical arguments from evil with D1(E)

---

[16]   Ibid., 192.

or something weaker than D1(E) as the datum. There are theorists – for example, Gleeson[17] – who think that serious arguments from evil must appeal to horrendous evils and that there is something deeply problematic about supposing that the slightest toothache is evidence against the existence of God. But if I am right, even the slightest toothache is a *prima facie* intellectual problem for perfect-being theists.

ROWE (1979)

Rowe[18] thinks that, while Lr2 is relatively uncontroversial and accepted by most theists, Lr1 is clearly controversial and something that many theists reject. This view is borne out in the subsequent literature, most of which focuses only on Lr1.

Anticipating that the argument with Lr1 and Lr2 as link is unsuccessful as it stands, Rowe suggests an alternative argument in which Lr1 is replaced with something like:

> Lr1*: We have thus far been unable to identify any greater good that would have been lost, or any equally bad or worse evil that would have been permitted, had an omnipotent, omniscient being acted on its power to prevent the truth of the datum.

Since the characterisation, the datum and the revised link do not form – and were not taken by Rowe to form – a logically inconsistent set of claims, the revised argument is not a logical argument from evil. Discussion of this revised argument is thus beyond the scope of the present chapter (but see Oppy[19] for some of my thoughts about it).

For theists who reject Lr1 because they think that some greater good would have been lost had an omnipotent, omniscient being acted on its power to prevent the truth of the datum, there are two options which preserve consistency: either they can identify the greater good they suppose would have been lost had an omnipotent, omniscient being acted on its power to prevent the truth of the datum, or they can insist that it is perfectly reasonable to reject Lr1 even if one cannot identify the greater good that would have been lost had an omnipotent, omniscient being acted on its power to prevent the truth of the datum.

[17] A. Gleeson, *A Frightening Love: Recasting the Problem of Evil* (New York: Palgrave-Macmillan, 2012).
[18] Ibid.
[19] 'Rowe's Evidential Argument from Evil.' In *A Companion to the Problem of Evil.* Ed. J. McBrayer and D. Howard-Snyder (Malden: Wiley-Blackwell, 2013), 52–70.

A free-will response to the logical argument of Rowe[20] says that freedom is the greater good that would have been lost had an omnipotent, omniscient being acted on its power to prevent the truth of the datum. This looks wrong. On its face, the suffering of other animals has nothing to do with freedom and moral responsibility, a fact that many theists will acknowledge. Perhaps there may be *some* theists who think that the suffering of other animals, where not the result of the actions of human agents, is all due to the malicious behaviour of demons and other malevolent supernatural beings. But quite apart from the implausible and *ad hoc* nature of this hypothesis, there is an assumption here that would require further justification: namely, that the freedom of those demons and other malevolent supernatural beings suffices to justify the often excruciating suffering that other animals have experienced for at least the past two hundred million years. Could the freedom of demons and other malevolent supernatural beings really be worth that much?

We have laws which make provision for the imprisonment of people who are found guilty of inflicting pain and suffering upon other animals. That is, we are prepared to take away from people their freedom to inflict pain and suffering on other animals rather than to allow them to go on inflicting pain and suffering on other animals. The value judgment that is implicit in these laws is that the disvalue of the pain and suffering of other animals outweighs the value of the freedom to inflict that pain and suffering on other animals. But given that we make this value judgment, it seems that we are committed to the further claim that the value of the freedom of demons and other malevolent supernatural beings to inflict pain and suffering on other animals does not outweigh the disvalue of the pain and suffering of those other animals. Even if the suffering of other animals, where not the result of the actions of human agents, were all due to the malicious behaviour of demons and other malevolent supernatural beings, the logical argument of Rowe[21] would pose a challenge to theists that is not answered merely by appealing to the value of freedom.

Of course, even if I am right in claiming that a free-will response to the logical argument of Rowe is inadequate, there are still two avenues of response that remain open to theists. On the one hand, perhaps they can identify some *other* greater good that would have been lost if all suffering – or all sufficiently severe suffering – of other animals not due to the actions of human agents were prevented. And on the other hand, perhaps they can claim that, while we do not know what greater good would have been lost if all suffering – or all sufficiently severe suffering – of other animals not due to the actions of human agents were prevented, it can nonetheless be reasonably believed that there is some such greater good.

It is perhaps worth emphasising the point that even Rowe's *logical* argument from evil might properly motivate consideration of sceptical theism. If you deny Lr1, then you are committed to the claim that, were an omnipotent, omniscient being to prevent the truth of the datum, some greater good would be lost (or some evil equally bad or worse would ensue). If you cannot say what is the greater good that would be lost (or what is the evil equally bad or worse that would ensue), then it seems to me that sceptical theism is likely to be an attractive option for you. For, plausibly, you need *some* explanation of how you come to accept an existential quantification when you are not prepared to point to a witnessing instance of that existential quantification. ('There is some greater good that would be lost, were an omnipotent, omniscient being to prevent the truth of the datum.')

HORRENDOUS EVIL

Earlier, I argued that there appears to be life left in logical arguments from evil based on quite weak data (e.g. the datum that there is evil or the datum that our universe is imperfect). I now turn attention to an argument that works with much stronger data. Consider *all* of the horrendous suffering in our universe that results from the actions of human agents and *all* of the horrendous suffering in our universe that does not result from the actions of human agents. Consider *all* of the horrendous suffering caused by floods, fires, tsunamis, tornadoes, earthquakes, hurricanes, droughts, viruses and bacteria. Consider, too, *all* of the horrendous suffering caused by war, genocide, torture, rape, sexual assault and forced prostitution. Don't overlook the horrendous suffering caused by mental illness, addiction, family violence, starvation, illness, poverty, injury and on and on. In short, take as our datum (D15 & D16).

Take as our characterisation some reasonably strong claim that is accepted by perfect being theists – for example, that, if God exists, God is the omnipotent, omniscient, perfectly good, perfectly free sole creator *ex nihilo* of our universe: (C1a & C1b & C1c & C1d & C1e).

Suppose, first, that, if God is to create a universe, then God's creative act involves the selection of a universe with its entire history: there is a range of universes with complete histories that are presented to God as feasible choices, and God selects from that range. On this way of thinking about things, God knows exactly how a chosen universe will unfold

once it is selected: creation occurs with full knowledge of any horrendous evils that belong to the created universe. In this case, the intuitive
basis for a logical argument from evil is that, if no feasible universes
were non-arbitrarily better than one in which (D15 & D16) are true, then
God would choose not to create any universe. In this case (L01 & L02) is
a candidate for the link in our logical argument from evil.

Perhaps we can support this argument by drawing an analogy
between God and human parents. It seems quite compelling to think that,
if human parents had foreknowledge that, were they to have a child, their
child would be raped, tortured and murdered before the age of two, then
those human parents would choose not to have a child. How, then, could
it be acceptable for God to choose to have *lots* of children in full knowledge that they will be raped, tortured and murdered before the age of two?

Suppose, instead, that, if God is to create a universe, then God's
creative act involves only the selection of an initial stage of the universe: there is a range of initial stages of universes that are presented
to God as feasible choices, and God selects from that range. On this
way of thinking about things, at creation God has merely probabilistic
knowledge about how chosen initial stages of universes will evolve: the
evolution of universes is chancy, and not even an omniscient being can
know in advance how a chosen initial stage of a universe will develop.
This might seem to leave a loophole for God: perhaps God made a world
in which it was unlikely that (D15 & D16) would turn out to be true and
was simply the victim of incredibly bad luck.

The problem with this proposal is that it seems manifestly untrue
that it was unlikely that (D15 & D16) would turn out to be true given
that creatures capable of suffering appeared in our universe. On the contrary, even if our universe is, in some respects, chancy, it seems more or
less inevitable that, once creatures capable of suffering appeared in our
universe, something like (D15 & D16) would become true. This suggests
something like the following link:

Lq1: If an omnipotent, omniscient, perfectly good, perfectly free being
made our universe, then it made a universe in which it was near
enough to certain that the facts about the distribution of evil would
turn out as they did.

Lq2: If an omnipotent, omniscient, perfectly good, perfectly free being
makes a universe, then it does not make a universe in which it is
near enough to certain that (D15 & D16) will turn out to be true.

In this case, too, we can support the argument by drawing an analogy
between God and human parents. It seems pretty compelling to think

that, if human parents recognised that it was near enough to certain that, were they to have a child, their child would be raped, tortured and murdered before the age of two, then those human parents would choose not to have a child.

One central focus of contention between theists and their critics, in connection with these logical arguments from horrendous evil, concerns the value judgments implicit in Lo2 and Lq2. The mooted analogies notwithstanding, I take it that theists will insist that there *are* goods that outweigh the evils described in (D15 & D16). Some theists may claim that they know what these goods are; other theists will maintain that it is perhaps impossible for us to form any conception of these goods, even though we can know that there are such goods. But I do not believe that any theists could seriously suggest that considerations about *freedom* suffice to justify the evils described in (D15 & D16). When it comes to a choice between the freedom of those who would be raping, torturing and murdering young children and the protection of young children from such people, we unhesitatingly agree that those who would be raping, torturing and murdering young children may be legitimately deprived of their freedom to act in that way. Freedom just isn't worth that much.

COMPARISON WITH LOGICAL ARGUMENTS FOR THEISM

Although it may seem to be flogging a dead horse, it is, I think, worth giving some more attention to the attitude, widely shared among contemporary theists, that logical arguments from evil are 'killed' by Plantinga's free-will defence. In order to think effectively about this claim, it will be useful to take a wider perspective. Rather than focus simply on theism, we shall think about the 'contest' between theism and naturalism. In particular, we are interested in the question whether there are logical arguments that advantage one particular side in the 'contest' between theism and naturalism.

If we think about the 'contest' between theism and naturalism as a matter of theory choice, then we should see this choice as a two-stage matter. The first question to be addressed is whether either theory can be decisively knocked out of the 'contest' on *non-comparative* grounds: is one of the theories such that, either taken on its own or taken in conjunction with data, it can be shown to be logically inconsistent or probabilistically inconsistent or the like? The second question to be addressed, assuming a negative answer to the first, is whether either theory is favoured on *comparative* grounds of theoretical virtue: does one theory score better than the other on an appropriate weighting of simplicity, explanation of data, fit with other established theory, explanatory scope, predictive accuracy and so forth?

Clearly enough, logical arguments bear on the first, non-comparative, question: a successful logical argument would show that the theory it targets is either internally logically inconsistent or else logically inconsistent with data. Of course, a given logical argument will address a particular formulation of a worldview; even if a given logical argument succeeds against a particular formulation of the theoretical content of a worldview, it remains open that proponents of the worldview may produce a revised theory that is not defeated by the logical argument in question. Nonetheless, if a particular theoretical formulation is widely held, then an argument which shows that that particular formulation is internally inconsistent or inconsistent with data does give *those* proponents of the worldview some intellectual work to do (and that seems to be the most that is likely to be achieved by a logical argument in this area).

In the 'contest' between theism and naturalism, there is no dearth of logical arguments involving data. On the naturalist side, apart from logical arguments from evil, there are logical arguments from divine hiddenness, logical arguments from unbelief, logical arguments from scale, logical arguments from cosmology and so forth. On the theist side, there are logical cosmological arguments, logical teleological arguments, logical arguments from consciousness, logical arguments from reason, logical moral arguments, logical evolutionary arguments and so on.

What is the current state of play with respect to this large body of logical arguments? In particular, what is the current standing of logical arguments from evil *in comparison with* the current standing of, say, logical cosmological arguments and logical teleological arguments? Is there *more* reason to say that logical arguments from evil are 'dead' than there is to say that logical cosmological arguments and logical teleological arguments and logical moral arguments and logical evolutionary arguments are 'dead'?

Suppose we think – as many contemporary theists do – that Plantinga's free-will defence 'kills' logical arguments from evil. The take-away lesson here would have to be that, in order to defeat a logical argument in which we can distinguish between characterising claim, datum and link, it is sufficient to find a claim, no matter how implausible you take it to be, that is consistent with the characterising claim and that entails the datum.

Consider logical cosmological arguments. In order to apply the strategy of Plantinga's free-will defence, we need to divide the premises of such arguments into characterising claim, data and link.

The characterising claim in logical cosmological arguments against naturalism might be some variant of the following claim: there are none but natural causes involving none but natural entities.

The data in logical cosmological arguments against naturalism are uncontroversial claims: for example, that some things are caused; and/or that there is a sum of natural causes; and/or that things do not cause themselves.

The link in logical cosmological arguments against naturalism is the remaining premises, that is the premises that, together with the characterising claim and the data generate – or are supposed to generate – logical inconsistency. Since we shall be following the strategy of Plantinga's free-will defence, we don't need to worry about exactly what these premises are. Nonetheless, it might be useful to have a particular example in front of us. So let's suppose that we have the following argument:

1. If naturalism is true, then there are none but natural causes involving none but natural entities. (Characterisation)
2. Some things are caused. (Datum)
3. Things do not cause themselves. (Datum)
4. There are no circles of causes. (Datum)
5. There are no infinite regresses of causes. (Datum)
6. There is no more than one first cause. (Datum)
7. If there is exactly one first cause, then that first cause is not natural. (Link)
8. (Therefore) Naturalism is false (from 1–7).

Of course, not all naturalists will accept that all of 2–6 are data. However, the more that is conceded to be data, the harder it will be for naturalists to defeat the argument.

Following the strategy of Plantinga's free-will defence, all that we need to do, in order to pronounce this argument 'dead', is to find a claim that is logically consistent with the characterising claim and which entails the data. Consider the conjunction of the following set of claims: *There is a network of global natural states. These global natural states are linearly ordered under the causal relation. There is an initial global natural state that has no cause; all other global natural states are caused by prior global natural states and by nothing other than prior global natural states. Local causal relations all align perfectly with global causal relations.* Since the conjunction of this set of claims is plainly logically consistent with the characterising claim and entails all of the data, the conjunction of this set of claims satisfies the conditions that Plantinga says suffice for a defence against a logical argument. Moreover, it doesn't matter whether naturalists suppose that the conjunction of this set of claims is plausible, though it may be that many naturalists will suppose that it is.

Perhaps it might be said that Plantinga himself is no friend of logical cosmological arguments and that he might be perfectly happy to have logical cosmological arguments pronounced 'dead'. However, in Plantinga,[22] there is a sketch of a cosmological argument from contingency that looks as though it is probably a logical cosmological argument. And in any case, there are certainly *other* contemporary theists who promote logical cosmological arguments and yet who also endorse Plantinga's free-will defence against logical arguments from evil. To give just one example, in Craig and Sinnott-Armstrong,[23] Craig enthusiastically endorses Plantinga's free-will defence[24] and also enthusiastically defends the following logical cosmological argument (recast to fit the format of the present chapter):[25]

1.   If naturalism is true, then Natural Reality has no cause.
2.   Natural Reality began to exist.
3.   Whatever began to exist has a cause.
4.   [Therefore] Naturalism is not true.

No naturalists will treat both 2 and 3 as data. Perhaps some will treat neither 2 nor 3 as data. Those naturalists who treat 2 as data can observe that the claim that Natural Reality began to exist uncaused is consistent with 1 and (when conjoined with 1) entails 2. And those naturalists who treat 3 as data can observe that the claim that everything other than Natural Reality both began to exist and had a cause, while Natural Reality neither began to exist nor had a cause is consistent with 1 and (when conjoined with 1) entails 3. Again, for the purposes of defence, it doesn't matter whether naturalists suppose that the specified claims are plausible, though perhaps many naturalists will suppose that they are.

While I have only considered a couple of examples here, I think that the discussion to this point already establishes that, if it were true that

22   Alvin Plantinga, "Two Dozen (or so) Theistic Arguments." In *Alvin Plantinga*. Ed. D. Baker (Cambridge: Cambridge University Press, 2007), 203–277.
23   William Lane Craig and W. Sinnott-Armstrong, *God? A Debate between a Christian and an Atheist* (Oxford: Oxford University Press, 2004).
24   Ibid., 113.
25   Ibid., 5.

Plantinga's free-will defence 'kills' logical arguments from evil, then the general strategy of that defence, suitably redeployed, also 'kills' logical arguments from data *for* the existence of God. Those many contemporary theists who suppose both that Plantinga's free-will defence 'kills' logical arguments from evil and that there are 'live' logical arguments for theism from data are simply kidding themselves. Moreover, *this* conclusion would stand even if Plantinga's free-will defence were in good order. But in fact, as we have seen in the previous sections of this chapter, it is actually not true that Plantinga's free-will defence 'kills' logical arguments from evil. So even if there were something wrong with my claim that the strategy of Plantinga's free-will defence can be applied equally successfully to logical arguments for the existence of God, it would still be true that Plantinga's free-will defence does not 'kill' logical arguments from evil. And so for all of the considerations that have been advanced thus far, it may be that logical arguments *about* the existence of God remain 'live', or it may be that logical arguments *about* the existence of God are 'dead'.

For what it's worth, my own view – which I have argued for at length elsewhere,[26] is that, while we currently have no good reason for thinking that there are successful *logical* arguments – or successful logical arguments from data – on either side of the dispute between naturalists and theists, we also currently have no good reason for thinking that it is *impossible* that we will someday come into possession of successful logical arguments – or successful logical arguments from data – on one side in this dispute. While logical arguments about the existence of God are not dead, all of the ones that we know about show no genuine signs of life.

(* I am grateful to audiences at CSU and UQ for feedback on presentations of the ideas contained in this chapter. Special thanks to Wiley Breckenridge, Steve Clarke, Dominic Hyde, Morgan Luck, Neil Manson and Graeme McLean. *)

FURTHER READING

Beebe, James. "Logical Problem of Evil." *Internet Encyclopedia of Philosophy* www.iep.utm.edu/evil-log/, 2016.
Dougherty, Trent. "Recent Work on the Problem of Evil" *Analysis* 71 (2011): 560–73.

---

[26] Including in *Arguing about Gods* and "Über die Aussichten erfolgreicher Beweise für Theismus oder Atheismus." In *Gottesbeweise von Anselm bis Gödel.* Ed. J. Bromand and G. Kreis (Frankfurt am Main: Suhrkamp Verlag, 2011).

Mackie, J. L. *The Miracle of Theism*. Oxford: Clarendon, 1982.

McBrayer, Justin and Howard-Snyder, D. (eds.) *The Blackwell Companion to the Problem of Evil*. Malden: Wiley-Blackwell, 2015.

Oppy, Graham. "Arguments from Moral Evil." *International Journal for Philosophy of Religion* 56 (2004): 59–87.

Tooley, Michael. "Alvin Plantinga and the Argument from Evil." *Australasian Journal of Philosophy* 58 (1981): 360–76.

4 God, Evil, and the Nature of Light

PAUL DRAPER

According to one version of theism, which I will call "Theism" with a capital "T," a personal God who is all powerful, all knowing, and perfectly good created the natural world. To hope that this version of theism is true is or at least should be easy, because no being could be better positioned to promote our well-being than one that is all powerful and all knowing, and no being could care more about promoting our well-being than one that is perfectly good. To actually believe, however, that Theism is true is made more difficult for some by the fact that terrestrial lives of low quality are far from rare. Countless human beings and animals suffer from intense or prolonged physical pain, by a failure to flourish either biologically or socially, by mental and physical decay in old age, and by the tragic frustration of their hearts' desires. Are such evils strong evidence against Theism? And if they are, should we conclude that the Theistic God does not, in all likelihood, exist? Many atheists believe that the correct answer to both of these questions is "yes." It is the job of philosophers, however, to test beliefs like this by argument, whether or not they share those beliefs. One way to do that is to construct and evaluate an "evidential argument from evil" against Theism. That is my project in this chapter. In constructing such an argument, I do not seek to convince anyone that belief in God is irrational or that God does not exist or even that the Theistic God does not exist. I'm no apologist for atheism. Argument construction and evaluation is, for me, a method of philosophical inquiry, not an attempt to persuade others to share my religious beliefs or disbeliefs.

POISSON'S SPOT

I would like to begin by telling one of my favorite stories from the history of physics. I will be using elements of this story throughout this essay to help clarify by analogy a variety of points about my argument from evil. Now it might be objected that it is a bad idea to use a *physics* example to try to make one's reasoning *easier* to follow. But don't worry. The physics is theoretical, but the fun is real.[1] The story takes place in France early in the nineteenth century. At that time, not unlike now, there was disagreement about the nature of light. The dominant theory had for some time been what is usually called the corpuscular theory of light but which I will simply call "particle-ism." According to this theory, light consists solely of particles. Isaac Newton favored this theory, which may be the main reason that it was dominant, since the available evidence at the time was rather ambiguous. The second-most-popular theory at the time was what I will call "wave-ism." According to this theory, light consists solely of waves.

In the year 1818, the French Academy of Sciences held a competition, to which a wave-ist by the name of Fresnel submitted his work on diffraction. Diffraction occurs when waves bend around small objects (or spread out as they pass through openings in objects). One of the judges for the competition, a well-known scientist by the name of Poisson, was convinced that light is composed of particles, not waves. He used Fresnel's model to show that, if light did consist of waves, then one should, given the right experimental setup, expect to see a spot of light in the middle of the shadow of a small illuminated disk. Part of the reason that wave-ism predicts such a spot is that, by orienting a point light source and disk properly, one can guarantee that every point on the disk's edge is equidistant from the center of the disk's shadow and from the light source. Thus, if light consists of waves and those waves simultaneously bend around the disk, then they will arrive in phase at the center of its shadow. Because they arrive in phase, they will reinforce each other (this is called constructive interference), resulting in the bright spot. Ironically, Poisson thought he had refuted wave-ism by showing that it had this "absurd" consequence. Another judge, however, a physicist by the name of Arago, actually performed the experiment, and to Poisson's chagrin, a spot of absurd light did in fact appear in the center of the shadow just as Fresnel's model had predicted. This spot came to be known as Poisson's spot or, for those with no sense of irony, as Arago's spot. Fresnel, by the way, won the competition.

Particle-ism fits this datum very badly. (By a "datum" I mean a fact that is known to obtain or a phenomenon that is known to be real.) If light consists solely of particles, then one would expect opaque objects properly oriented relative to a light source to perfectly shade anything

---

[1]   I borrow this line from an episode of the television comedy series *The Big Bang Theory*.

directly behind them. Analogously, if someone is firing bullets at you, just stay behind a sufficiently large and strong shield and you need not worry, because bullets, being particles, will not bend around the shield and hit you. Of course, you may want to wear hearing protection, since the sound waves generated by the firing of the gun will bend around the shield and strike your ears, even if the shield itself is perfectly soundproof.

So here we have a classic case in which one theory, wave-ism, fits a datum, Poisson's spot, better than another theory, particle-ism. More specifically, it predicted that datum while particle-ism made the opposite prediction, but there's nothing special about prediction here. If the experiment had taken place before anyone had ever postulated wave-ism or even if wave-ism were formulated precisely in order to account for this datum, the datum would have favored wave-ism over particle-ism to precisely the same degree. The key is that, given our background information, we have much more reason to expect the datum in question if we assume the one theory to be true than if we assume the other theory to be true.

Notice the role of background information here. Wave-ism does not all by itself entail or even make likely the appearance of Poisson's spot. Given, however, the background information possessed by Poisson and Arago, including crucial knowledge about how particles and waves of various sorts behave and of course Fresnel's specific work on diffraction and Poisson's calculations based on that work, there is good reason to expect the spot if wave-ism is true, while it is very surprising (though not impossible) given particle-ism. In short, wave-ism fits the datum of Poisson's spot much better than particle-ism does. Further, wave-ism and particle-ism appear to make symmetrical claims of equal logical strength and coherence; so it would be hard to defend the claim that wave-ism is intrinsically less probable than particle-ism. For these reasons, particle-ists in the nineteenth century faced a serious "problem of Poisson's spot." Partly because of this problem and partly because of other similar problems, most scientists in the nineteenth century eventually abandoned particle-ism (though the theory famously made a comeback early in the twentieth century).

THE ARGUMENT

Scientific debates about the nature of light have nothing to do with the philosophical problem of evil if you focus on the subject matter of those debates but quite a bit to do with it if you focus on the structure of the reasoning in those debates. My argument from evil has a similar structure. It compares Theism to an alternative theory that I will call "source physicalism," focusing in part on which of these two theories better fits the relevant data. Here is my official statement of the argument:

1. Source physicalism is much (that is, many times) more probable intrinsically than Theism.
2. Source physicalism fits the data of good and evil much better than Theism does.
    It follows from 1 and 2 that
3. Other evidence held equal, Theism is very probably false.

Neither of the premises of this argument is obviously true. Each needs defense. In addition, an explanation of how the argument's conclusion is related logically to its two premises is needed.

Before doing all that, however, it is important to define two of the key terms in the argument, namely, "source physicalism" and "Theism." I won't abbreviate "source physicalism" as "physicalism," because philosophers generally use the term "physicalism" to abbreviate "ontological physicalism," which is the view that everything – or, to be redundant, every *existing* thing – is physical. Appearances do not universally support ontological physicalism (which is not to say that it appears to be false), because mental entities – that is, minds and things located in minds – do not appear to be physical – that is, they do not appear to be regions of space or things located in regions of space. Even if ontological physicalism is false, however, source physicalism might still be true, because it is a claim about the source of mental entities, not about their nature. Source physicalists, whether they are ontological physicalists or ontological dualists, believe that the physical world existed before the mental world and caused the mental world to come into existence, which implies that all mental entities are causally dependent on physical entities. Further, even if they are ontological dualists, source physicalists need not claim that mental entities never cause physical entities or other mental entities, but they must claim that there would be no mental entities were it not for the prior existence (and causal powers) of one or more physical entities.

The distinction between source physicalism and ontological physicalism exactly parallels another distinction, namely, one between source idealism and ontological idealism. Ontological idealism is the view that everything is mental. Once again, appearances do not universally support it (which is not to say that it appears to be false), because physical entities do not appear to be minds or things located in minds. Even if ontological idealism is false, however, source idealism might still be true, because source idealism is a claim about the source of physical entities, not about their nature. Source idealists believe that the mental world existed before the physical world and caused the physical world to come into existence. This view is consistent with both ontological idealism and ontological dualism and also with physical entities having both physical and mental effects. It entails, however, that all physical entities are, ultimately, causally dependent on one or more mental entities and so is not consistent with ontological physicalism.

Theism is a form of source idealism. It takes God to be or to have a mind and holds that God intentionally brought into existence the physical world for some purpose. Thus, according to Theism, God is a person like us. Unlike us, however, God possesses power, knowledge, and goodness perfectly or to an optimal degree, from which a further inference is made (at least implicitly) to the conclusion that God possesses them to a maximal degree. That there are maxima here is controversial, but Theists seem to be confident that there are, and so they maintain that God is omnipotent (all powerful), omniscient (all knowing), and omnibenevolent (perfectly good).

Obviously source physicalism and source idealism cannot both be true. It is at least conceivable, however, that both are false. For example, perhaps a sort of panpsychism is true according to which every existing thing (except for abstract objects if any such objects *exist*) consists of a single sort of "stuff" that has both physical and mental aspects. Or perhaps something that transcends all but our most general categories and so is neither physical nor mental is the source of both physical and mental reality. (Some theists – but not Theists with a capital "T" of course – believe that God is like this.) Or perhaps (in some very weak sense of "perhaps") eliminative physicalism or eliminative idealism is true, in which case either the mental world or the physical world doesn't even exist. Let us group together all of the possible alternatives to source physicalism and source idealism under the single banner of "otherism." Given these definitions, exactly one of source physicalism, source idealism, and otherism must be true.

INTRINSIC PROBABILITY

With this terminology in place, I am now ready to examine the first premise of my argument, which says that source physicalism is intrinsically much more probable than Theism. By way of introduction, I will return as promised to the story of Poisson's spot. Switching from actual history to hypothetical history, suppose that, faced with the problem of Poisson's spot, particle-ists at the time had expanded their theory instead of abandoning it, perhaps calling their expanded theory "particle-ism plus." This new theory, like the original one, states that light consists solely of particles, but it adds to this core theory the claim that the trajectories of those particles, unlike the trajectories of most other particles, are guided by waves. Particle-ism plus arguably fits the datum of Poisson's spot just as well as wave-ism. And since it entails particle-ism, a defense of particle-ism plus is in effect a defense of particle-ism. An interesting question, then, is this. Why didn't Poisson and other particle-ists in the early nineteenth century employ this strategy? Why should anyone back then have abandoned particle-ism given that particle-ism plus fits the datum of Poisson's spot just as well as wave-ism does?

The answer, of course, is that how well a theory fits the data is not the only thing that affects the credibility of scientific hypotheses. The probability of a theory depends not only on evidence – that is, on factors extrinsic to the theory that raise or lower its probability from some prior or initial probability – but also on intrinsic factors, factors that determine a theory's "intrinsic probability" – that is, its probability prior to all evidence. The problem with particle-ism plus is that it is intrinsically far less probable than wave-ism. But what is it about particle-ism plus that makes it less probable intrinsically than wave-ism? Two answers strike me as fairly obvious, which is not to say that they are uncontroversial.

First and foremost, particle-ism plus is much less modest than wave-ism. When I say that it is less modest, I mean that it has more "content" in the sense that it says "more" about the world that is not known by rational intuition to be true, where saying more involves making more claims or making claims that are broader in scope or that are more specific. The less one says about the world in this sense, the less room there is for error, and hence the more likely it is that what one says is true. So modesty is rather obviously a theoretical virtue: it makes a theory more likely to be true. Applying this to our theories of light, wave-ism and particle-ism are highly symmetrical. Both assert that light consists solely of one sort of entity. This suggests (and I will assume for the purposes of this chapter) that the two theories are equally modest. Particle-ism plus, however, says everything that particle-ism says and more. Thus, it is less modest than particle-ism and for that reason must be less modest than wave-ism.

A second reason that particle-ism plus is less probable intrinsically than wave-ism is that what it adds to particle-ism does not cohere very well with particle-ism. Just as a theory can fit the data to different degrees, its parts (that is, the statements it is known to entail) can fit each other to different degrees. One part of a theory can support other parts, or it can be irrelevant to other parts, or it can count against other parts. Clearly, the more coherent a theory is – the better its parts fit together – the more likely it is to be true. So coherence, like modesty, is a theoretical virtue. Again, because of their symmetry and because there is no more or less internal tension in saying that light is a particle than in saying that it is a wave, it would seem that wave-ism and particle-ism are equally coherent. But the added claim that the trajectories of light particles, unlike the trajectories of most other particles, are guided by waves does not fit well with particle-ism for two reasons. First, it postulates the existence not of more particles interacting with light particles but of waves. Second, particle-ism plus implies that, while most other particles are not guided by waves, light particles are, which introduces even more probabilistic tension into the theory. One could, of course, remove the clause about most other particles not being guided by waves, but that would just shift the problem from one of poor intrinsic fit to one of poor extrinsic fit with the datum that most other particles are not guided by waves. So the lack of coherence of particle-ism plus – the fact that its parts, though consistent with each other, don't fit together well – is another reason that it is so much less probable independent of the data than wave-ism.

Now let's use these two theoretical virtues, modesty and coherence, to compare source physicalism, source idealism, and Theism. Source physicalism and source idealism, even more than wave-ism and particle-ism, are highly symmetrical positions.[2] Both theories postulate the existence of mental and physical entities, and both assert that one of these two sorts of entities explains why there are any entities of the other sort. Further, for any position that a source physicalist takes on how the mental and physical worlds are related ontologically, there is a parallel, equally modest and equally coherent position that a source idealist might take, and vice versa. For example, while source physicalists might hold that mental entities are constituted by physical entities, source idealists might hold that physical entities are constituted by mental entities. Alternatively, both source physicalists and source

[2] This symmetry is deeper than surface grammar and invariant across perspectives. I note this because syntactical symmetry is not all that is important here (as Goodman's paradox makes clear), and sometimes symmetries considered from one (objective) perspective are asymmetries considered from another (equally objective) perspective (as Bertrand's paradox suggests).

idealists might, as I already mentioned, be mind–body dualists of various sorts. Of course, there are source idealists who are ontological physicalists about local minds including human minds but ontological dualists at a broader metaphysical level.[3] Similarly, a source physicalist might be an idealist about local physical objects, including tables and rocks and atoms, but a dualist at a broader level. I find both of these views quite strained – obviously their parts are far from a perfect fit – but the key point is that they are equally so. Neither is more or less coherent than the other. I conclude that the symmetry between source physicalism and source idealism is deep enough to justify the position that these two theories are equally modest and equally coherent.

This implies that Theism is analogous to particle-ism plus. I could even call it "source idealism plus" (but I won't). Just as particle-ism plus is much less probable intrinsically than particle-ism and so much less probable intrinsically than wave-ism, Theism is much less probable intrinsically than source idealism and so much less probable intrinsically than source physicalism. Theism is much less probable intrinsically than source idealism because it claims that source idealism is true and then adds two other claims to source idealism, namely, the claim that the mental reality responsible for the existence of physical reality is a person and the further very immodest claim that this person is omnipotent, omniscient, and omnibenevolent. Even granting that these additional claims fit well with each other and with source idealism, their specificity makes them risky even if source idealism is assumed to be true. Therefore, since source physicalism is just as probable intrinsically as source idealism, it follows that source physicalism, because of its greater modesty, is much more probable intrinsically than Theism. Figure 1 illustrates this argument. The amount of space occupied by otherism in this figure was chosen arbitrarily. It makes no difference to the argument. All that is important is that source physicalism and source idealism occupy equal amounts of space and that Theism occupies a relatively small portion of the space occupied by source idealism.

Of course, this argument for my first premise depends on the assumption that intrinsic probability depends only on modesty and coherence. This seems fairly obvious to me. If we abstract from all factors that are extrinsic to a hypothesis (e.g., all confirming and disconfirming data,

---

3   Peter van Inwagen is one notable example. He believes that God exists and that God is a nonphysical person, but he also is a physicalist about human persons. For his defense of local physicalism, see chapter 9 of his *Metaphysics*, 3rd edition (Boulder, CO: Westview Press, 2009).

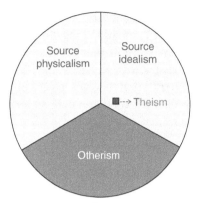

Figure 1

arguments, perceptions, etc.), focusing only on what is intrinsic to the hypothesis, then what else could its probability depend on other than how little it says and how well what it says fits together? Still, some philosophers deny this assumption, claiming either that intrinsic probability is largely subjective or that it depends primarily on how simple a theory is.4 I reject the first claim because it implies falsely that theory choice in science and elsewhere is radically subjective. I am sympathetic to the second claim because I agree that simplicity (whether understood as ontological parsimony, linguistic elegance, or intelligibility) is a theoretical virtue. This reveals no defect in my argument, however, because, as I have argued elsewhere,5 the reason that certain facets of simplicity make a theory more likely to be true is that they are either identical to or correlated with greater modesty or greater coherence.

Suppose, however, that I am wrong about that. Suppose, in other words, that intrinsic probability depends on something besides modesty and coherence. Because of the symmetry of source physicalism and source idealism, it's very unlikely that this would undermine the first premise of my argument. For example, each hypothesis is committed to the existence of both physical and mental entities and nothing else, so Occam's razor won't cut in favor of one theory over the other. In addition, neither theory can be stated more concisely than the other, so considerations of "elegance" can't be used to justify assigning one of the two

4   For a defense of the latter view, see R. Swinburne, *Epistemic Justification* (Oxford, Clarendon Press, 2001), 83–102.
5   Paul Draper, "Simplicity and Natural Theology." In *Reason and Faith: New Essays in Honor of Richard Swinburne*. Ed. M. Bergmann and J. E. Brower (Oxford University Press, 2016), 63–80.

theories a higher intrinsic probability. Thus, it is with a considerable amount of confidence that I conclude that the first premise of my argument is true. Further, the truth of that premise is itself a strong *prima facie* reason to believe that source physicalism is much more likely to be true than Theism and hence that Theism is very probably false. But this reason has nothing to do with good and evil, so let's turn to the second premise of the argument.

THE DATA OF GOOD AND EVIL

The heart of the problem of evil for Theism is very similar in structure to the heart of the problem of Poisson's spot for particle-ism. In both cases, at least one serious alternative theory (where seriousness depends in part on relative intrinsic probability) fits a certain body of data far better. In the case of particle-ism, the relevant alternative was, at least in France in 1818, wave-ism, and the datum in question was Poisson's spot. In the case of Theism, that alternative is source physicalism, and the data in question are the data of good and evil. By the "data of good and evil" I mean to include a variety of known facts about the quality of the lives led by human beings and any other living things capable of being benefited or harmed from their own internal point of view. I do not mean to include information about the existence or nature of the living things on earth or about the various conditions that make life of that sort possible in the first place. Such information should not be ignored in evaluating premise 2 of my argument. But it has the status of background information rather than evidence. Treated as evidence, it is relevant to the issue of how significant the conclusion of the argument is, including as it does the clause "other evidence held equal." Even with these restrictions on what counts as part of the data of good and evil, my space in this chapter is too limited to discuss all of those data. I will, however, discuss three very important sets of facts, one about (physical) pleasure and pain, one about flourishing and languishing, and one about what Eleonore Stump has called the "desires of the heart."[6] Premise 2 of my argument from evil should be interpreted as the claim that source physicalism fits these particular facts much better than Theism does. In other words, we have much more reason to expect these facts to obtain if we assume that source physicalism is true than if we assume that Theism is true.

---

[6] E. Stump, *Wandering in Darkness: Narrative and the Problem of Suffering* (Oxford: Oxford University Press, 2010). See especially chaps. 11 and 14.

To see that this is so, imagine two alien beings much like us in intellectual ability and gradually learning everything we know (and nothing more) about our biosphere. To make them even more similar to us, let us also suppose that these two beings know as little about themselves as possible and don't take into account what they do know when they engage in theoretical reasoning. One of these alien beings is named Sophy, spelled S-o (which is the first two letters of "source") p-h-y (which is the first three letters of "physicalism"); Sophy, surprise surprise, is convinced that source physicalism is true. The other alien is Theo. Theo, of course, is equally confident that Theism is true. Having already acquired a great deal of information about Earth and its inhabitants, Sophy and Theo begin to acquire the data of good and evil. As these data slowly trickle in, Sophy and Theo quite reasonably form different expectations based on their respective worldviews about what they will soon learn about the conscious beings that they already know to exist on Earth. I contend that Sophy's expectations will be confounded much less often and much less severely than Theo's. One reason for this – the only reason I will emphasize in this book – is that the assumption that Theism is true, unlike the assumption that source physicalism is true, undermines certain inferences based on background information that Sophy and Theo share.

The first set of facts I intend to discuss concerns, as I said, pleasure and pain.[7] After learning that human beings and some other animals feel (physical) pain and pleasure, Sophy and Theo may consider the question of what role pain and pleasure play in the lives of human beings and animals. Having previously learned that many other parts of living organisms play a biological role – they systematically promote survival and reproduction – Sophy may expect to learn, or at least not be surprised to learn, that pain and pleasure play a similar role, especially since they are so well suited to function in that way. Theo has much less reason to make such a prediction. He will note that pain and pleasure have a special sort of moral significance that other parts of organic systems do not have. There is good reason for Sophy to ignore this difference, to regard it as an irrelevant dissimilarity when she reasons analogically about what role pain and pleasure are likely to play in the world. Theo, however, believes in a perfectly good God, a powerful and wise God who presumably cares about the happiness of his creatures. Thus, he should not be confident at all

[7] For a much more detailed discussion of these facts than is possible here, see my "Pain and Pleasure: An Evidential Problem for Theism," *Nous* 23 (1989): 331–50.

that the moral difference between pain and pleasure on the one hand and other parts of living things on the other is not important. Because of this difference, Theo will reason, God might very well treat pain and pleasure differently from other parts of organic systems. So Theo has much less reason than Sophy to expect to learn that pain and pleasure play the biological role that in fact it turns out they do play. Further, given that human beings are moral agents, Theo no doubt has some reason to expect pain and pleasure to play some systematic and discernible moral role in human lives. While they certainly do play a moral role, it is so far as we can tell hardly a systematic one. For example, pain and pleasure do not systematically function as punishment and rewards promoting the moral goal of justice. Nor do they systematically promote moral or spiritual development. Sophy, by contrast, expects to find and does in fact find that the rain on the planet Earth falls on both the just and the unjust and that pain and pleasure are for the most part incompetent moral trainers and spiritual guides, and not just because people freely resist such training and guidance.

Of course, facts about physical pleasure and pain hardly settle the issue of whether source physicalism or Theism is a better fit with the data of good and evil. For it is possible to suffer much from physical pain and still flourish, and it is also possible to suffer little, feel much physical pleasure, and yet never flourish. Thus, we may suppose that, after Sophy and Theo learn a great deal about the distribution of pain and pleasure on earth, they still do not yet know anything substantive about how flourishing and languishing are distributed among the sentient beings in the world. We may also suppose that, prior to learning anything about that, they learn that very many plants die before they ever have a chance to flourish, that very many others languish for much or all of their lives, and that even plants that flourish for much of their lives eventually wither and die. They then consider the question of whether the sentient beings on earth (including of course human beings) suffer the same fate as plants. Is death at a very young age common? Do very many animals barely survive, languishing for most or all of their lives? Do the ones that manage to flourish for a time still face decay and death in old age?

Being a source physicalist and (like Theo) seeing a connection between these ecological facts and the operation of natural selection, Sophy expects to learn that the answers to these questions are all "yes." Of course, there is an interesting moral difference between plants and conscious animals, since the latter, unlike the former, can be made worse off from their own internal point of view; and when Sophy reasons analogically from facts about plants to the likelihood of similar facts obtaining in the case of animals, she will ask herself whether her inference is undermined by this difference. In other words, does she have any reason to believe that this dissimilarity between conscious animals and plants is a relevant one? Because she is a source physicalist, she will with good reason answer this question negatively. For relative to source physicalism combined with all of the information Sophy and Theo already have about the physical (and mental) world, there is no good reason to believe that terrestrial evolution is guided or that it is sensitive to moral considerations.

Theo's Theism, on the other hand, gives him substantial *prima facie* reason to believe that these dissimilarities are relevant; for he believes that the ultimate cause of evolution and of all ecological, botanical, and zoological facts is an omnipotent, omniscient, and omnibenevolent God. Such a God, being omniscient, would be well aware that flourishing in the biological sense can benefit some animals (but no plants), and languishing can harm them. Being omnipotent, such a being would be as well positioned as possible to ensure, either by directly intervening in the world or by manipulating the laws and initial conditions of the universe, that all or almost all sentient animals flourish for at least most if not all of their lives. And being omnibenevolent, such a being would, other moral considerations held equal, want such beings to flourish. So Theo, if he is reasonable, will regard the analogical reasoning that Sophy used when she inferred that sentient life fares no better than nonsentient life to be virtually worthless. Clearly he would be foolish to believe that what he knows about plants provides significant support for the prediction that large numbers of conscious animals either die young or survive but languish for most or all of their lives. Notice that my argument here assumes the truth of experientialism, which is the view that only conscious beings have moral standing because only they can be literally benefited or harmed – that is, made better or worse off from their own internal point of view. If this assumption is correct (and the vast majority of moral philosophers believe it is), then one important objection to my argument fails, namely, the objection that if God has a moral justification for allowing many plants to languish (which he must if Theism is true and many plants do in fact, as Theo knows, languish), then it is likely that God also has a moral justification for allowing many animals to languish.

Of course, Theo recognizes that both his knowledge of possible goods and evils and his knowledge of entailment relations between goods and evils are very limited. Thus, he realizes that there might be moral reasons unknown to him for the Theistic God he believes in to bring about a biosphere in which virtually all conscious beings feel a significant amount of physical pain and in which many conscious beings fail to flourish and so fail to achieve one of the goods for which they appear to be designed. He also recognizes, however, that he has at least as much reason to believe that God would have reasons *unknown* to him *not* to create a world of that sort. Thus, it is the known reasons that must break the tie,[8] and those are reasons to create an animal world in which physical pain is rare and in which extended flourishing is the rule rather than the exception. So even though Theo is not sure what his God will do, he certainly cannot simply dismiss as irrelevant either the moral differences between pain (or pleasure) and other parts of organic systems or the moral differences between conscious animals and nonconscious living things; but this means that he should not be even close to as confident as Sophy is in the relevant analogical arguments that Sophy uses to make her predictions. Of course, the conclusions of those arguments are true. So when the relevant data comes in, Sophy will turn to Theo and say, "See? I told you so. Source physicalism fits this body of data much better than Theism does." A bit snotty, perhaps, but logic and reason are on her side.

Theo, however, may not yet be convinced. In fact, the poor performance of his theory thus far may make him more confident than ever that a third set of facts will at least partially redeem him. For even someone who never flourishes in the biological sense and who suffers greatly from physical pain might still obtain the desires of their heart – the things they want most of all from life. Even though Theo has by now inferred from Theism and the data he has thus far obtained that God has morally good reasons to permit great evils like intense pain and chronic poor health, he still has much more reason than Sophy has to be optimistic about the balance of good and evil in this third dimension of value. For satisfying one's heart's desires increases well-being, at least other factors held equal, and the assumption that God, who (being morally perfect) has a *pro tanto* desire to increase our well-being, has unknown good reasons not to prevent the pain and languishing we observe in the

---

[8]   It is important to keep in mind that Theo is making predictions here. Once he acquires the relevant data, he may, *if* he has inferential or noninferential evidence for Theism that makes Theism probable in spite of my argument (and other reasons to believe that Theism is false), reasonably infer from the evils in the world and the failure of theodicy that God has unknown reasons to permit those evils. This is why the conclusion of my argument includes the clause "other evidence held equal."

world does not make it likely that God has unknown reasons to allow desires of the heart to be routinely frustrated. Imagine Theo's surprise, then, when the data once again confound his expectations and he learns that, when it comes to the desires of the heart, tragedy and heartbreak are more common on earth than triumph and the fulfillment of one's dreams and aspirations.

THEODICIES AND SKEPTICAL THEISM

At this point, Theo may be experiencing a significant amount of cognitive dissonance, which he will, if he is psychologically similar to human beings, try to reduce, most likely in one of at least two ways. First, he might construct theodicies – that is, he might try to formulate auxiliary hypotheses about God's purposes and how their accomplishment allegedly depends on God's allowing evil. The goal here is to boost Theism's fit with the data, which is a perfectly reasonable project unless of course Theo biases his inquiry by seeking only auxiliary hypotheses that boost Theism's fit with the data and not also hypotheses that reduce it or that boost (or reduce) source physicalism's fit with the data. (Fortunately, knowing Theo like I do, I'm sure he would never be as one sided as human theodicists seem to be.) Second, if he (correctly) comes to believe that all of his efforts at theodicy are, to quote Alvin Plantinga, "shallow, tepid, and ultimately frivolous,"[9] he may be tempted by the idea that, given how little we know about what goods and evils there are and what logical relations goods and evils bear to each other, we can't really judge how well or poorly Theism fits the data of good and evil, and so we can't really judge that source physicalism fits those data better than Theism does. If he likes oxymorons, he might even call his new position "skeptical Theism."[10]

Switching stories, notice that particle-ists in the nineteenth century could have made a similar skeptical move in response to the problem of

---

[9] Alvin Plantinga, "Epistemic Probability and Evil." In *The Evidential Argument from Evil*. Ed. D. Howard-Snyder (Bloomington: Indiana University Press), 70. Plantinga says here only that "most" theodicies strike him this way. He now defends a theodicy of his own.

[10] I coined the term "skeptical theism" in my 1996 paper, "The Skeptical Theist." In *The Evidential Argument from Evil*. Ed. Howard-Snyder (Indianapolis, IN: Indiana University Press, 1996), 175–92. I did not, of course, invent the position, nor did I defend it. My 1996 paper was primarily a response to Peter van Inwagen's version of skeptical theism. See his "The Problem of Evil, the Problem of Air, and the Problem of Suffering." In *The Evidential Argument from Evil*, 151–74.

Poisson's spot. After failing at the project of particlodicy, they might have defended skeptical particle-ism, claiming that we know so little about what physical forces there are and how they might affect the trajectory of light particles that we can't really judge whether or not or how well particle-ism fits the datum of Poisson's spot, and thus there is no good reason to believe that wave-ism fits that datum better than particle-ism does. Indeed, I recently discovered the writings of a nineteenth-century Spanish physicist who defended precisely this position. His name was Pedro van Outwagen. (Yes, I know, I too was surprised to learn that "van Outwagen" is a Spanish surname.) Van Outwagen claimed that, for all we know now (remember van Outwagen was writing in the nineteenth century), particle-ism plus is true and if it is true, then particle-ism does predict the datum of Poisson's spot after all; so for all we know, particle-ism fits the datum of Poisson's spot just as well as wave-ism does. In addition, a contemporary of van Outwagen's named Esteban Lykstra (also a Spaniard, strangely enough) reasoned that, if there is some physically sufficient reason why light, in spite of its corpuscular nature, bends around the edges of objects, then given the current state of physical science, it is not likely that we would know what that reason is. Lykstra concluded in his original paper on this topic that Poisson's spot is no evidence at all against particle-ism. In his later work, he only denied that it is *serious* evidence against particle-ism.

Skeptical particle-ism is mistaken for multiple reasons. Van Outwagen erred by confusing "epistemic" fit, which is relative to one's current evidential situation, with some absolute notion of fit. Lykstra made a less subtle mistake, one that devout particle-ists repeated *ad nauseam* for decades after he made it. From the fact that, if particle-ism were true, we would be unlikely to know the reason why light particles bend around the edges of objects, all that follows is that our ignorance of that reason (that is, the failure of the project of particlodicy) is not strong evidence against particle-ism. It does not follow that the datum of Poisson's spot itself is not strong evidence against particle-ism.

Transferring these points to skeptical Theism, even if Peter van Inwagen is right that we can tell an epistemically possible story in which God allows the evils we find in the world, it hardly follows that for all we know Theism fits – in the relevant *epistemic* sense of "fit" – the data of evil as well as source physicalism does.[11] Unless such a story is, *independent of our knowledge of the data of good and evil*, sufficiently likely given Theism, it will not undermine the second premise

---

[11]   P. Van Inwagen, *The Problem of Evil* (Oxford: Oxford University Press, 2006).

of my argument.[12] Further, from the alleged fact that, even if there were good reasons for a Theistic God to create a world like ours, we wouldn't expect to know what they are, all that follows is that our ignorance of those reasons (that is, the failure of the project of theodicy) is not strong evidence against Theism. It obviously does not follow that the evils themselves are not strong evidence against Theism, contrary to what Stephen Wykstra and many other philosophers of religion have been claiming for more than a quarter of a century.[13]

THE INFERENCE

Part of the idea of my argument is that the probability of a theory being true, whether that theory is scientific or historical or metaphysical, depends in part on how well it fits the data and in part on its intrinsic probability. Fit with data is a matter of how likely or expectable or predictable a theory makes that data (or would make it in the right sort of idealized circumstances). Intrinsic probability is a function of modesty and coherence. Frequently there is tension between intrinsic probability and fit with data: one is often forced to choose between two theories, one of which is intrinsically more probable and the other of which fits the data better. This is inevitable, since by complicating a theory and thus making it less modest (and perhaps less coherent as well), it can often be made to fit the data.

The two premises in my argument claim that, when we compare source physicalism and Theism in light of the data of good and evil, we have a rare case in which one theory, source physicalism, has a large advantage both in fit with a significant body of data and in probability

---

[12]   The failure to meet this standard is one of the reasons that Eleonore Stump's theodicy, for example, fails to undermine my argument. See her *Wandering in Darkness* and my critical study of that book in *Notre Dame Philosophical Reviews*, 2011.

[13]   Wykstra makes this mistake in the final section of his important essay, "The Humean Obstacle to Evidential Arguments from Suffering: On Avoiding the Evils of 'Appearance,'" *International Journal for Philosophy of Religion* 16 (1984), 73–93. I point out and explain this mistake in "Confirmation Theory and the Core of CORNEA." In *Skeptical Theism: New Essays.* Ed. T. Dougherty and J. P. McBrayer (Oxford: Oxford University Press, 2014), 132–41. Wykstra now recognizes his mistake, defending a new version of skeptical Theism to deal with arguments like mine: see Timothy Perrine's and his "Skeptical Theism, Abductive Atheology, and Theory Versioning." In *Skeptical Theism.* Eds. Dougherty and McBrayer (Oxford: Oxford University Press, 2014), 142–63. This new version, however, is no more successful than the old version, or so I argue in "Meet the New Skeptical Theism, Same as the Old Skeptical Theism." *Skeptical Theism* Eds. Dougherty and McBrayer (Oxford: Oxford University Press, 2014), 164–77.

independent of data. In technical terms, this is called the "wow factor" of my argument. The upshot is that we have an unusually strong reason to believe that source physicalism is much more likely to be true than Theism. But it is only a *prima facie* reason. For we have other data besides the data of good and evil that must be taken into account, and what's more, it is at least possible that the probabilities of source physicalism and Theism, perhaps unlike many scientific theories, depend on more than just fit with data and intrinsic probability. This is why the conclusion of my argument includes the clause "other evidence held equal." By "evidence," I mean anything extrinsic to a theory (experiences, arguments, known facts, etc.) that raises or lowers the probability of that theory.

Again, consider the case of Poisson's spot. Even if wave-ism fits the datum of Poisson's spot much better than particle-ism does and is also just as probable intrinsically as particle-ism, it doesn't follow that wave-ism is more probable, all things considered, than particle-ism, because there are other data to be considered besides Poisson's spot, including data about shadows, reflection, refraction, and so on. Indeed, a serious blow came to wave-ism in the early twentieth century when Einstein showed that, if light is made up of photons (which qualify as particles in a broad sense), then the photoelectric effect could be explained. This was a victory for particle-ism over wave-ism, though scientists ultimately rejected both theories in favor of a third theory that attributes some sort of wave–particle duality to light and to other physical things as well.

Similarly, before we can conclude that Theism is very probably false or even that it is probably false, we need to compare how well Theism and source physicalism fit other data besides the data of good and evil. For example, it might be argued that Theism, unlike source physicalism, fits well with data like consciousness, libertarian free will, and deontic (as opposed to merely evaluative) moral facts. I believe that some of this evidence does favor Theism over source physicalism but that, once undercutting defeaters and additional evidence favoring source physicalism over Theism are taken into account, no significant overall advantage for Theism remains.

Also motivating the "other evidence held equal" clause in the conclusion of my argument is the fact that some philosophers deny that intrinsic probability and fit with data are the only factors affecting the probabilities of Theism and its alternatives. So-called Reformed epistemologists, for example, claim that we have a special cognitive faculty called a *sensus divinitatis* that gives some of us direct evidence for God's existence. Indeed, some Reformed epistemologists (e.g. Alvin Plantinga) believe that, for a number of lucky epistemic elites, that evidence is so powerful that it overwhelms any advantage in intrinsic probability and fit with data that source physicalism has over Theism, even if that advantage is large.

While I find the assertion that all of this is true as opposed to just true for all we know epistemically reckless, Reformed epistemologists are certainly correct that direct or noninferential evidence can be very powerful. Also, if cognitive scientists of religion are to be believed, forming beliefs about invisible agents including gods is very natural for human beings in certain common circumstances. We tend to form such beliefs instinctively, without inferential evidence, and our tendency to do so is not culture specific but species specific, contrary to what most social scientists seem to believe. Obviously, we have no similar tendency to form the belief that light consists solely of particles. So we should take the Reformed epistemologist's appeal to a *sensus divinitatis* more seriously than we would take a particle-ist's appeal to a *sensus illuminatis*.

Still, there are at least three good reasons to doubt that Reformed epistemology solves the problem of evil. First, an inclination to believe in some sort of god or gods is not an inclination to believe in the God of Theism. This doesn't show that such an inclination doesn't support Theism over source physicalism, but it limits how strong that support can be. Second, even if the inclination to form beliefs about gods in certain circumstances is widespread, it is not close to as strong or as universal as the inclination to form beliefs about the past or about physical objects or about other human minds. (Indeed, in many cases, it merely causes theists to consciously entertain beliefs about God that they already have.) This renders doubtful the Reformed epistemologists' claim that many Theists have *very strong* offsetting evidence supporting Theism. Third, even if everything Reformed epistemologists say about the *sensus divinitatis* were correct, it would be a mistake to conclude categorically that my argument from evil is unsound, because the probabilities in my argument are relative to evidential situations. Thus, my argument might still establish its conclusion relative to the evidential situations of those of us who do not have a properly functioning *sensus divinitatis*, and this includes, I think most Reformed epistemologists would be willing to grant, many Theists as well as non-Theists. Those engaged in the sort of philosophical inquiry in which I am engaged may find the claims of others to have special faculties or ways of knowing interesting, but, lacking evidence for those claims, they will not find them relevant or useful. After all, if one is trying to determine by philosophical inquiry whether or not God exists, then it does not help to learn that *if* God exists, then some people probably have a special faculty that enables them to know he does.

I draw two conclusions in this chapter. First, if additional evidence does not on the whole favor Theism over source physicalism, then premises 1 and 2 of my argument establish that source physicalism is *much* more probable than Theism. This does not imply that source physicalism is probably true, but it does imply that Theism is *very* probably false. Second, even if additional evidence on the whole favors Theism but fails to favor it *strongly*, then my premises still show that Theism is *probably* false.

FURTHER READING

On evidential arguments from evil:

Tooley, Michael. "The Problem of Evil." *The Stanford Encyclopedia of Philosophy* (Fall 2015 Edition), Edward N. Zalta (ed.), http://plato.stanford.edu/archives/fall2015/entries/evil/.

On theodicies:

Collins, Robin. "The Connection-Building Theodicy," in *The Blackwell Companion to the Problem of Evil*, ed. Justin P. McBrayer and Daniel Howard-Snyder. Hoboken, NJ: John Wiley & Sons, Inc., 2015, 222–35.
Swinburne, Richard. *Providence and the Problem of Evil*. Oxford: Clarendon Press, 1998.

On skeptical theism:

Bergmann, Michael. "Skeptical Theism and the Problem of Evil," in *The Oxford Handbook of Philosophical Theology*, ed. Thomas P. Flint and Michael Rea. New York: Oxford University Press, 2008, 374–402.
Draper, Paul. "The Limitations of Pure Skeptical Theism," *Res Philosophica* 90 (2003): 97–111.

5 Skeptical Theism

TIMOTHY PERRINE AND STEPHEN J. WYKSTRA

Skeptical theism emerged in the 1980s in response to the *evidential* problem of evil, itself emerging out of the apparent collapse of the *logical* problem of evil.[1] While the seeds of evidential arguments can be found in Hume's *Dialogues*, they were brought into the limelight by the pioneering work of the late William Rowe and Paul Draper. But these sophisticated formulations of evidential atheological arguments gave rise – and continue to give rise – to "skeptical theistic responses" by William Alston, Michael Bergmann, Daniel Howard-Snyder, Alvin Plantinga, Peter van Inwagen, Stephen Wykstra, and others.

The dialectic between evidential atheology and skeptical theism, because of its ever-increasing connections to other perplexing issues in mainstream philosophy, has become a rich and lively one. With limited space, our aim is to pinpoint the key ways in which skeptical theists have sought to defuse the evidential arguments from evil, to spotlight problems central to current debates among philosophers of religion, bringing out how these intertwine with issues within mainstream philosophy, and to offer some new ideas, including a proposal for taking skeptical theism into new waters of "constructive worldview theorizing."[2]

---

[1] This paper is fully coauthored, with last names listed alphabetically.

[2] Existential, Biblical, and theological roots of skeptical theism are explored in Stephen J. Wykstra, "A Skeptical Theist View" and "The Skeptical Theist Response," in Chad Meister and James K. Drew Jr., eds., *God and the Problem of Evil: Five Views* (Downer Grove, IL: IVP Academic, 2017), 99–127, 173–184. Noteworthy here are writings of Nicholas Wolterstorff following the death of his son Eric in a climbing accident. He writes, "Job's friends tried out on him their explanations...I have read the theodicies to justify the ways of God to man. I find them unconvincing. To the most agonized question I have ever asked, I do not know the answer. I do not know why God watched him fall. I do not know why God would watch me wounded. I cannot even guess...." Nicholas Wolterstorff, *Lament for a Son* (Grand Rapids: Eerdmans Publ. Co., 1987). For his further reflections, see Nicholas Wolterstorff, *Inquiring about God*. Ed. Terence Cuneo (Cambridge: Cambridge University Press, 2010).

THE CORE CLAIMS OF SKEPTICAL THEISM

Skeptical theism – like the evidential problem of evil to which it responds – comes in many versions, with many roots. We propose that two core claims form the root of all lines of the family tree:

(I) *The Core Conditional:* If the theistic God does exist, then very likely there is a divine–human gap such that we humans should, for many evils in our world, not expect to grasp the divine purposes and reckonings behind God's allowing these evils.

And:

(II) *The Core Implication:* The *Core Conditional* entails the failure of a variety of important antitheistic evidential arguments from evil.

Various skeptical theists take these core claims in different directions, reflecting both their varying philosophical orientations and the variety of atheological arguments being targeted. Before looking at the differences, however, we underscore three points.

First, the *Core Conditional* is *not* seen by skeptical theists as precluding knowledge (or reasonable belief) of God's existence, attributes, or capacity for self-revelation to humans in a way suited to their capacities. It is seen as expressing a *conditional epistemic humility* about the scope of our grasp of God's cosmic purposes and plans. For if God exists, we should not expect to grasp more than a small *fraction* of either the goods which lead God to act as God acts (including divine acts of allowing evil) or the constraints that make such divine allowings needful. A corollary of this conditional epistemic humility is that even if God were to exist, we nevertheless should not expect to be able to fully explain or predict anywhere near all the features of good and evil in the world around us.

Regarding the second core claim – *Core Implication* – we stress that skeptical theism is fully compatible with affirming that *some* features of evil in our world decrease to *some* extent the probability or reasonableness of theism.[3] What is essential to contemporary skeptical theism is

[3]   Construing skeptical theism as this stronger claim is not baseless, as it can be found in skeptical-theist writings (cf. Stephen J. Wykstra, "The Humean Obstacle to Evidential Arguments from Suffering: On Avoiding the Evils of 'Appearance.'" *International Journal for Philosophy of Religion* 16.2 (1984): 73–93; Daniel Howard-Snyder and Michael Bergmann, "Evil Does Not Make Atheism More Reasonable Than Theism." In *Contemporary Debates in the Philosophy of Religion*. Ed. Michael L. Peterson and Raymond J. VanArragon (Cambridge: Blackwell Publishing, 2004, 13–25). But we see it as limit-theses not universally accepted, cf. Stephen J. Wykstra, "Rowe's Noseeum

the claim that "conditional epistemic humility" takes the steam out of many evidential arguments from evil against theism on offer.

Taken together, we note, the two core claims suggest that the label "skeptical theism" is a misnomer.[4] As conditionals, both claims can be fully embraced not only by theists but by atheists, agnostics, pantheists, panentheists, and all manner of nontheists. Moreover, there's nothing especially "skeptical" about epistemic humility. As even Dirty Harry Callahan had to regularly if unsuccessfully remind himself, "a man's got to know his limits."

THE VARIETIES OF SKEPTICAL THEISM

CORNEA–Based Skeptical Theism

In the contemporary literature, an early version of skeptical theism was Wykstra's "CORNEA" response to William Rowe's 1979 paper that opened the floodgates of evidential arguments from evil. Rowe's case culminates in a two-premise argument that, slightly simplified, goes like this:

> *Rowe-1:* If God exists, then God will prevent any instance of intense suffering unless doing so would lose some greater good (or permit some evil equally bad or worse).[5]
>
> *Rowe-2:* There exist instances of intense suffering the divine allowing of which do not serve any God-justifying good.
>
> *Rowe-3:* Therefore, God does not exist.[6]

This argument is deductively valid. What makes the case "evidential" is Rowe's way of supporting the second premise. (Rowe sees Rowe-1 as a conceptual truth on which theists and nontheists should agree.[7]) Rowe here relies on the story – one he takes to have prolific

Arguments from Evil." In *The Evidential Argument from Evil*. Ed. Daniel Howard-Snyder (Bloomington: Indiana University Press, 1996), 137.

[4]   Cf. Daniel Howard-Snyder, "Epistemic Humility, Arguments from Evil, and Moral Skepticism." *Oxford Studies in Philosophy of Religion*. Ed. Jonathan Kvanvig (Oxford: Clarendon Press, 2009), 20.

[5]   For simplicity's sake, we omit this last disjunct in what follows.

[6]   William Rowe, "The Problem of Evil and Some Varieties of Atheism." *American Philosophical Quarterly* 16.4 (1979): 335–41.

[7]   Though many theists accept Rowe's claim, there's a lively dispute over what could be a God-justifying good, specifically, the relationship between a God-justifying good and the person who suffers for it. See Marilyn McCord Adams, *Horrendous Evils and the Goodness of God* (Ithaca, NY: Cornell University Press, 1999) and the resulting literature for discussion.

instantiations – of a fawn who, burned in a forest fire, perishes after days of agonizing pain. Rowe's argument – FAWN, we'll call it – goes like this:

> *Fawn-1*: No matter how hard we look, we *see no* God-justifying purpose served by this suffering;
> *Fawn-2*: Hence, it appears that there is *no* good that would justify God in allowing this evil.
> *Fawn-3*: Hence, probably there *is no* good that would so justify God.

Rowe urged that FAWN, coupled with its multiple realizations in our world, gives us good inductive reason for accepting his crucial second premise and thus Rowe-3 as well.

Fawn-2, Wykstra argued, uses "appear" in an epistemic sense, meaning (roughly) that barring defeaters, it is reasonable to believe the clause following "appears." Wykstra thus analyzed the logic of epistemic "appears" claims and proposed an evidential norm for evaluating such claims – dubbing that norm by the unprincipled acronym CORNEA, the *"Condition Of ReasoNable Epistemic Access"*:

> On the basis of cognized situation s, human H is entitled to claim "it appears that p" only if it is reasonable for H to believe that given her cognitive faculties and the use she has made of them, if p were not the case, s would likely be different than it is in some way discernible by her.[8]

CORNEA, Wykstra argued, helps diagnose fallacies in inferences involving appears-claims. Imagine a doctor who, after close visual inspection of a hypodermic needle picked up off the floor, reports

> *Germ-1*: I see no viruses or germs on the needle.

On this basis, the doctor then asserts

> *Germ-2*: It appears that there are no germs on this needle.

And from this concludes that

> *Germ-3*: Probably, there are no germs on the needle.

Wykstra sees Germ-2 as overstepping and uses CORNEA to challenge the move from Germ-1 to Germ-2. By CORNEA, Germ-1 entitles the doctor to assert Germ-2 only if it is reasonable for her to believe:

> If there were germs on the needle, the doctor's perceptual experience (or "cognized situation") would likely be different than it is.

---

[8]   Wykstra, "The Humean Obstacle," 85.

But this is clearly not reasonable for her to believe given the limits of unaided human visual perception. While entitled to say that she *sees no* germs, she is not – by CORNEA – entitled to infer the appears claim. Her visual evidence is, after all, just what she should expect if there *were* germs on it.

CORNEA gives exactly the right verdict in this and many other cases; Rowe thus wholeheartedly endorsed it. The issue is then what verdict it yields when applied to FAWN-2. In his application, Wykstra's distinctive moves are prototypical of skeptical theism. Is it at all reasonable to think that if there were a justifying good for a particular evil, then we would likely discern it? In answering this question, Wykstra claims that the outweighing good at issue here is

> ... of a special sort: one purposed by the Creator of all that is, whose vision and wisdom are therefore somewhat greater than ours. How much greater? A modest proposal might be that his wisdom is to ours, roughly as an adult human's is to a one-month old infant's ...

Wykstra then joins this with CORNEA, using a parent/child analogy:

> But if outweighing goods of the sort at issue exist in connection with instances of suffering, that we should discern most of them seems about as likely as that a one-month old should discern most of his parents' purposes for those pains they allow him to suffer – which is to say, it is not likely at all.[9]

But this means that Rowe's FAWN argument (and with it his main argument) fails, for we are – by CORNEA – not entitled to Fawn-2: "it *appears* that there is no good that would justify God in allowing this evil" and thus not entitled to Rowe-2. If we shouldn't expect to see the justifying good even if it is there – if our failure to see it is pretty much what we'd expect if it were there – then not seeing such goods doesn't warrant us in claiming that the goods do not appear to be present.[10]

Representativeness-Based Skeptical Theism

While not conceding that theism itself implies so unfavorable an estimate of our ability to discern outweighing divine goods, Rowe bypassed the subtleties of the "appears" idiom by shifting to a more plainly

[9]   Ibid., 88.
[10]   Ibid., 89.

inductive formulation.[11] Just as it is reasonable to inductively infer from "all iron we've observed does not float in water" to "all iron does not float in water," so also, Rowe claimed, we can reasonably make the following inference:

> *Inductive-1:* No good we know of justifies God in permitting E1 and E2.
>
> *Inductive-2:* Therefore, it is probable that no good at all justified God in permitting E1 and E2.

(where "E1" and "E2" designate two horrific evils). Combing these claims with his earlier conceptual principle that God will prevent any instance of intense suffering unless doing so would lose some greater good, we again get the conclusion that it is probable that God does not exist.[12]

Focusing on the inference from Inductive-1 to Inductive-2, William Alston and Michael Bergmann urged that the inductive strength of that inference depends heavily on whether we can be reasonably confident that our premise reflects testing of a "representative sample" of Xs of the entire population of Xs.[13] Whether our confidence is well placed or ill placed will often depend on what *sort* of thing Xs are and how much we know about them. For example, if we do not know whether some chemical element (say, carbon) has allotropes, then we may not be well placed even to judge whether our sample from the carbon population contains a sufficient variety of cases to be deemed representative of *all* carbon – and so to infer a conclusion like "Probably, all carbon is soft."

With this point in hand, Alston and Bergmann argue that Rowe's inference from Inductive-1 to Inductive-2 is defective. Bergmann,[14] specifically, advocates for these two theses:

> (ST1): We have no good reason for thinking that the possible goods we know of are representative of the possible goods there are.

---

[11]   William Rowe, "The Evidential Argument from Evil: A Second Look." In *The Evidential Argument from Evil*. Ed. Daniel Howard-Snyder (Bloomington: Indiana University Press, 1996), 267.

[12]   This is a slightly revised version of the argument in Rowe's "The Evidential Argument from Evil: A Second Look," 263.

[13]   See William Alston, "The Inductive Argument from Evil and the Human Cognitive Condition." Reprinted in Howard-Snyder (1996); Michael Bergmann, "Skeptical Theism and Rowe's New Evidential Argument from Evil." *Nous* 35.2 (2001): 278–96; Michael Bergmann, "Skeptical Theism and the Problem of Evil." In *The Oxford Handbook of Philosophical Theology*. Ed. Thomas P. Flint and Michael C. Rea (Oxford: Oxford University Press, 2009), 374–99.

[14]   We focus on his (2009) reconstruction in Michael Bergmann, "Skeptical Theism and the Problem of Evil," 374–99.

(ST2): We have no good reason for thinking that the possible evils we know of are representative of the possible evils there are.[15]

Bergmann argues that, given (ST1) and (ST2), Rowe's new inference is defective. But this is not the only problem with the argument. Bergmann also submits two additional claims:

(ST3): We have no good reason for thinking that the entailment relations we know of between possible goods and the permission of possible evils are representative of the entailment relations there are between possible goods and the permission of possible evils.[16]

(ST4): We have no good reason for thinking that the total moral value or disvalue we perceive in certain complex states of affairs accurately reflects the total moral value or disvalue they really have.[17]

Bergmann argues that given these additional claims, we have no good reason to think Inductive-1 is true.[18] Rowe's revised argument thus continues to be undercut by skeptical-theist considerations.

Modal-Based Skeptical Theism

A third important representative of skeptical theism is the "modal skepticism" by which Peter van Inwagen argues that important atheistic arguments – specifically, arguments like Paul Draper's – depend on dubious assumptions about the epistemic status of crucial modal propositions. While granting we can be pretty confident about some ordinary modal claims – that, for example, there might have been more dogs in Paris in 1933 than there actually were – van Inwagen has long advocated a general "modal skepticism" coming, he says, to this:

If the subject matter of p is remote from the concerns of everyday life, then our ordinary human powers of modalizations are not reliable guides to the modal status of p.

For instance, as van Inwagen sees it, while I may be in a position to assert "I could've been a janitor," I'm in no position to assert "I could've existed while nothing material exists."[19]

---

[15] Ibid., 376.

[16] Ibid., 376.

[17] Ibid., 379.

[18] Cf. William Alston, "The Inductive Argument from Evil and the Human Cognitive Condition," 102–8.

[19] Cf. Peter Van Inwagen, "Modal Epistemology." Reprinted in *Ontology, Identity, and Modality* (Cambridge: Cambridge University Press, 1998 [2001]), 244.

Failure to admit limitations of our "powers of modalization" is endemic to contemporary professional philosophers. We are, says van Inwagen, like

> ... a Greek mariner in Homeric times who thinks that his [well-grounded] belief that the mountain that has just appeared on the horizon is about thirty miles away and his belief that the sun is about thirty miles away stem from the same source, to wit, his ability to judge distances by eye.

Of particular importance is van Inwagen's application of modal skepticism to Paul Draper's evidential argument. Draper concedes that the skeptical theists' critique has effectively undermined Rowe-style inductive arguments, but he does not think they thereby undermine *all* evidential arguments from evil, specifically *abductive* arguments from evil.[20] Using Bayes's theorem and simplicity considerations as tools of choice, Draper pioneered abductive approaches for comparing theism and naturalism against a broad range of "Humean data" about both good and evil. To illustrate the dialectic between them, we begin with a minimalist sketch of Draper's approach.[21]

Draper compares theism with the "Hypothesis of Indifference":

(HI): "Neither the nature nor the condition of sentient beings on earth is the result of benevolent or malevolent actions performed by non-human persons."[22]

Draper compares HI to theism *vis-à-vis* their ability to explain a full range of empirical data that he calls "O," formulated as

O: "A statement reporting both the observations one has made of humans and animals experiencing pain or pleasure and the testimony one has encountered concerning the observations others have made of sentient beings experiencing pain or pleasure."[23]

Draper's overall strategy is then to argue *abductively* that HI is much more probable than theism on O. We can formulate his argument as:

---

[20]   Paul Draper, "The Skeptical Theist." In Howard-Snyder (1996: 176).
[21]   Draper's argument has changed in the last 25 years; we focus only on the earliest presentation. We discuss a more recent presentation in our "Skeptical Theism, Abductive Atheology, and Theory Versioning." In *Skeptical Theism: New Essays*, ed. Trent Dougherty and Justin McBrayer (Oxford: Oxford University Press, 2014).
[22]   Paul Draper, "Pain and Pleasure: An Evidential Problem for Theists" Reprinted in Howard-Snyder (Bloomington, IN: Indiana University Press, 1989 [1996]: 13).
[23]   Ibid., 13.

Draper-1: HI explains the facts O reports much better than theism does.
Draper-2: So, there is *prima facie* good reason for thinking theism is less probable than HI.[24]

To contest the argument's sole premise, van Inwagen deploys his modal skepticism against a parallel premise of a parallel argument that is simpler but of the same sort – what we may call a Draper-*Style* argument. The thought here – accepted by Draper[25] – is that the modal issues brought to light will apply *mutatis mutandi* to Draper-1. In the place of Draper's data O (covering both good and bad), van Inwagen substitutes:

S: A proposition that describes "in some detail the amount, kinds, and distribution of suffering."[26]

The parallel argument is then

(Draper-Style-1): HI explains S much better than theism does.
(Draper-Style-2): So, there is *prima facie* good reason for thinking theism is less probable than HI.[27]

Here van Inwagen claims that a sufficient condition for showing *Draper-Style-1* false is to find a *version* of theism – that is, theism conjoined with further claims, H – that meets the following two conditions:

(Cond-1) the probability of H given theism is high, and
(Cond-2) the conditional probability of S, given theism and H is high (or at least not too low).[28]

Taking an indirect route, van Inwagen does not provide a version of theism that, he thinks, meets these conditions. Instead, he proposes the following principle, which we'll call *PvI's Condition*:

We are in no position to evaluate whether the HI explains the data of (good and) evil, if there is a version of theism such that (i) the probability of the data, given that version, is high and (ii) we are in no position to determine how likely that version is, given theism.

---

[24] Ibid., 14.
[25] (1996: 179).
[26] (1991 [1996]: 153).
[27] Ibid., 153.
[28] Strictly speaking, it is neither necessary nor sufficient for showing *Draper-Style-1* false that a version of theism meets these conditions (cf. our (2014: 148–50)). Nevertheless, van Inwagen and Draper appear to agree that, as a matter of fact, if some version met these conditions, Draper-1 would be false, perhaps because neither think that HI explains the relevant data very well.

Otherwise put, *PvI's Condition* states that if there is a version of theism
that meets Cond-1, but we are in no position to say it meets Cond-2,
then we are in no position to say Draper-Style-1 is true.[29] Using his
modal skepticism, van Inwagen constructs a "defense" of theism – a
version of theism that meets Cond-1 *and* is such that, *for all we know*,
also meets Cond-2.[30]

For his Defense, van Inwagen offers the following threefold
proposition:

Defense-1: Every possible world that contains higher-level sentient
creatures either contains patterns of suffering morally equivalent to
those recorded by S or else is massively irregular.

Defense-2: Some important intrinsic or extrinsic good depends on
the existence of higher-level sentient creatures; this good is of
sufficient magnitude that it outweighs the patterns of suffering
recorded by S.

Defense-3: Being massively irregular is a defect in a world, a defect at
least as great as the defect of containing patterns of suffering morally
equivalent to those recorded by S.[31]

Now van Inwagen's key claim here is that we are simply in no position to evaluate whether, on the Defense, (Cond-2) is satisfied, that
is, whether the conditional probability of S is high, low, or middling.
We're in no such position, van Inwagen argues, in multiple ways: to
think Defense-1 is false or unlikely, we'd need to be (but are not) in
a position to construct an extremely detailed story of how a world
could go;[32] to think Defense-3 false, we'd need to be (but are not) in
a position to have reliable moral intuitions regarding the comparison
of extremely complex cosmic states of affairs; and so on.[33] But if we
are in no position to judge S is improbable on the Defense, and the
Defense is itself not very improbable on theism, we have every reason to admit we are not in a position to assert Draper-Style-1, and so
mutatis mutandi Draper-1.

[29]   van Inwagen, Peter. "Reflections on the Chapters by Draper, Russell, and Gale." In
The Evidential Argument from Evil, ed. Daniel Howard-Snyder (Bloomington: Indiana
University Press, 1996: 228).

[30]   van Inwagen, Peter. "The Problem of Evil, the Problem of Air, and the Problem of
Silence." Reprinted in *The Evidential Argument from Evil*, ed. Daniel Howard-Snyder
(Bloomington: Indiana University Press, 1991 [1996]: 156).

[31]   Ibid., 157.

[32]   Ibid., 159.

[33]   Ibid., 161–2.

ISSUES AND BRIDGES

A second aim of our chapter is to review the rich issues provoked by
skeptical theism among philosophers of religion and to describe these
issues so as to bring out their connection to current topics in mainstream philosophy.

The Analogical-Inference Puzzles

Wykstra argues for *Core Conditional* by appeal to a parent/child analogy
and for *Core Implication* by appeal to CORNEA. Here we present two
lines of response to the first argument pressed by Rowe and Russell.[34]

Rowe objects that Wykstra's parent/child analogy does not support
Core Conditional.[35] The parent/child analogy, Rowe concedes, does
show that if God exists, then God likely grasps many goods (and bads)
beyond our ken – goods in the distant future, for example. But what it
needs (but fails) to show is that if God exists, God allows those evils we
are aware of for the sake of this class of inscrutable goods.

Wykstra, in response, refined the parent/child analogy and supplemented it with a new line of reasoning. The refinement compared parents on a continuum of intelligence and goodness, arguing that as we
get parents with more intelligence and goodness, we also get increased
likelihood that they will allow things (savings accounts for college,
say) for the sake of future goods that are beyond the child's ken.[36] By
extension, God would also allow many things in the present for the
sake of our distant future. Supplementing this, Wykstra also argued
that if God exists, we have considerable reason to think that our universe will have a depth reflecting God's own depth. And this moral
depth, Wykstra argued, finds some independent confirmation in the
way in which scientific revolutions disclose new physical depths of
the universe.

---

[34] Some have criticized the second argument by claiming that CORNEA is false, either
because it violates closure principles (Andrew Graham and Stephen Maitzen, CORNEA
and Closure. *Faith and Philosophy* 24.1 [2007]: 83–6) or is incompatible with inductive
evidence (Justin McBrayer, "CORNEA and Inductive Evidence." *Faith and Philosophy*
26.1 [2009]: 77–86) As these issues have been treated elsewhere – (Wykstra, "CORNEA,
Carnap, and Current Closure Befuddlement." *Faith and Philosophy* 24.1 [2007]: 87–98)
and Wykstra and Perrine, "The Foundations of Skeptical Theism: CORNEA, CORE,
and Conditional Probabilities." *Faith and Philosophy* 29.4 [2012]: 375–99), respectively – we won't repeat discussion.

[35] William Rowe, "Evil and the Theistic Hypothesis: A Response to Wykstra." *International Journal for the Philosophy of Religion* 16.2 (1984): 97–8.

[36] Wykstra, "Rowe's Noseeum Arguments from Evil."

These further considerations are, however, opposed by countercon-siderations. Perhaps, given theism, it is probable that *either* the universe has great moral depth *or* that we human beings have cognitive limita-tions limiting how deeply we can see into the actual depth. But it does not follow from that, given theism, we should expect *both* an axiological depth in which the "deep goods" play an essential role in God's permis-sion of evil *and* an inscrutability of those deep goods for those who are suffering for the sake of them. In support of this point, Rowe argues that Wykstra's parent/child analogy backfires: for when a loving parent allows a dearly beloved child to suffer (in, say, a medical procedure), the parent will do her best to mitigate the suffering by being personally pres-ent to the child as much as possible rather than, in the midst of such human suffering, remaining hidden, distant, and unavailable.[37]

In evaluating these analogies, it is important to keep in mind that good analogical reasoning demands finely tuned holistic judgment that weights dis-analogies and counterconsiderations. One puzzling consid-eration is Rowe's usage of (as it has come to be called) "divine hidden-ness" in his appeal to the parent analogy. Rowe clearly deployed it to show that Wykstra's parent/child analogy fails to undercut his original argument. But whether it can be deployed to do more than this – in particular, to fortify Rowe's original evidence with further atheological evidence – is a topic of ongoing investigation.[38]

The Modal Skepticism Puzzles

Peter van Inwagen, responding to Draper-style arguments, appeals both to his more general "modal skepticism" position and to a plausible prin-ciple regarding epistemic probabilities:

PvI's Condition: We are in no position to evaluate whether the HI explains the data of (good and) evil, if there is a version of theism such that (i) the probability of the data, given that version, is high and (ii) we are in no position to determine how likely that version is, given theism.

---

[37] See Rowe, 1996: 275–6; 2006. For an analysis and response, see Wykstra, "Suffering, Evidence, and Analogy: Noseeum Arguments Versus Skeptical Gambits," in *Philosophy Through Science Fiction*. Ed. Ryan Nichols, Fred Miller and Nicholas Smith (New York and London: Routledge, 2008), 184–85.

[38] Here the problem of divine hiddenness impinges on evidential arguments from evil. On this, see Schellenberg's contribution to this volume, Bergmann, "Skeptical Theism and the Problem of Evil," 382–3, and Peter van Inwagen, "What Is the Problem of the Hiddenness of God?" In *Divine Hiddenness*. Ed. Dan Howard-Snyder and Paul Moser (Cambridge: Cambridge University Press, 2002), 24–32.

But Bruce Russell argues that, even given his modal skepticism and PvI's Condition, the critique fails: van Inwagen's Defense, Russell thinks, fails to meet PvI's Condition because, even given theism, we do have reason to think the Defense *unlikely* (or even *false*). This is because the first claim in the Defense is unlikely:

> Defense-1: Every possible world that contains higher-level sentient creatures either contains patterns of suffering morally equivalent to those recorded by S or else is massively irregular.

This is highly unlikely because given the vast amount of suffering in our world, we can easily imagine – in some detail – a world that contains higher-level beings with *less* suffering, where (for some particular evil) God miraculously intervenes to prevent *that* evil. And such a world, Russell argues, is not "morally equivalent" to our world: God thus has "decisive reason" for preferring that imagined world to our own[39] – and this, for (roughly) the reason that was specified in *Rowe-1*: a person is obligated to (and a perfectly good being would) prevent any evil it can if this does not sacrifice some greater good (such as the regularities of a world). Since Defense cannot be more probable that any claim it contains, and Defense-1 is unlikely given theism, Defense fails to meet *PvI's Condition*.

Van Inwagen is not without reply: Rowe-1, he thinks, is a weak reason for thinking Russell's world is morally equivalent to our world. Even if God could prevent some suffering without loss of a greater good, sorities considerations should keep us from thinking this gives God decisive reason for doing so. Here van Inwagen offers analogies: a 10-year prison sentence for a criminal might be no less effective if it was one day shorter, but we quickly end in absurdities if we think a just judge is therefore required to shorten the sentence by a day rather than choose an arbitrary cut-off point. Similarly, a just God may choose an arbitrary cut-off for the amount of suffering allowed to achieve a set of cosmic goods. The mere fact that we can conceive of a world that, without loss of goods, has one less bit of suffering does not suffice to show that world fails to be morally equivalent to the actual world. Russell's argument does not show Defense-1 unlikely given theism.

Draper resists van Inwagen's critique by arguing that even conceding modal skepticism, van Inwagen's Defense does not undermine *Draper-1*. As

---

[39] Russell here uses van Inwagen's definition of "morally equivalent" in van Inwagen, "The Problem of Evil, the Problem of Air, and the Problem of Silence." Reprinted in Howard-Snyder (Indianapolis, IN: Indiana University Press, 1991 [1996]): 158.

Draper reads him, van Inwagen is granting that we have some initial reason for thinking that the pleasure and pain we observe is more likely given the hypothesis of indifference than theism; van Inwagen is merely trying to tip the scales back in favor of theism by using his Defense. Draper urges this "tipping" fails because we can construct counterdefenses which neutralize van Inwagen's defense where a "counterdefense" is, roughly, a version of theism such that the version makes the relevant data really *improbable* and are such that we are in no position to judge how likely it is given theism.

Draper's discussion of counterexamples is probabilistically quite complex, and we lack space to fully articulate it. But insofar as his discussion of counterdefenses incorporates this reading of van Inwagen, detailed discussion is not needed. For van Inwagen is not urging that defenses give us reason to shift the initial value that Draper gives. He is arguing that defenses give us a sufficient reason to *not assign even an initial value* to Draper's comparative claim.[40]

The key issue in this exchange, as we see it, is whether *PvI's condition* is true. Even if Draper's initial criticism misses its mark, it might be that some revised criticism does show that principle false. A full discussion of the principle would take us deep into complex issues about defeaters for comparative epistemic probabilities – something we lack the space to discuss.

A different response than either Russell or Draper is to criticize van Inwagen's argument at the first stage.[41] For example, one might argue that van Inwagen's modal skepticism compromises *ordinary* modal knowledge. For instance, van Inwagen claims that his Defense would fail if we could, with good reason, say that there are possible worlds with nomological regularity comparable to ours, in which high-level organisms live in utopia.[42] But to say such worlds are even possible, we'd need detailed insight into the laws of nature that would hold in them and how the evolutionary story would then go and so on. Filling in such cosmic details is not remotely within our cognitive capacities.

It might be objected that the same inability holds for claims that van Inwagen thinks do fall within our modal knowledge – for example, that JFK could have died of natural causes instead of being assassinated in 1963.[43] None of us can imagine in any great detail a possible world

40 Paul Draper, "The Skeptical Theist."
41 Here we rely on the work of H. Geirsson, "Conceivability and Defeasible Modal Justification." *Philosophical Studies* 122.3 (2005): 279–304.
42 Peter Van Inwagen, "The Problem of Evil, the Problem of Air."
43 Peter Van Inwagen, "Modal Epistemology." Reprinted in *Ontology, Identity, and Modality* (Cambridge: Cambridge University Press, 1998 [2001]), 246.

in which JFK is merely wounded and lives to a ripe old age. So, it may seem, van Inwagen's requirements for modal knowledge undercut much ordinary modal knowledge. Consequently, there might be reasons (independent of arguments from evil) for thinking that van Inwagen's modal skepticism is suspect and thus that his criticism of Draper's argument fails.[44]

The Hellish-World-Immunity Problem

Some have claimed that Core Implication has an absurd consequence: if the expectable hiddenness of God's cosmic purposes means the evil in our world does not seriously disconfirm theism, then virtually *no* amount of evil – not even the universe being utterly hellish, with all creatures in intense suffering during their entire endless existence – can do so either.[45]

Whether this is a consequence, however, turns on the particulars of *why*, according to some version of skeptical theism, a particular atheological argument fails to provide the intended support for atheism. After all, the claim that some particular argument (e.g., Rowe's) fails to show an evil to be gratuitous does not entail that *any* argument for that conclusion likewise fails. An analogy may help here. Balancing the budget of some large state university with more than a hundred thousand employees and multiple satellite campuses is a complex matter for which most of us are ill equipped. It requires knowing the particularities of the different campuses, the university tax codes, the details of large-scale loans for construction of new buildings and maintenance of old ones, the expected demographics over the coming decade … and a slew of other things that don't even occur to most of us. Given such ignorance, we ordinary folks might often – even usually – be in no position to second-guess most financial decisions by a college president or Board of Trustees as cases of irresponsible management. But it doesn't follow from this that we'd be unable to deem as irresponsible *any* possible managerial decision – say, a decision to eliminate the entire chemistry department and use the laboratory spaces for arcades of video games.

Moreover, Michael Bergmann has argued that skeptical theism is consistent with other principles which, if conjoined to theism, would make the hellish world precluded by theism. One such principle is

---

[44] For further discussion, see Geirsson (2005) and Peter Hawke, "van Inwagen's Modal Skepticism." *Philosophical Studies* 153.3 (2011): 351–64.

[45] Cf. Ian Wilks, "Skeptical Theism and Empirical Unfalsifiability." *Faith and Philosophy* 26.1 (2009): 68–9; William Rowe, "Skeptical Theism: A Response to Bergmann." *Nous* 35.2 (2001): 298.

that a good God would not create a world such that each of its sentient creatures had, on balance, a bad life. Since nothing in skeptical theism rules out conjoining theism with such a principle, it is false that skeptical theism entails that theism could not be seriously disconfirmed – even decisively falsified – were our evidence to be that our world is a hellish world.[46]

The Entails-Moral-Skepticism Problem
Critics of skeptical theism sometimes object that the position entails some odious kind of *moral skepticism*. Now not all kinds of skepticism are odious: some moral truths, like some mathematical truths, might be beyond the limits of human understanding. But many theists suppose that humans have a God-given "commonsense faculty" for grasping some important moral truths; if skeptical theism threatens important regions of such "moral common sense," we have a source of serious worry.

The objection here, as usual, can assume many forms, depending on what region of commonsense moral knowing is seen as under threat. Perhaps the most plausible threat is that skeptical theism undercuts – in a way that would lead to objectionable paralysis – judgments resting on practical moral reasoning in which consequential considerations play a decisive role (which even deontologists recognize can occur). Suppose, for example, that I face a situation in which I alone (among human beings) can prevent some instance of suffering (a child drowning, say) about to occur and can do so without – so far as I can tell – any adverse consequences. Moral common sense dictates that I ought to act so as to prevent that suffering. But suppose I, as a theist, believe both that God regularly fails to intervene for similar instances of evil and this is because God sees that such nonintervention is essential to promoting to some inscrutable greater good. If I hold this, must I not worry about whether I know, or can even reasonably judge, whether the good that leads God to fail to intervene will be compromised by *my* intervening?[47]

---

[46] Bergmann (2009: 390). Bergmann's point is correct: skeptical theism does not entail P if it is consistent with some other principle Q, and together they do not entail P. Nevertheless, he does not point out, as perhaps he should, that to provide a convincing response, it must also be the case that the skeptical theist's reason for holding Q is not undercut by that skeptical theism.

[47] Cf. Mark Piper, "Skeptical Theism and the Problem of Moral Aporia." *International Journal for Philosophy of Religion* 62.2 (2007): 65–79; Jeff Jordan, "Does Skeptical Theism Lead to Moral Skepticism?" *Philosophy and Phenomenological Research* 72.2 (2006): 403–17; Bruce Russell, "Defenseless" in Daniel Howard-Snyder, ed., *The Evidential Argument from Evil* (Bloomington, IN: Indiana University Press, 1996); Michael Almeida & Graham Oppy, "Sceptical Theism and Evidential Arguments from Evil," *Australasian Journal of Philosophy*, 81.4: 496–516.

Note that this problem does not just arise given the strong assumption (accepted by Rowe and Wykstra but contested by van Inwagen) that God's allowing of each and every evil is due to God's seeing (as we cannot) that doing so is essential for promoting certain God-intended outweighing goods. It also arises on the more modest assumption that God permits *some* evils because doing so is in this way essential – and that these include evils that, by "moral common sense," we judge that it would be *morally wrong* for *us* not to prevent. So even van Inwagen's weaker view will not escape the problem.

A proper solution to this problem will require attention to relevant work in contemporary moral theory.[48] To illustrate that relevance, consider Derek Parfit's distinctions between three senses in which an action may be said to be "morally wrong."[49] One is the "objective" sense: an action is morally wrong for an agent in this objective sense if (roughly put) the agent would correctly judge it morally wrong in the ordinary sense, were the agent aware of all of the morally relevant consequences of the action (and of its live alternatives). Now, on some consequentialist theories, the morally relevant consequences include any outcome of an agent's acting – no matter how inscrutable that outcome might be to the agent.[50] But in Parfit, we find the suggestion that the morally relevant consequences are a function of – as one of us has put it elsewhere – the "optimal axiological horizon" of that agent (or that sort of agent).[51] This offers a cue to how skeptical theists might address this problem. That God the divine agent sees vastly many good and bad consequences that we human agents can't see does not entail that we are in no position to know, in situations in which consequential reasoning plays a deciding role, what the objectively right thing for us to do is. For that knowledge will require us to weigh the good and bad consequences falling within *our* own optimal axiological horizon as human moral cognizers. The skeptical theistic proposal that God's horizon is infinitely greater need

---

48 For one approach, see Michael Bergmann, "Commonsense Skeptical Theism." In *Reason, Metaphysics, and Mind: New Essays on the Philosophy of Alvin Plantinga.* Eds. Michael Rea and Kelly James Clark (Oxford University Press, 2012). For worries about Bergmann and a Parfitean approach to resolving them, see Wykstra (2012) and Stephen J. Wykstra,"Beyond the Impasse: Contemporary Moral Theory and the Crisis of Skeptical Theism." In *Ethics and the Problem of Evil*, ed. James P. Sterba (Bloomington: Indiana University Press, 2017: 108–140).

49 Derek Parfit, *On What Matters* (Oxford: Clarendon Press, 2011).

50 Cf. David Sosa, "Consequences of Consequentialism." *Mind* 102.405 (1993): 101–2.

51 See Stephen J. Wykstra,"Beyond the Impasse: Contemporary Moral Theory and the Crisis of Skeptical Theism." In *Ethics and the Problem of Evil*, ed. James P. Sterba (Bloomington: Indiana University Press, 2017: 108–40).

not, given the cue we find in Parfit, imperil our common sense practical reasoning about what the morally right and morally wrong thing – in Parfit's objective sense – is for us to do.

The Entails-Other-Skepticisms Problem

Beyond moral beliefs, skeptical theism can also seem to threaten the epistemic status often accorded to other sorts of beliefs as well,[52] ranging from external-world claims like

A.   I am sitting on a chair

through well-established scientific claims like

B.   The earth is very old

to claims central to major religious traditions like

C.   God chose Israel to bless all nations.

One source of threat here is that the skeptical-theistic strategy seems to open serious possibilities of divine lies and deception. Does not the strategy ask us to hold that horrific suffering in our world may – contrary to how things seem – serve God-justifying goods that are beyond our ken? If we hold that, won't we need to say that for all we know, God may well equally be deceiving us on matters like (A) through (C) for God justifying purposes which are inscrutable to us for similar reasons?

For these to be more than mere pesky questions, they must be morphed into disciplined arguments. Thus, we will here explore how a critic might craft a challenging argument that skeptical theism of the CORNEA type threatens an untoward skepticism about the scientific claim that the earth is old.[53] Does the CORNEA strategy indeed create a threat for this claim?

Let E be the pool of accumulated scientific data favoring the Old-Earth theory – data including such things as carbon-14 testing, ordered geological strata, tectonic plate rates of motion, and so on. Let Y be the

---

[52]   Cf. Hud Hudson, "The Father of Lies?" In *Oxford Studies in the Philosophy of Religion*, volume 5 Ed. Jonathan Kvanvig, 2014; Erik Wielenberg, "Skeptical Theism and Divine Lies." *Religious Studies* 46.4: 509–23; Wilks (2009); Stephen Maitzen, "Skeptical Theism and God's Commands." *Sophia* 46(2007): 237–43; Russell (1996).

[53]   Russell (1996) has been an important stimulus to the argument we develop. For a discussion of the CORNEA strategy applied to beliefs like (A), see Kenneth Boyce, "Some Considerations Concerning CORNEA, Global Skepticism, and Trust." In *Skeptical Theism: New Essays*. Ed. Trent Dougherty and Justin McBrayer (Oxford: Oxford University Press, 2014).

hypothesis that the earth is very young. Now according to CORNEA, E entitles us to claim that it appears that

(~Y) The earth is not young

only if it is reasonable for us to believe what we'll call:

> *Y-Crux:* If Y were true (i.e., the earth was a young earth), then E – the scientific data – would likely be different in a way we can discern.

So far, CORNEA seems to pose no problem: the scientific community, after all, would endorse Y-Crux, noting that a young-earth hypothesis makes (e.g.) the results of carbon-14 tests far less expectable than does the Old Earth theory. The Critic's intuition, however, is that if we accept CORNEA-style skeptical theism, this endorsement is somehow no longer open to us. What lies behind this intuition is by no means obvious – skeptical theism does not, after all, have much to say about what to expect from a Young Earth hypothesis. The Critic's underlying idea becomes clearer, however, if we use the weighted average principle. For the Critic can note that we can flesh out two different versions of theism relative to the presumptions of scientific testing:

> T1: If God exists, he would make a veridical universe in which scientific inquiry gets at the truth, or
> T2: If God exists, God would create a universe in which the evidence systematically points to hypotheses that are in fact false for reasons beyond our ken.

If we combine Y with T1, we remain in accord with the commonsense presumptions of normal scientific reasoning, making it reasonable to accept Y-Crux. After all, given Y&T1, there is still a high conditional probability that the evidence would be different from what it is so that the probability of ~E, given Y&T1 is high (or in probabilistic notation: Pr (~E | Y & T1 & k) > .5).[54]

However, if we accept T2, things are different. For on Y&T2, it does *not* seem so likely that the evidence will differ from E (if only because we now have a hard time knowing what to expect from *any* hypothesis).

Here the weighted average importantly enters.[55] It tells us that what Y *itself* "probabilistically predicts" regarding E will be the weighted

---

[54]   We here assume what we've discussed elsewhere (Wykstra and Perrine, 2012), namely that conditionals that are grammatical subjunctives – like Y-Crux – can be understood as expressing conditional probabilities.

[55]   For more on this principle, see Wykstra and Perrine (2012).

average of how likely E is on each of these two conflicting conjunctive hypotheses, each one weighted by, respectively, the antecedent probability of T1 and of T2. And a lot will turn on these antecedent probabilities. In particular, if T2 is very probable, then the low probability of E on Y&T2 will swamp the weighted average, so Pr (~ E | Y & k) will turn out to be low, making Y-Crux unreasonable to accept. So for the CORNEA-style skeptical theist to be reasonable in believing Y-Crux – and, by it, reasonable in believing, based on E, that the earth is not very young – it must be reasonable for her to believe that T2 is not very probable at all. But – and here is the linchpin of the Critic's argument – skeptical theism makes this problematic: by espousing diffidence about what to expect from God, it blocks us from assigning to T2 a low probability and so undermines our standard way of confirming scientific hypotheses.

The argument we've developed has no obvious satisfactory response, and we offer none here. However, an important question here is whether entails-skepticism objections like this one dependent at all on its being *God* – rather than an evil demon or envatting alien of epistemological lore – doing the deceiving. If not, wielders of the objection (insofar as they are themselves not radical skeptics) are making an assumption: that of the many current respectable responses to standard evil-demon arguments for skepticism, none – when transposed into the context here – will be equally availing to the skeptical theist. It is not clear to us that this assumption will survive serious scrutiny. In any case, the issue here once again intertwines with mainstream issues at the cutting edge of current epistemology.

SKEPTICAL THEISM AND WORLDVIEW EXPANSION

What unifies skeptical theists are two things. The first – *Core Conditional* – is an insistence that for finite human knowers, conditional epistemic humility is the appropriate stance for a reasonable person to take toward the full range of goods and constraints that would inform divine decision making. The second – *Core Implication* – is that such conditional epistemic humility brings to light serious defects in at least some important versions of the evidential argument from evil. While the "at least some" may seem a retreat from the bolder claims of early skeptical theism,[56] evidential arguments have evolved beyond Rowe-style arguments of the 1980s, and no "one-size-fits-all" response handles all of them.

---

56   E.g., Wykstra (1984).

Indeed, quite varied strategies now seem in order. Against Rowe-style *inductive* arguments, it was useful to use a "minimalist" strategy urging that if God exists, then it is – considering just the core claim of theism – relatively unsurprising that finite human cognizers should often fail to see the goods or constraints comprising God's rationale for allowing suffering. But against Draper-style *abductive* arguments, a more "expansive" strategy seems needed, by which we explore the various "best extensions" of core theism that may best outfit it for an explanatory rough and tumble with naturalism on its own best extensions.

We see this expansive strategy as avoiding two temptations.[57] The first – call it Indulgent Adhocery – is to suppose that when certain data E has a problematic fit with mere theism (relative to some rival like "mere naturalism"), we can immediately solve the problem by plumping for *any* expanded version of theism, T^* – no matter how *ad hoc* – that fits this data well. Such success is illusory: the expanded hypothesis T^* may not, by E, be *made* more improbable than it was prior to E. Nevertheless, while T^* is not made improbable by E, it still becomes improbable by its increased content and complexity.[58]

The second temptation – call it Compulsive Timidity – is to overcorrect, by supposing that if we are to avoid *ad hoc* expansion, we must never look at how some plausibly expanded version of theism might fit and illuminate the data. We find this temptation belied by the history of scientific theorizing, which shows us that it is only by a disciplined expansion of core claims that we gain deeper insight into reality. The search for insight proceeds precisely by taking a vague or unadorned core hypothesis – Darwin's vague conception of pangenesis, say, or an unadorned wave conception of light – and, by sustained trial and error, using new incoming data to expand that core conception into its best versions, comparing these with the best versions of rival core claims. Such after-the-fact expansions, by increasing the complexity and content of the theory, do indeed represent an initial price. But if the new supplement has new theoretical content, the price may be right – an investment in extra content may quickly pay for itself and more by reshaping our expectations in ways that yield high explanatory or predictive dividends. In worldview theorizing as well, we think, theory expansion is central to the only process by which the core claims of any worldview can, through the rough and tumble of worldview competition, eventually prove its mettle in the long run.[59]

[57] Cf. Wykstra (1984: 91), Russell and Wykstra (1988: 155–60), and Rowe (1991: 79).
[58] Cf. Perrine and Wykstra (2014: 148–50).
[59] A useful model for this is a broadly Lakatosian approach, on which mere theism functions as the "hard core" of a research program, just as mere naturalism is the "hard

As we see it, the past several decades of analytic philosophy can naturally be seen as attempts to work out coherent and systematic worldviews. In areas as diverse as philosophy of mind, epistemology, and ethics, philosophers have sought to let the detailed results of scientific research guide their effort to produce so-far-best version of an overarching worldview and to let such a so-far-best-versioned worldview heuristically shape and illuminate further inquiry. In its newer approaches to the problem of evil, contemporary evidential atheology is squarely within this trend, and theistic responses will need to complement their earlier minimalist "undercutting" projects with that disciplined expansion of a theistic core worldview, by which it can best be "versioned" so as to harmonize with and heuristically guide our empirical inquiry into this world.

THE COHERENCE QUESTION

Our proposal that skeptical-theistic responses of the old-fashioned "minimalist" sort be supplemented with a more positive "worldview research program" may raise some skeptical eyebrows. To some, the proposal may seem in tension with skeptical theism; to others, it may seem incoherent, contradicting its very essence. We see neither tension nor incoherence. The skeptical theists' substantive claim is that if God exists, it is not likely that we should grasp the full range of God's purposes for current divine actions. This claim is entirely compatible with affirming that we are nevertheless capable of seeing and grasping a good many truths about God and God's purposes.

Many analogies model this compatibility. One earlier analogy was a university budget: It is perfectly consistent to expect to understand some but not all of the reasoning behind a university budget. The consistency remains even when there are more fundamental sources for our lack of full epistemic access. For example, while gazing at the heavens on a clear night, one could fully grant that innumerable celestial objects may lie beyond our vision and that many celestial mechanisms are beyond our current comprehension or imagination. But such humility about the limits of our perception, comprehension, and imagination is consistent

core" of a rival research program. There will be differences between worldview theorizing understood this way and scientific theorizing, as worldview inquiry would not dismiss modes of access other than the scientific (including, perhaps, divine revelation and divine illumination within theistic traditions). But while we lack the same to do so here, we think an adequate model could be developed. We've tried our hand at this, albeit somewhat indirectly, in our 2014 work.

with full confidence that an amazing number of celestial objects are in plain sight and that we have a good grasp of many of the mechanisms behind them (e.g., those behind the super-eclipse in September 2015). Moreover, epistemic humility about celestial objects and mechanisms is fully compatible with a passionate quest, in matters astronomical, to push beyond the current limits of what we can observe, comprehend, and imagine. In the same way, there is neither contradiction nor tension, in matters theological, between affirming that a divine axiology will have fathomless depth while also affirming that many things lie within our current grasp, and many more may, on passionate investigation, come into cognitive focus.

The dialectical challenges we have here surveyed are, to be sure, both intricate and formidable. They are, however, intertwined with – and a backdoor entrance into – issues within mainstream philosophy that are equally thorny. While granting that skeptical theism gives no one-size-fits-all answer to evidential atheology and needs to be incorporated within a broader "worldview research program," we judge that it will remain a keen resource in that worldview competition that must ineluctably engage all reflective human beings, from world-class philosophers and Nobel-laureate physicists to the janitors who sweep their floors and empty their wastebaskets.

FURTHER READING

Howard-Snyder, Daniel. "Epistemic Humility, Arguments from Evil, and Moral Skepticism." In *Oxford Studies in Philosophy of Religion.* Ed. Jonathan Kvanvig. Oxford: Clarendon Press, 2009.

Howard-Snyder, Daniel (ed.). *The Evidential Argument from Evil.* Bloomington: Indiana University Press, 1996.

Jordan, Jeff. "Does Skeptical Theism Lead to Moral Skepticism?" *Philosophy and Phenomenological Research* 72.2 (2006): 403–17.

McBrayer, Justin and Daniel Howard-Snyder (eds.). *The Blackwell Companion to the Problem of Evil.* Malden, MA: Wiley-Blackwell, 2013.

Rowe, William. "Friendly Atheism, Skeptical Theism, and the Problem of Evil." *International Journal for Philosophy of Religion* 59.2 (2006): 79–92.

Van Inwagen, Peter. *The Problem of Evil.* Oxford: Clarendon Press, 2006.

6 Evil, Hiddenness, and Atheism

J. L. SCHELLENBERG

In recent years, a new way of reasoning in support of atheism has arisen in philosophy: it is called the hiddenness argument. But some have wondered whether this way of reasoning is really so new. In particular, certain features of the hiddenness argument have reminded philosophers of atheism's argument from evil. A number of philosophers, indeed, have concluded that what hiddenness arguers are concerned with comes down to some fact or facts about evil in the world – perhaps intellectual facts, and ones we're not used to thinking of in this way, but still facts about evil.

In this chapter, I consider whether any such view is correct. I conclude that none is. The hiddenness argument stands firmly on its own two feet. In the course of this discussion, I set out and briefly defend a version of the most widely discussed instance of hiddenness reasoning, which I developed in 1993.[1] Readers will thus gain a sense of the issues raised by the hiddenness problem, whether or not they agree with me about its relation to the problem of evil. (I treat 'the problem of evil' and 'the argument from evil' synonymously, as most philosophers do, and will adopt the same practice on the hiddenness side.) It should be noted that even if the older problem does not include the newer, there may be other connections between the problem of evil and the hiddenness problem that are worth exploring and that have a bearing on the status of atheism. I will touch on some of these before concluding.

WHAT HIDDENNESS IS

The problem of evil is well known, the hiddenness problem less so. Thus before getting into the thick of things, we need to set the stage, beginning with an issue about what that term 'hiddenness' means when it is

[1] J. L. Schellenberg, *Divine Hiddenness and Human Reason* (Ithaca, NY: Cornell University Press, 1993).

used to refer to a basis for concluding that God does not exist. It obviously isn't meant to be taken literally, for when we speak of something as hidden, meaning this literally, we assume that the thing in question exists. (Think of the hidden locket or the statue hidden from view just around the corner or your mother's hidden fear that you don't love her.) And so God, if hidden, exists, and no atheistic argument can, without contradiction, report in its premises that God literally is hidden. Why, then, is the term used?

To see, it may help to notice that no argument arises in a cultural vacuum. Hiddenness reasoning arose in a context in which theologians, guided by thinking that goes back at least to the book of Psalms in the Hebrew Bible, were accustomed to using the concept of God's hiddenness in the interpretation of various facts – including especially the experience of spiritual darkness, of being bereft of God's presence, that believers sometimes have. When widespread nonbelief in God started to become noticeable, it seemed appropriate to use the language of hiddenness for that too. God's hiddenness, on this view, means not just that believers will sometimes not feel God's presence but also that some people won't be able to see that God exists at all.

But this practice of the theologians came to be challenged when it was observed that their most recent use of 'hiddenness' provided a clue to a new way of reasoning in support of atheism: an argument against God's existence from such things as the failure of arguments *for* God to convince even many who were ready to believe. While not expecting that God would be completely nonhidden (that is to say, revealed) if God existed – for a simple example, we should surely not expect to understand every thought of an omniscient being – the hiddenness arguer is nonetheless inclined to say that some of the nonbelief-related facts to which theologians have applied the language of hiddenness would not *be* facts were there to be a God. Given the context as set by theology, it is natural for the arguer to say: God would not be hidden *in this way*. By the same token, it is natural to speak of the relevant sort of divine hiddenness as a problem and of any atheistic argument exploiting this problem as an argument from divine hiddenness, when what people really have in mind is again *those facts*, which *would* hide God in a certain way if there were a God. When atheists say or imply that God is hidden, therefore, what they should be taken to mean is that the world contains such facts.

The image of a hidden God is a powerful image, and we have just seen how discussion of whether God would be hidden or not, were God to exist, naturally occurs when hiddenness arguers try to make their case for atheism. So we should probably not expect to find other terminology completely taking the place of hiddenness terminology anytime soon. But, having said that, to really understand what the hiddenness discussion is all about, we need to become better acquainted with the facts that the hiddenness arguer has discovered under the linguistic blanket of theology and finds problematic. Various facts can be and have been cited in this discussion, but, as suggested, they seem all to be tied up, in one way or another, with *nonbelief in the existence of God* or evidential circumstances conducive to such nonbelief.

THE HIDDENNESS ARGUMENT

Let's continue our stage setting by thinking about how nonbelief can come to be taken as evidence in this context. Usually when people find themselves in a state of nonbelief with respect to a proposition, either in doubt about whether it is true or believing it to be false, that very state of nonbelief, or the weak evidence provoking it, won't be viewed as evidence supporting the falsehood of the proposition. If you're in doubt about whether the Stampeders will win the Cup or whether there's any ice cream left in the fridge, it would be odd for someone to say: "Okay, and what about the very fact that you don't believe this – isn't that *itself* evidence that it isn't true?"

But it isn't at all odd to say such a thing when it comes to the question whether God exists. The possibility of a hiddenness argument comes into view when one sees this. If God exists, God has control over whether people believe in the existence of God and over the evidence of God that appears in the world. So we can always ask whether things in relation to belief and nonbelief in the world, and the evidence pertaining thereto, are as they *would* be if God had control over these facts. When asking such questions, philosophers are not presumptuously applying their own standards to God's behavior or presuming to know the mind of God but rather thinking about what the claim that there *is* a God *implies* in this regard. That claim has content, it is not empty, and so we can think about what follows from it: what *else* would have to be true if *it* were true? Perhaps among the things that follow is that certain facts about nonbelief or theistic evidence won't obtain. We can't assume from the outset that this *won't* follow. (If we do assume this, we are doing theology, not philosophy.) Rather, we have to look and see.

In the past twenty-five years or so, a number of different facts about nonbelief and theistic evidence have been put forward as having this character – as facts we wouldn't find if there were a God. They include the fact that there is inculpable nonbelief, that is, nonbelief for which the nonbeliever is not to blame; that there is any persistent nonbelief of any kind at all; that the evidence relevant to belief in God is objectively indecisive or ambiguous; that nonbelief is very unevenly distributed in the world; that there is nonbelief that arises not from resistance of God; and that certain particular forms of nonresistant nonbelief occur, namely those exemplified by former believers, lifelong seekers, converts to nontheistic religion, and isolated nontheists. (Works developing these ideas will be found listed under the Guide to Further Reading at the end of this chapter.)

So how can such facts be made to support the nonexistence of God? Well, as might be expected, in various ways. But let me pick the form of reasoning I think is strongest, which is also very close to the one that has received the most discussion. Setting aside some complications that would require treatment in a fuller discussion, it can be stated quite simply as follows:

(1) If a perfectly loving God exists, then there exists a God who is always open to a personal relationship (i.e., an explicit, conscious, interactive relationship) with any finite person.

(2) If there exists a God who is always open to a personal relationship with any finite person, then no finite person is ever nonresistantly in a state of nonbelief in relation to the proposition that God exists.

(3) If a perfectly loving God exists, then no finite person is ever nonresistantly in a state of nonbelief in relation to the proposition that God exists (from 1 & 2).

(4) Some finite persons are or have been nonresistantly in a state of nonbelief in relation to the proposition that God exists.

(5) No perfectly loving God exists (from 3 & 4).

(6) If no perfectly loving God exists, then God does not exist.

(7) God does not exist (from 5 & 6).

To show how the terminology of hiddenness may be applied: if, as this argument has it, many people who have not caused this condition themselves by resisting God still fail to believe in the existence of God, then we can say that, if God were to exist in these circumstances, God's existence would be *hidden* from these people. And if, as the argument claims, we should think that God would prevent nonresistant nonbelief, then we can say that God would not be hidden in this way.

DEFENDING THE HIDDENNESS ARGUMENT

My main aim in this chapter is not to show the cogency of this reasoning but instead to explore its relations to arguments from evil. However, it may be appropriate to highlight a few of its strengths before moving on, if only to show that the question we're focusing on is significant and should be of interest.

It may be fairly easy to see how an unsurpassably great personal being – which is what God is said to be – could not be less than perfectly loving and disposed to express that love for its own sake, in a simple expression of the divine nature, as well as because of the great good it would bring to the lives of creatures. This means that, as premise (6) of the argument has it, anything showing there to be no perfectly loving God shows there to be no God, period. Here we see something of what I was mentioning earlier about how philosophers think about the content of the claim that there is a God and about what follows from it: part of the content of the claim that there is a God is that God is an unsurpassably great *personal* being, and what follows from this is that God is perfectly loving. The hiddenness argument simply takes things a step further, spelling out what follows from *that*, and arguing that this includes consequences not realized in the world as we find it, so that in this world, no perfectly loving God exists.

What follows from divine love, the argument's first premise says, is that God would always be open to personal relationship with any finite person, understood as a creature able to form the belief that there is a God, identify an experience as that of God's presence, respond to it appropriately, and so on. (Most humans have such abilities or capacities. You might think that more should, citing the debilitating emotional and intellectual handicaps from which some humans suffer, but that would make for a *different* hiddenness argument.) How should we understand such perennial openness? More than one characterization suggests itself, but the argument chooses the weakest – the one that claims the least. For God always to be open to personal relationship with a finite person P is for God *never to be closed to it*, which is to say for God to ensure that there is never something *God* does at a time that puts such relationship out of reach for P at that time. Openness to personal relationship thus defined is, it may be noted, decidedly a *minimal* condition of perfect divine love. (One might well think that even mediocre or humdrum love would have *this* feature!) Yet it is substantial enough to allow us to make serious headway with it, intellectually speaking.

This is because of the plausibility of a certain general principle about openness and nonopenness. I call it *Not Open* because it identifies a condition in which, at a certain time, a person B clearly is not open to personal relationship with a second person A:

Not Open
If a person A, without having brought about this condition through resistance of relationship with a person B, is at some time in a state of nonbelief in relation to the proposition that B exists, *where B at that time knows this and could ensure that A's nonbelief is at that time changed to belief*, then it is not the case that B is open at the time in question to having a personal relationship with A then.

After all, given that one clearly cannot even get started in a personal relationship (an explicit, conscious, interactive relationship, as defined earlier) without believing that the other party exists, by not revealing himself B is doing something that makes it impossible for such a relationship with A to exist at the relevant time, and this, according to our definition, is precisely what is involved in not being open to it then.

Now you might think that even if A doesn't *believe* that B exists, A might still *hope* or have *faith* (in some nonbelieving sense) that B exists. And you might further think that at least some movement toward a relationship is possible under these circumstances, so that B could in such circumstances still be considered open to a relationship with A. But the problem with this view is twofold: (i) although B might in such circumstances be open to having a relationship with A at some time in the future, B is not open to having such a relationship with A *now*, and this is because (ii) we're talking about a *conscious* relationship, which, as mentioned, cannot exist unless each party believes in the other's existence. Not just any relationship is good enough for the best love, and neither is openness to conscious relationship *at one time or another* but not always. Think about it: which admirably loving person you know would be content with that?

The plausibility of *Not Open* explains why not just premise (1) of the argument but also premise (2) is true and why the first conclusion of the argument, (3), can be drawn. And it's all downhill from here, because nonresistant nonbelief is plentiful in the world. Theistic critics of the argument have sometimes denied this, focusing only on examples of *reflective* nonbelief – the nonbelief of people who have thought about the issue of God's existence. As it happens, many examples of nonresistant nonbelief can be found even in this context. Some nonbelievers are former believers who had a strong love for the God they believed to exist, when careful examination of the relevant evidence took their belief in God away. (It is important in this connection to see that belief is not voluntary, not something you can choose to have, just like that. If you doubt what I say, try voluntarily to believe it. Whatever the result, you'll see my point!) But ultimately the dispute over reflective nonbelief threatens to be a waste of time, since even if reflective nonbelief were never resistant, the hiddenness arguer would still be able to appeal to the nonbelief of all those, down the evolutionary ages, whose nonbelief was nonresistant simply by virtue of the fact that circumstances prevented them from even getting the idea of Western theism squarely before their minds, let alone reflecting on it. Premise (4) is therefore quite secure and, with (3), leads immediately to the conclusion – devastating for theism, as we saw before – that no perfectly loving God exists.

Because of the force of its other claims, most people who resist the hiddenness argument have come back around to the idea embodied by premise (1), arguing that there might be some great good for the sake of which even a perfectly loving God would reluctantly choose not to be open to personal relationship with some beloved creature for some period of time, permitting their nonresistant nonbelief. But such arguments are not as plausible here as they are when used similarly in connection with the problem of evil – more on this in the fifth section, "Is the Hiddenness Argument 'Close Enough' to Being an Argument from Evil?" Moreover, a powerful general strategy is available to those who defend this premise of the argument. They can say that the idea of an unending, ever-growing personal relationship with *God*, who is after all described as an unsurpassably great personal reality, is sufficiently commodious to allow for the realization, *within such relationship*, of the very goods God is said to be unable to achieve without postponing or interrupting it or of other goods belonging to the same type. And if this is the case, we shouldn't expect a perfectly loving God – a God biased toward personal relationship – ever to permit such a postponement or interruption. For example, if the idea is that God must permit nonresistant nonbelief and postpone relationship to enable our desire for God to grow through the search for God, it is necessary to point out that there would be no end of moving, within a divine–creature relationship, from one level to another, with each spiritual discovery calling forth more yearning for yet deeper acquaintance with the infinite richness of God and presenting more opportunities for its pursuit.

So much for a brief indication as to how the various moves of the hiddenness argument can be defended. We are now ready to turn to a fuller consideration of how this argument is related to the problem of evil. It shouldn't be hard to see that if the hiddenness problem is included among arguments from evil, then *this argument* had better be – however implicitly or incipiently – an argument from evil. After all, this is the hiddenness argument that is most widely discussed. If anything, we should, given the realization of the possibility in question, find it to be *more obviously* realized here than elsewhere. But is that the case?

THE HIDDENNESS ARGUMENT IS NOT
AN ARGUMENT FROM EVIL

It is not. And here is why. Although nonresistant nonbelief *can* be viewed as evil, especially by theists (and this is the source of the confusion), it is *not* viewed as evil by the hiddenness arguer, who rather takes nonresistant nonbelief as a signal that there is no being in the world who has the relational aspirations that a loving divine being would have. It should be noted that I'm approaching this matter on the generous philosophical assumption that *anything bad* may rightly receive the label 'evil.' So it's not because I'm in some way restricting the use of that word that I'm led to the view defended here. Take it as broadly as you like and you'll still find that what makes nonresistant nonbelief problematic by the lights of our hiddenness argument is not something that ties the argument to facts about evil.

Just about anything can be viewed as making for badness in one set of circumstances or another. And the same goes for nonresistant nonbelief. Perhaps if a person really wants to believe in God but can't, then by not getting what she wants, we might think she is experiencing something bad. Or maybe as a former believer, her nonbelief causes her great suffering. Then it is tied to badness – not bad in itself, perhaps, but bad because of the suffering to which her loss of belief has led. However, none of this matters in the present context if these are not the reasons why the hiddenness arguer thinks God would not permit nonresistant nonbelief. And they are not.

But perhaps the connection to badness can be made in another way. Perhaps we should think about a kind of badness that would exist only if there were a God, the badness of not being aware of so great a truth as the truth that there *is* a God, and moreover the badness of being in a situation in which through no fault of one's own, one is for a time unable to participate in personal relationship with God. *God* at least would think of these things as bad, and so we can imagine the atheist noticing this and thinking that for these evil-related reasons, God would prevent non-resistant nonbelief.

One might wonder, on reflection, just how bad these things are. Presumably that would depend on what other truths were available to nonresistant nonbelievers and how diminished were the circumstances in which they found themselves unable to participate in personal rela-tionship with God. But all of this is beside the point. Again we have a way in which the argument *could* be interpreted but not the way it *is* interpreted by the hiddenness arguer. Perhaps it is unsurprising that the-ists especially should be attracted to what is in fact beside the point here. As an evil, nonresistant nonbelief is not so impressive. Adding this one extra evil of hiddenness to all the other horrible things that happen in the world doesn't make for a significant change to the force of the prob-lem. And for a theist defending the existence of God, that has to be seen as a good thing! But the philosopher's perspective must be completely different. A philosopher is committed to making even arguments against positions she's fond of as strong as they can be to see whether some new insight might be generated by them. She is asked to scour all of the infor-mation relevant to an argument's interpretation to make sure she isn't getting anything wrong. And when this approach is taken, it won't be so hard to see that the argument from nonresistant nonbelief is introducing something new, which may provide a basis for atheism even if nonresis-tant nonbelief is not regarded as bad at all.

IS THE HIDDENNESS ARGUMENT 'CLOSE ENOUGH' TO BEING AN ARGUMENT FROM EVIL?

But maybe a related point can still be defended by the critic. Look, she might say, God's opposition to evil stems from a divine attribute called benevolence, which involves a desire for the *well-being* of others. It's not hard to see how somebody with this attribute will oppose bad things happening to others. But the very same attribute will of course lead to doing *good* things for others. These are two sides of the same coin. So if we can show that the hiddenness argument, whatever it says about evil, still depends on God wanting good for creatures – specifically, the very great good of a relationship with God – we will show that the argument is 'close enough' to being an argument from evil. For the same consider-ations about good and evil, about God needing to give up certain goods in order to have others, and so on, will arise when dealing with it. And perhaps it won't be so hard to see how God might be willing to give up a short period of divine–creaturely relationship for the sake of some other great good. Certainly theists who consider themselves able to deal with the fact that God has given up the great goods associated with preventing holocausts won't think there to be – nor should they think there to be – something fundamentally different from the problem of evil or more difficult to handle in the hiddenness problem.

What should we say about this? I suggest we distinguish three motives that might be attributed to God here: the *anti-bad* motive, the *pro-good* motive, and the *pro-relationship* motive. The critic has so far been focused on the first two of these, but it is the third that we will need to think about if we want to see the hiddenness problem for what it truly is. And then we will also see how it should clearly and carefully be distinguished from the problem of evil.

Consider this quotation from the philosopher Robert Adams: "The ideal of Christian love includes not only benevolence but also desire for certain kinds of personal relationship, for their own sake. Were that not so, it would be strange to call it 'love.' It is an abuse of the word 'love' to say that one *loves* a person...if one does not care, except instrumentally, about one's relation to that object." And again: "The Bible depicts a God who seems at least as interested in divine-human relationships as in human happiness per se."[2]

Reflecting on these points will get us into the right neighborhood. We shouldn't expect God to be open to relationship with creatures just because it would be good for them any more than we should expect a loving mother to behave in this way in relation to her children. The fullness of love, which God obviously would have to have, involves valuing personal relationship for its own sake. And when we have distinguished the pro-relationship motive from the pro-good motive in this way, we are able to see something else about love and relationship: that openness to personal relationship, properly understood, is just *written into* love. I would add to the Adams observation that it is an abuse of the word 'love' to say that one *loves* a person at a time if one is not open to relationship with that person at that time. Certainly the motives of benevolence may *add* force to the atheist's claim that God would prevent nonresistant nonbelief, but the latter's fundamental basis lies elsewhere.

There are various reasons for even serious thinkers to miss this point, and thus to miss the new challenge presented by the hiddenness argument. Of course, some of these thinkers are, as suggested earlier,

---

[2]   Robert M. Adams, *The Virtue of Faith and Other Essays in Philosophical Theology* (New York: Oxford University Press, 1987), 188, 189.

motivated to defend the existence of God against new challenges – what better way to do this than by suggesting that the challenge isn't new at all! But this temptation may be overcome by some or all who experience it, and in other thinkers isn't going to be present. So it is worth noting another factor: the tradition in philosophy of favoring such 'hard' attributes of God as omnipotence and omniscience. Benevolence may also come into consideration, but usually it is with an emphasis on a desire for the well-being of creatures that could be exercised from afar. Some might say that the neglect of 'softer' qualities such as relational love by philosophers stems from the fact that most of them are male. I venture no such conjecture here, though I think the neglect in question is clear. When it is remedied, and when theists stop to consider what the hiddenness arguer is actually emphasizing rather than being influenced only by what they themselves might emphasize, the hiddenness argument as stated earlier will better be able to stand out as distinct from the problem of evil.

A final point that needs to be made here fills out an observation from the third section, "Defending the Hiddenness Argument": in part precisely because of the pro-relationship emphasis that is central to the hiddenness argument, 'greater good' theodicies of the type that have been used from time immemorial for the problem of evil do not work nearly as well for the hiddenness problem, and so in this way too we see how the latter is not 'close enough' to the problem of evil in the way suggested by the critic. For example, consider how free will is brought into play when the question is whether God might permit some *pain and suffering* despite being perfectly *benevolent*. There is no obvious way to extend this move to the hiddenness problem. For one thing, free will could be exercised in innumerable ways even if no one ever had any choice on the matter of whether to believe in God. Indeed, it could be exercised precisely in response to God's openness! For one would still have to choose whether (and to what extent) to react positively to such openness. Here it's important to remember that awareness of God need not come from some blinding display of divine power. Subtly modulated religious experience is also possible. And so the possibility of a rejection of God need not be ruled out when nonresistant nonbelief is prevented.

More to the present point: as we saw earlier, the idea of an unending, ever-growing personal relationship with God is sufficiently commodious to allow for the realization, within such relationship, of the very goods God is often said to be unable to achieve without postponing or interrupting it or of other goods belonging to the same type. A special instance of this strategy is also noteworthy. It points us to the fact that *belief* in God and *experience* of God are not to be conflated; it is possible for God to feel far away even for one whose reasons for believing in the existence of God are many and forceful. Thus there is the possibility, within a relationship with God, of something like what mystics have called 'the dark night of the soul' – a kind of *secondary* hiddenness that would be conducive to whatever goods of testing or courage (and so on) are thought to require God to be hidden in the *primary* way that would deprive creatures of belief in God, shutting the door to a personal relationship with God. Perhaps this kind of point, which emphasizes all that is available within a relationship with God, could be used by those who advance arguments from evil too, but it will be evident that it emerges more 'organically' in the context of the hiddenness argument, and also that it provides resources that may leave the hiddenness arguer in a good position vis-à-vis 'greater good' arguments, even if the argument from evil is here vulnerable. So once again we see how a clear distinction between the problem of evil and the problem of hiddenness is warranted.

MIGHT THE HIDDENNESS ARGUMENT AND THE ARGUMENT FROM EVIL PROFITABLY JOIN FORCES?

It is important that we see how the two arguments are distinct. But after having seen this, there may be intellectual benefit in considering how they could work together to produce a *third* argument that is stronger than either of the two on its own. Let's take a moment to explore how this could work.

The most obvious way would involve the suggestion that divine motives of interest to each argument are together applicable either to nonresistant nonbelief or to some fact about evil, thus providing added reason to suppose that it would not exist or occur if there were a God. For example, the pro-relationship motive provides an *extra* reason for God to be *anti-bad* – hurting people can drive them away! On the other side, our earlier discussion has already taken note of how not just the pro-relationship motive but also the pro-good motive and the anti-bad motive might be appealed to when arguing that God would not permit nonresistant nonbelief or some particular type or instance thereof. Although the hiddenness argument doesn't need any such move to get it going, there is nothing in principle to prevent it from being applied, and perhaps the result would be the stronger for it.

Perhaps. But a more interesting way of having the two arguments join forces will take us in another direction, I think. Consider people nonresistant to God who experience horrific suffering and *also* lack conscious access to God. Should such people exist, of any one of them, the following structural point about God's motives might be made.

A perfectly loving God would not only have motives sufficient to prevent the horrific suffering of this person and sufficient to prevent this person's nonresistant nonbelief but also would have the more complex or meta-motive to ensure that, if it was impossible to act on the former motive, the latter would be acted on instead. Wherever someone's horrific suffering was impossible to avoid, a perfectly loving God would grant the person conscious access to the divine. (Notice that we can understand 'if' and 'wherever' here in such a way as to allow for the possibility that horrific suffering never in fact *is* impossible to avoid.) Should this point go through, we could argue for atheism from any case in which someone experiences the dreadful combined condition in question, even if both the hiddenness argument and the argument from horrors as developed in the literature were to be quite unsuccessful. We would then say that even if God were to permit cases of hiddenness and even if God were to permit cases of horrors, hiddenness and horrors would never be combined in any individual person's life in the manner in question.

What should we say of such an argument, which emphasizes not a multiplicity of motives applied to a single case of evil or nonresistant nonbelief but rather a meta-motive rendering problematic any single case in which evil of a certain sort and nonresistant nonbelief are combined? I will not venture a judgment as to its success or failure here. But that it is of interest and worthy of further investigation is supported by a number of points. First, it should not be hard to find evidence that hiddenness and horrors sometimes *are* combined in the way mentioned, if not in the present then in the long evolutionary history of hominin species like our own. Second, the benevolent motive of compassion must surely respond more strongly (if such is possible) to the thought of someone undergoing horrors without even the assurance of belief in God than to horrors alone, and the relational motive of love must respond even more strongly (if such is possible) to the thought of being closed to relationship with the one loved when the beloved is undergoing horrors than to being closed off from relationship alone. Third, it may well be an uphill battle in the extreme to combat an atheistic argument from hiddenness and horrors that is able to allow that God might well permit hiddenness and that God might well permit horrors!

OTHER RELATIONSHIPS BETWEEN THE HIDDENNESS PROBLEM AND THE PROBLEM OF EVIL

In this final section of the chapter, I will briefly address a motley set of further relationships between the two problems that might seem to invite attention. Here I will not always restrict myself to the single argument that I have set out and called 'the hiddenness argument' when referring to the corresponding problem.

(1) The problem of evil is often said to allow for both logical and evidential formulations, and the same is true of the hiddenness problem. The hiddenness argument discussed earlier falls into the former category, and there are various ways, actual and imaginable, of producing a similar argument that falls into the latter. All that's required for an argument of the latter type is a more modest aspiration: the *probability* that inductive arguments seek instead of the certainty that deductive arguments can provide. Something often overlooked here, however, is that the domain of probability is murky and poorly understood and that this murkiness can rub off on probability arguments. So even if in a certain sense they are more modest, they often do require that formidable obstacles not faced by deductive arguments be overcome before a great deal of confidence can be reposed in them. In consequence of this fact, sound deductive arguments must have a great deal of value when they can be found. Today in philosophy, there is not much confidence in the ideal of deduction, but I myself am inclined to think that there may be many good deductive arguments we have not yet found, since in evolutionary terms, we are still at a very early stage of investigation. Perhaps, until recently, the hiddenness argument discussed earlier was one of them.

(2) Both problems introduce phenomena that are said to be in some way contrary to the moral character of God – and, specifically, to the love of God. For this reason, in my 1993 book, which first developed the hiddenness problem as an argument for atheism, I spoke of that problem as a 'special instance' of the problem of evil.[3] I therefore bear some of the responsibility for this confusion entering the literature. As this remark makes obvious, I subsequently decided that this was a misleading way of talking, and the previous parts of this chapter explain why. Here it might be added that 'moral character of God' is a very broad expression: it's hard to imagine any phenomenon someone might put forward as indicating the nonexistence of God that would not properly be said to be, in one way or another, in conflict with the moral character of God. Even divine love is too broad to allow for a convincing assimilation of the newer problem to the older one, given the distinction that we have found between the benevolence and the relational motives that equally belong to love.

---

[3]   Schellenberg, *Divine Hiddenness and Human Reason*, 7.

(3) In my view, of the two problems, the hiddenness problem as set out in the second section, "The Hiddenness Argument," is the more *fundamental*. This third relationship is more controversial than the others, but here is how it may be defended. That there is this hiddenness problem – in particular, that the nonresistant nonbelief making it possible actually occurs – in an important sense explains why there is a problem of evil. If God's existence were clear enough to make nonresistant nonbelief an impossibility, then *only those disposed to resist God would be found suggesting that facts about evil threaten to disprove God's existence*. As it is, everyone who thinks hard about the issue – including theists – can see the intellectual threat presented by evil, and so it is an important problem. It might still be a problem of a different kind if there were no hiddenness problem. Theists, in particular, would be spending time trying to figure out why God permits evil. But no one who came to these issues with true philosophical openness, ready and willing to believe in God, would see in the argument from evil a good reason to be an atheist.

Why would this be so? For surely the argument from evil could still be formulated. The reason is this. Everyone open and willing to believe whatever the evidence shows would, in that other world, in which there is no nonresistant nonbelief, believe in the existence of God. The available evidence would include strong evidence of the existence of God not actually available to us today that outweighs any evidence against the existence of God, including any evidence provided by the problem of evil. Perhaps this would be theoretical evidence of God's existence widely distributed among creaturely minds; perhaps instead it would be experiential evidence of the existence of God available to all (though also resistible by those with the relevant motives, as explained in connection with the idea of 'subtle modulation' in the fifth section). It doesn't really matter. The point is that the problem of evil only gets to be as intellectually impressive as it is today because of the existence of the problematic phenomenon emphasized by the hiddenness argument. Thus the latter argument gets at something more basic, more fundamental, in the domain of atheistic reasoning than the former.

There are, then, various connections between hiddenness and evil. But the most important point to take away from this discussion, on which many of the others rest, is that quite distinct ways of arguing to the nonexistence of God are represented by hiddenness and evil, not just one. The hiddenness problem is a *new* challenge to belief in God, and quite a formidable one, as we have seen. Therefore, even if a solution to the venerable old problem of evil should one day present itself, traditional theists would not be in a position to breathe easy.

FURTHER READING

Drange, Theodore. *Nonbelief and Evil: Two Arguments for the Nonexistence of God*. Amherst: Prometheus Books, 1998.

Draper, Paul. "Seeking But Not Believing: Confessions of a Practicing Agnostic." In *Divine Hiddenness: New Essays*. Ed. D. Howard-Snyder and P. Moser. New York: Cambridge University Press, 2002, 197–214.

Evans, C. Stephen. *Natural Signs and Knowledge of God: A New Look at Theistic Arguments*. Oxford: Oxford University Press, 2010.

"Is the Argument from Hiddenness a Stronger Challenge to Theism than the Argument from Evil?" http://dudeexmachina.wordpress.com/2012/02/22/is-the-argument-fromhiddenness-a-stronger-challenge-to-theism-than-the-argument-from-evil/ (Accessed 24 July, 2014).

Maitzen, Stephen. "Divine Hiddenness and the Demographics of Theism." *Religious Studies* 42 (2006): 177–91.

Schellenberg, J. L. *Divine Hiddenness and Human Reason*. Ithaca, NY: Cornell University Press, 1993/2006.

The Hiddenness Argument. Oxford: Oxford University Press, 2015.

The Wisdom to Doubt: A Justification of Religious Skepticism. Ithaca, NY: Cornell University Press, 2007.

"The Hiddenness Problem and the Problem of Evil." *Faith and Philosophy* 27 (2010): 41–57.

7 Anti-Theodicy

N. N. TRAKAKIS

WHAT IS ANTI-THEODICY?

Anti-theodicy is a relatively new contender in contemporary discussions on the problem of evil, at least within analytic (Anglo-American) philosophy of religion. Although anti-theodical views have a long and venerable history in philosophical and religious thought, proponents today usually come from outside analytic circles, particularly from theological and so-called Continental quarters. Given the comparative novelty of the anti-theodicy position, and given also the increasing attention that is being paid to it, it will be helpful to clarify as precisely as possible its central ideas and commitments.

Anti-theodicy, however, is not a uniform doctrine, having been developed in various ways by different proponents. Nonetheless, it is possible to single out some prominent themes, both critical or negative and positive or constructive. Negatively, as its prefix suggests, anti-theodicy stands in opposition to a certain way of responding to the problem of evil, above all (but not only) the tradition of 'theodicy'. A theodicy, roughly speaking, is a reasonable or plausible justification of God's permission of evil, where this consists in delineating what might be (or what are likely to be) God's purposes for allowing evil. These purposes are the 'greater goods' for the sake of which God allows evil, and there is typically thought to be a necessary (and not merely contingent) connection between the evil and the greater good, so that the eradication of the former would necessitate the loss of the latter. To illustrate with a well-known theodicy, that developed by John Hick: nothing less than a risky, dangerous and religiously ambiguous 'soul-making' environment, as our world appears to be, is required for the fulfilment of God's overriding purpose of bringing his human creatures to freely transcend their natural self-centredness and to develop the most desirable qualities of moral character and, especially, to enter into loving communion with others and their Maker. If the world did not bear the marks of soul shaping (if, for instance, the world were a hedonistic paradise whose inhabitants experience a maximum of pleasure and a minimum of pain), then God's goal of eliciting the finest characteristics of human personality – particularly the capacity to love – could not be realized. By thus tracing a necessary connection between evil and the greater good of soul making, Hick's theodicy helps to vindicate the justice or goodness of God in the face of evil.

Anti-theodicists obviously reject theodicy, but not for the reasons philosophers of religion typically do so. Hick's theodicy, for example, might be criticized on the grounds that it does not account for natural evil – that is, suffering that results from natural processes (e.g. an earthquake, a tsunami) that cannot be attributed to the misuse of any human being's free will; or one may object that, even if some suffering serves the purposes of soul making, much suffering does not and instead only debilitates people's capacity to lead a loving and meaningful life. But for the anti-theodicist, all such objections are beside the point. It is always open to Hick and other theodicists to provide a supplement or emendation that will cover the relevant lacuna. The anti-theodicist, however, claims that theodicies are by nature defective in various respects and that these are not the kinds of deficiencies that could be remedied if only we knew more about, say, God's intentions or the workings of the world.

It is along these lines that Zachary Braiterman introduced the term 'anti-theodicy' in *(God) After Auschwitz: Tradition and Change in Post-Holocaust Jewish Thought*, where he defined it as "any religious response to the problem of evil whose proponents refuse to justify, explain, or accept as somehow meaningful the relationship between God and suffering."[1] As this makes clear, anti-theodicy is for Braiterman a specifically *religious* response to the problem of evil, though I do not see any reason why the anti-theodicy position could not also be employed in a non-religious or anti-theist manner, with the aim of showing that the problem of evil renders theistic belief false or irrational.[2]

The very project of theodicy, on this view, is a non-starter, and this is because theodicies invariably rest on a range of deeply problematic presuppositions, framework principles, and categories and styles of thought. The specific flaws may be moral, conceptual, metaphysical, or methodological

---

[1]   Zachary Braiterman, *(God) After Auschwitz: Tradition and Change in Post-Holocaust Jewish Thought* (Princeton, NJ: Princeton University Press, 1998), 31.
[2]   The term 'anti-theodicy' can also be found in other writers, including John Roth, "Theistic Antitheodicy," *American Journal of Theology and Philosophy* 25 (2004): 276–93.

in nature. Again, we should not seek to present the anti-theodicy program
in a uniform way, as different aspects of the theodical enterprise will come
under fire by different anti-theodicists. However, some characteristic criticisms of theodicy can be identified so as to at least give an indication of
the trajectory of thinking espoused by anti-theodicists.

A typical anti-theodical claim is that theodicy subverts aspects of
morality or specific moral concepts we would not wish to do without.
One such concept is that of 'evil', and it is sometimes argued that certain
streams in theodicy trivialize and diminish the reality and horror of evil
and thus surreptitiously end up altering, if not disfiguring or destroying, our moral compass. John Hick and Marilyn McCord Adams, for
example, argue that God is not exonerated in the face of evil unless a
certain eschatology is posited, one in which (and here I follow Adams's
formulation) everyone is afforded everlasting, post-mortem beatific
intimacy with God, this in turn providing them with good reason for
considering their life – in spite of any evils it may have contained – as
a great good on the whole, thus removing any grounds of complaint
against God. Since beatific relationship with God is an incommensurable good (more precisely, it is incommensurable with respect to any
merely temporal evils or goods), it does not simply outweigh any evil
that someone may suffer but renders the suffering trivial by comparison.[3] The anti-theodicist detects here a subtle but definite shift in
moral perspective, one that brings the very reality or at least the horror
of much evil under doubt. Consider, again, what Adams is proposing.
The time will come when we will be able to view our sufferings *sub
specie aeternitatis*. This will be the perspective we will enjoy in the
eschaton when we find ourselves experiencing beatific intimacy with
God, and moreover it will provide us with the *correct* perspective on
our sufferings – it's not as though we will then be looking at our earthly
lives through 'rose-coloured glasses', but rather we will finally be seeing things as they truly are (indeed, for Adams, we would not, at that
future time, even wish that the past were different). What this means,
however, is that what we initially regarded as evil is not so bad after all.[4]

---

[3]   See Marilyn McCord Adams, "Redemptive Suffering: A Christian Solution to the
Problem of Evil." In *Rationality, Religious Belief, and Moral Commitment*. Ed. Robert
Audi and William J. Wainwright (Ithaca, NY: Cornell University Press, 1996), 262–3;
and Adams, *Horrendous Evils and the Goodness of God* (Melbourne: Melbourne
University Press, 1999), 162–3. Adams, however, does not seek to provide a theodicy
but only a way of showing how God can be good to created persons despite the evil
they experience.

[4]   Consider also the view of Stephen T. Davis (a proponent of the free-will theodicy) that
"in the kingdom of God, all evil will be overcome. People will be able to look back

But to come to see earthly evils in this way is to end up with a moral perspective on the world wherein evil does not really exist or at least where the moral categories we customarily deploy have been radically displaced and reconfigured. For evil that is 'not so bad after all' is not genuinely evil.

Another typical anti-theodical view targets the theodicist's denial of even the possibility of gratuitous evil. Theodicists hold, in other words, that every evil is always connected to a greater good and that we ought to believe (or can come to know) this to be so. For the anti-theodicist, however, this has the objectionable consequence of reducing us to an attitude of passivity and fatalism in the face of evil. For why fight to eradicate evil if evil is a necessary or unavoidable part or by-product in God's providential plan for the world? The teleological or instrumentalist conception of evil presupposed in theodicies, where evil is permitted by God *for the sake of* some higher end, is also open to the Kantian criticism that it negates the inherent worth and dignity of persons by treating them as mere means to some end rather than as ends in themselves. D. Z. Phillips expresses this point by saying that theodicy undermines our usual (non-instrumental) way of relating to those who are undergoing some suffering.[5] To highlight this, Phillips concentrates on theodicies which make appeal to the good of moral responsibility and schematises the line of reasoning employed in such theodicies as follows: "Suffering prompts moral responsibility. That people are morally responsible is a good thing. Therefore, this justifies the suffering." But, as Phillips pointedly and humorously remarks, such thinking is subject to a *reductio*: "The argument leads to a grotesque inversion of moral relations to the sufferings of others. Instead of our concern being directed towards the suffering, the suffering is said to have its point in the concern. It would have the Good Samaritan saying, 'Thank you, God, for another opportunity for my moral development.'"[6]

Various other objections to the project of theodicy have been offered by anti-theodicists. The anti-theodical position, however, is not merely a negative one but also has a constructive dimension, and this may well be its most appealing feature. Consider, for example, the anti-theodical

from the perspective of the kingdom of God and see that their past sufferings, no matter how severe, prolonged, or undeserved, have been overcome and *no longer matter*" ("Free Will and Evil." In *Encountering Evil: Live Options in Theodicy*, 2nd edition, ed. Stephen T. Davis. Louisville, KY: Westminster John Knox Press), 84, emphasis mine.
[5] See Phillips, "Theism without Theodicy," 148: 'first bee sting'.
[6] Phillips, "Theism without Theodicy," 148.

view of the customary distinction made between the 'theoretical problem of evil' and the 'practical problem of evil', where the theoretical
problem is the intellectual matter of determining the rationality or
truth of theistic belief in light of the facts about evil, while the practical problem concerns the existential and experiential difficulties evil
creates for love and trust towards God (or the difficulties in combating
evil and alleviating suffering). Theodicists tend to uphold a distinction
of this sort, and they usually offer their work as a solution to the theoretical problem of evil only – the practical problem is regarded as the
business of priests and healthcare workers. But if, as anti-theodicists
suggest, such dichotomies are artificial and pernicious, reducing philosophy to a technical and disinterested exercise, rather than a holistic enterprise involving the whole person (body and mind, passion and
intellect) and calling forth the resources and insights of the arts as well
as the sciences, then not only a very different approach to the problem
of evil than the well-worn theodical one may result but, more fundamentally, an alternative way of thinking about and practicing philosophy itself will be made possible. Anti-theodicy thus quickly leads down
the path of metaphilosophy.

Equally significantly and just as constructively, anti-theodicy opens
the way to alternative understandings of reality, particularly the ultimate or divine reality. Sometimes this is put in terms of the historically
contingent character of theodicy, where it is held that the problem of
evil (as conceptualized by contemporary philosophers) and the atten-
dant project of theodicy represent a uniquely 'modern' preoccupation.
On this view, theodicy has a particular historical pedigree: it is a way of
understanding God and the world that arose out of the historical circumstances and philosophical ideas of the modern period and thus reflects
the worldview of 'modernism' (where 'modernism' refers to the values,
practices, and institutions of the West that begin to emerge at the end
of the medieval period in the 15th century and become dominant in the
18th and 19th centuries). It is therefore anachronistic to trace the problem of evil back to pre-modern times, as though the ideas and assumptions of modern philosophers of religion about God and evil must have
been upheld also by (say) the church fathers in the medieval period or the
authors of the books of the Bible. Karen Kilby gives expression to this
view when writing that

> It is clear that the problem of evil as presented by philosophers of
> religion is not an ahistorical, timeless question, a universal human
> conundrum, but that in different societies and in different parts

of the Christian tradition people have, in the face of various evils, asked very different kinds of questions.[7]

Kilby highlights the ways in which contemporary analytic discussions on the problem of evil are deeply coloured by Enlightenment thought on religion, observing that

> the God whose compatibility with evil they [contemporary theodicists such as Hick and Swinburne] discuss is presented as an abstract entity with a number of characteristics, a God who can be described without reference to any particular narratives, without any discussion of Incarnation, Christology, Trinity.[8]

But, for Kilby, this is not necessarily an objection (or a fatal objection) to the practice of theodicy, though she adds that "the strong Enlightenment overtones of theodicy are enough to make a Christian theologian begin to wonder whether something *might* have gone wrong here – to raise the theological hackles, as it were."[9] Arguably, what has gone wrong is that the theodicist has got God wrong (or: they have got the wrong god). The implications may be far reaching, giving rise to the challenging opportunities of speculative metaphysics (still decried by some philosophers), with the aim of re-envisioning the nature of God and reality. But in seeking alternative models of God or returning to more traditional ones, it is necessary to remain true to the realities of evil while also avoiding the pitfalls of modernist conceptions (e.g. a narrow theistic framework or what Rowe called 'restricted standard theism', as well as a tendency towards anthropomorphism) and preferably without renouncing a commitment to divine providence – that is, the idea of God being actively involved in and lovingly governing the world. There is, to be sure, a plethora of such models, including the Thomist notion of God as 'pure act' and *ipsum esse subsistens* (subsistent being itself); or the process reconceptualization of divine power as persuasive,

[7]   Karen Kilby, "Evil and the Limits of Theology," *New Blackfriars* 84 (2003): 22. For similar views, see Kenneth Surin, *Theology and the Problem of Evil* (Oxford: Basil Blackwell, 1986), 39–46, and John Swinton, *Raging with Compassion: Pastoral Responses to the Problem of Evil* (Grand Rapids: William B. Eerdmands Publishing Company, 2007), ch. 2.

[8]   Kilby, "Evil and the Limits of Theology," 14. Kilby adds, "also the way evil is discussed, and the way evil is discussed in relation to God, are detached from any wider theological context" (14).

[9]   Kilby, "Evil and the Limits of Theology," 14, emphasis in original. Kilby, however, also contends that even suitably 'expanded' versions of theism – such as those that provide a distinctly Christian account of God and creation – may well still face a problem of evil of their own (22–23).

not coercive, thus rejecting the 'monarchical' model of God found in classical theism (where God, as 'ruling Caesar', has the capacity to coercively control any detail of our historical trajectory);[10] or, moving further away from traditional theism, the pantheist identification of God with the world or all-there-is, and the Advaita ('non-dual') Vedanta view of Brahman as the supreme (singular and featureless) reality. This is not to say that these models are guaranteed to succeed where Enlightenment models have failed, but it does at least offer the possibility of seeing anew the relationship between God, humanity and evil.[11]

It is interesting in this context to compare how responses to evil or suffering have changed from medieval to modern times. Thomas G. Long, in *What Shall We Say? Evil, Suffering, and the Crisis of Faith*,[12] highlights the paradigm shift that has taken place by considering how a leading contemporary scholar of the New Testament and early Christianity, Bart D. Ehrman, came to give up belief in God as a result of finding the existence of God incompatible with the realities of suffering.[13] Long invites an interesting thought-experiment: Suppose Ehrman lived in the Middle Ages, would he have responded in this way? Most likely not. But then, how can we account for Ehrman's response, replicated as it is in countless modern lives? Long writes:

> If Ehrman had lived in the fourteenth century, his sense of injustice about suffering might have provoked him to prayerful lament, to ever-greater cries to heaven for God to come and save. But Ehrman lives on this side of modernity's ditch, and his crisis of faith leads him not to his knees in prayer but to his mind in thinking things through rationally. A fourteenth-century mind would encounter terrible suffering and say, "This is from the hand of God. What is God

---

[10] See David Ray Griffin, in his exchange with Phillips, in "Theism without Theodicy," 164–5, where Griffin holds that the process view avoids the anthropomorphism inherent in the traditional theistic picture of God as "having the power to control worldly events" (165).

[11] Kilby's paper, "Evil and the Limits of Theology," 17–18, provides some salutary suggestions on how to understand the way in which divine agency relates to human agency without succumbing to the common theodical fallacy of seeing the two as in a kind of competitive relationship.

[12] Thomas G. Long, *What Shall We Say? Evil, Suffering, and the Crisis of Faith* (Grand Rapids: William B. Eerdmans Publishing Company, 2011).

[13] Ehrman recounts this in his book, *God's Problem: How the Bible Fails to Answer Our Most Important Question – Why We Suffer* (New York: HarperCollins, 2008). Thomas Long, in ch. 1 of *What Shall We Say?*, similarly compares Leibniz's response to the problem of evil with Voltaire's reaction to the Lisbon earthquake (of November 1, 1755), seeing in this a move from an 'enchanted' world to a 'disenchanted' and deistic world.

saying to us?" A contemporary mind encounters suffering and asks, "How does the reality of this suffering fit into my worldview? How do the pieces of reality I think of as true fit together logically?"[14]

This may not get matters entirely right, insofar as medievals, as much as moderns, sought to 'think things through rationally'. Medievals, however, operated with a different kind of rationality, one that was embedded in religious commitment (famously expressed in Anselm's 'faith seeking understanding' dictum), while moderns have a relatively autonomous conception of rationality that seeks to question or authenticate religious beliefs from the outside, as it were, or from a purportedly objective or neutral point of view. Nonetheless, Long makes a significant point, which could also be put by asking: Why does no biblical author or medieval theologian regard suffering as even posing *prima facie* evidence against the existence of God, whereas today philosophers and theologians routinely view suffering in this way? The answer, it seems, will lie in large part in our metaphysics, the way we construe the world and God's relationship to it. Anti-theodicy, in short, calls for a reconsideration of questions not only in metaphilosophy but also in metaphysics.

ANTI-THEODICY AND PESSIMISM

Anti-theodicy, as a relative newcomer on the analytic philosophical scene, is beginning to receive a greater amount of attention and scrutiny, in comparison with the swift dismissals that were common previously. A number of journal articles, for example, have recently appeared, offering lengthy and rigorous treatments of the anti-theodicy position, and it is one of these that I will concentrate upon here: Samuel Shearn's "Moral Critique and Defence of Theodicy," published in a 2013 issue of *Religious Studies* and the recipient of the journal's Postgraduate Essay Prize for that year.[15]

The focus of Shearn's paper is what he calls *moral anti-theodicy*: "objections to the practice of theoretical theodicy on moral grounds."[16] Shearn goes on to add that "such objections have been

---

[14] Long, *What Shall We Say?* 23, emphasis in original.
[15] Samuel Shearn, "Moral Critique and Defence of Theodicy," *Religious Studies* 49 (2013): 439–58. See also Atle O. Søvik, "Why Almost All Moral Critique of Theodicies Is Misplaced," *Religious Studies* 44 (2008): 479–86, and Robert Mark Simpson, "Moral Antitheodicy: Prospects and Problems," *International Journal for Philosophy of Religion* 65 (2009): 153–69.
[16] Shearn, "Moral Critique and Defence of Theodicy," 439.

presented by both atheists and theists.''[17] In a somewhat circuitous trajectory, Shearn considers various arguments both for and against (moral) anti-theodicy and ends up offering a partial defence of (moral) anti-theodicy. Specifically, he contends that anti-theodicy is persuasive when viewed as a critique of 'ambitious theodicies' but not when taken as targeting 'low-ambition theodicies'. More precisely still, "*ambitious theodicies*, which claim God has good reason for allowing horrendous evil because he intends greater goods to emerge from those evils, will be implausible to people suffering acutely and therefore always be a trivialization of their experience – a reinterpretation they cannot accept."[18] *Less ambitious theodicies*, by contrast, are theodicies that "do not reinterpret suffering as being advantageous in itself but promise that, from the perspective of the eschaton, life will be judged to be overall good,"[19] and Shearn places Hick's soul-making theodicy and Plantinga's free-will defence in this category.[20]

Although my focus will be on the connection Shearn draws between less ambitious theodicies and a morally problematic form of pessimism, it might be helpful to consider some general features of Shearn's discussion, as these unfortunately betray prevalent misconceptions regarding the anti-theodicy view. To begin with, there is the reduction of anti-theodicy to *moral* anti-theodicy. It is perfectly in order, of course, to circumscribe the object of one's study in a short journal paper, but it is regrettable that the anti-theodicy view is regularly limited or narrowed in this fashion. For what is thereby overlooked are the various non-moral – for example, metaphilosophical and metaphysical – dimensions of the anti-theodicy position adumbrated earlier.

But even the moral dimension is unduly restricted by Shearn. Moral anti-theodicy, as Shearn understands it, consists in the main in the charge of 'the trivialization of suffering'. He explains that "theodicy trivializes suffering if it reinterprets suffering in a way the sufferer cannot

[17]   Shearn, "Moral Critique and Defence of Theodicy," 439.

[18]   Shearn, "Moral Critique and Defence of Theodicy," 446, emphasis in original.

[19]   Shearn, "Moral Critique and Defence of Theodicy," 446. It is questionable whether the mere judgement that life is overall good despite the evils it may have contained is sufficient to constitute a *theodicy*. A theodicy (as standardly understood) is an explanation for God's permission of suffering, and the mere fact that the goodness of life is not undermined by evil does not provide any explanation for God's permission of evil.

[20]   Later, Shearn draws the distinction between ambitious and less ambitious theodicies by way of "a qualitative difference between justifying horrendous suffering and justifying the creation of the world as a place containing conditions which make horrendous evils possible (as in the free-will defence)" ("Moral Critique and Defence of Theodicy," 452).

accept."[21] And he claims to detect such a charge in "a set of complaints regularly made against theodicy, such as that theodicy makes light of suffering, does not give horrific experiences due weight, and fails to take the devastating impact of great evils seriously."[22] So as to render the charge of trivialization more plausible, Shearn restricts it to cases of *horrendous evil* only, so that if the sufferer insists that a mild discomfort (Shearn gives the example of feeling hunger before dinner) is a terrible evil that could not be interpreted as on balance good, then we would not be obliged to follow suit and regard the discomfort as an evil.[23] However, one might wish to present the anti-theodicy critique as a *global* one, in that it rules out all theodicies, not merely theodicies of a certain sort (e.g. theodicies for horrendous evils). Be that as it may, the moral criticisms anti-theodicists wish to make cannot all be grouped under the charge of trivialization. Moral anti-theodicy should allow for more, including some of the criticisms outlined earlier: the subversion of moral practice, and in particular the motivation to resist and oppose evil, and the instrumentalization of human persons. Finally, anti-theodicy need not be linked with the prioritization of the sufferer's point of view, as it is by Shearn. The problem here is that, even though the sufferer's perspective must be accorded great weight, there is no need to accord it absolute or incontrovertible authority. Even in cases of horrific evil, first-person accounts may get matters significantly wrong – for example, failing to recognize the gravity of the situation, or misdescribing certain features of the experience, or being wounded by the traumatic experience in such a way as not being able to see the connections between (say) one's suffering and some higher good. It would be preferable, then, to formulate the trivialization charge in a way that does not place undue weight on the sufferer's perspective.

Nonetheless, in an intriguing move towards the close of his paper, Shearn considers the possibility that the debate between the theodicist and the anti-theodicist runs much deeper than is apparent at first glance, being at bottom a clash of worldviews. Initially, Shearn presents this clash as follows:

> Thus far it seems there are grounds for considering this conflict [between the theodicist and the anti-theodicist] as about competing visions of the world. The overall positive or negative 'picture' within which one interprets evils is not merely a matter of evident goods

---

[21] Shearn, "Moral Critique and Defence of Theodicy," 441.
[22] Shearn, "Moral Critique and Defence of Theodicy," 440.
[23] Shearn, "Moral Critique and Defence of Theodicy," 441–2.

which emerge from those evils, or a counting up of goods and evils, but a way of seeing the world. The theodicist insists that the good outweighs the bad. The anti-theodicist insists the bad is so weighty it could never be matched or overcome. This seems like an aesthetic impasse, and not simply a moral issue.[24]

This may not be the most felicitous way of representing the conflict, for why should the impasse be considered an *aesthetic* one? The differences between the two mutually incompatible ways of seeing the world might be conceptual, metaphysical, or moral, as well as aesthetic, or a combination of all these.[25] It is also unclear why the anti-theodicist is described as claiming that "the bad is so weighty it could never be matched or overcome." This is a matter I will return to later, for it is important to recognize that even the anti-theodicist may hold that all evil is overcome, redeemed, or defeated, even if it is not overcome in the specific way envisaged by the theodicist.

Shearn then turns to 'Karamazov's Challenge', in which Ivan in Dostoyevsky's *The Brothers Karamazov* invites his pious brother Alyosha to consider the following now-famous scenario:

> Imagine that you yourself are erecting the edifice of human fortune with the goal of, at the finale, making people happy, of at last giving them peace and quiet, but that in order to do it it would be necessary and unavoidable to torture to death only one tiny little creature, that same little child that beat its breast with its little fist, and on its unavenged tears to found that edifice, would you agree to be the architect on those conditions, tell me and tell me truly?[26]

Ivan's contention is that a heavenly afterlife of bliss built upon torturing to death a single child cannot be morally justified. And so, if this is the way in which God has created our world, then God's creation cannot be morally justified but must be rejected. Ivan would rather 'return his entry ticket' than enter into an eternal harmony achieved in that way. Shearn detects, first, a structural parallel with the Free Will Defence: As with the scenario depicted by Ivan, so too in the Free Will Defence, God creates a world in which humans are capable of freely bringing about horrendous evil. Importantly, both display an *all-or-nothing* structure: either we

---

24 Shearn, "Moral Critique and Defence of Theodicy," 452.

25 Even a clear-cut distinction between morality and aesthetics is problematic, as Shearn himself acknowledges – see "Moral Critique and Defence of Theodicy," 458, n17.

26 Dostoyevsky, *The Brothers Karamazov*, book V, ch. 4; quoted in Shearn, "Moral Critique and Defence of Theodicy," 452–3.

have it all (creation, freedom, and horrific evil), or we have nothing (no creation, no free will, and no horrific evil).[27] Shearn then identifies a further parallel, this time with Schopenhauer's Pessimism (or 'SP' for short):

> SP: Given the suffering the world contains, even given any amount of suffering, it would have been better had the world not existed.

Shearn goes on to state:

> Ivan effectively endorses a similar pessimism about this world as it is, since, according to Ivan, given the existence of one child who endured horrendous suffering, it would be better that the world had never been.[28]

The conclusion Shearn draws is that "moral anti-theodicy is equivalent to philosophical pessimism."[29] This is presented as a *reductio* of anti-theodicy, since SP is taken to be objectionable on at least two grounds. First, SP is "over-demanding, asking that the moral outrage at incidences of suffering so colour our perception of all of reality as to render human existence on balance harm."[30] Second, SP is self-defeating. The idea here is that SP is grounded in the conviction that life is of great value and that this value is diminished by the experience of suffering (it is this conviction that gives Ivan's Challenge its great force). But SP is just the thesis that life is not to be affirmed but is to be rejected. Hence, SP is internally inconsistent.[31]

Assuming that we do not wish to follow Schopenhauer's lead in subscribing to SP, how can the anti-theodicist avoid such gloomy pessimism?[32] Shearn has posed a significant challenge (aimed, he notes, only at anti-theodicists who oppose 'less ambitious' theodicies), underscoring in the process the intimate relationship between theodicy construction and the pervasive human longing for meaning. Theodicies seek to outline the providential plan God has for his creatures and, in doing so,

---

27 Shearn, "Moral Critique and Defence of Theodicy," 453.
28 Shearn, "Moral Critique and Defence of Theodicy," 453.
29 Shearn, "Moral Critique and Defence of Theodicy," 454.
30 Shearn, "Moral Critique and Defence of Theodicy," 454.
31 Shearn, "Moral Critique and Defence of Theodicy," 454.
32 Interestingly, Schopenhauer himself did not see any incompatibility between a religious outlook and a pessimistic one, and indeed he took Christianity (at its best!) to be a *pessimistic* religion. See Christopher Janaway, "Schopenhauer's Pessimism." In *The Cambridge Companion to Schopenhauer.* Ed. Janaway (Cambridge: Cambridge University Press, 1999), 319–20. Any stark opposition, therefore, between religious faith and Schopenhauerian pessimism may be untenable, without thereby assuming that all aspects of the one can be reconciled with the other.

help to give meaning, hope, and consolation to sufferers. By contrast, the anti-theodicist, by refusing the very practice of theodicy, appears to lack the resources to address sufferers in terms of meaning and hope, and may even be committed to a nihilistic picture of the world as utterly random and chaotic and of human life as lacking any intrinsic worth or purpose. But such a literally hope-less view of life can only undermine rather than strengthen one's will to actively respond to evil, reducing one to fatalistic resignation or indifference in the face of evil. It may seem, then, that the anti-theodicy view only adds to rather than alleviates the contemporary sense of nihilism and meaninglessness, expressed best by Nietzsche's madman as 'the death of God', where the horizon of meaning is wiped away as we plunge continually through an infinite expanse of nothingness. Anti-theodicy thus becomes radically subversive, overturning not only our most cherished beliefs and hopes but even our will to live. In short, anti-theodicy is bad ethics and poor pastoral care.[33]

In light of such charges, the anti-theodicist is well advised not to reject the project of theodicy as obviously detestable or outrageous. For the attempt to cast light on the ways of God is, in some respects at least, an entirely natural (if not honourable) response to the suffering we see around us. As Leszek Kolakowski has stated, "the problem of theodicy, far from being invented for the amusement of speculative minds, has strong and unwithering roots in the everyday experience of those who refuse to admit that suffering and evil are just suffering and evil, plain facts meaning nothing, related to nothing, justified by nothing."[34] We seem to be by nature meaning-seeking creatures, and so the very idea that there is no meaning or point to suffering has the potential to leave us debilitated and despairing.[35]

Albert Camus addressed a similar challenge in *The Myth of Sisyphus*, where he famously stated at the very beginning: "There is but one truly

---

[33]   To be clear, this is my attempt to state an objection to anti-theodicy in the strongest terms; it is not a view endorsed by Shearn (in fact, he rejects it: see "Moral Critique and Defence of Theodicy," 447–8).

[34]   Leszek Kolakowski, *Religion, if There Is No God...On God, the Devil, Sin and Other Worries of the So-Called Philosophy of Religion* (New York: Oxford University Press, 1982), 35. Borrowing from Freud, theodicy construction might also be regarded as the attempt to make one feel "at home in the unhomely." See Beverley Clack, "Distortion, Dishonesty and the Problem of Evil." In *Wrestling with God and with Evil: Philosophical Reflections.* Ed. Hendrik M. Vroom (Amsterdam: Rodopi, 2007), 211.

[35]   The connection between theodicy-construction and meaning-making is also brought out in many sociological accounts of religion, such as those developed by Max Weber, Peter Berger, and Clifford Geertz.

serious philosophical problem and that is suicide."[36] The question, in particular, for Camus is whether life is worth living *given that* life is (in some sense, teased out in the remainder of his essay) meaningless and 'absurd'. And the conclusion he reaches – perhaps surprising for someone so seemingly and relentlessly dark and despairing – is that suicide is not the only or even the most logical option in an absurd world, and so he offers his essay as "a lucid invitation to live and to create, in the very midst of the desert."[37] Camus, I have elsewhere argued, provides the anti-theodicist with the resources for showing that life can be lived (indeed, can only be lived) passionately and meaningfully in complete consciousness of the 'absurdity' of existence and the consequent lack of 'theodical' explanations.[38] However, an alternative, and perhaps more traditionally religious, set of responses to suffering that avoids the perils of theodicy, Schopenhauerian pessimism and Leibnizian optimism has recently been suggested by John Swinton, and it is to this that I now turn.

ANTI-THEODICY AND REDEMPTION

Specializing in practical theology and pastoral care, and with a background in nursing, ministry and healthcare chaplaincy, John Swinton brings these areas of research and experience to bear on the subject of theodicy in *Raging with Compassion: Pastoral Responses to the Problem of Evil*. Much like anti-theodicists, Swinton rejects theodicy, presenting the main thesis of his book in these terms: "I argue that standard philosophical and theological approaches to theodicy not only do not work, but can also be dangerous and have the potential to become sources of evil in and of themselves."[39] In place of traditional or theoretical theodicy, Swinton seeks to offer an alternative perspective, a 'practical theodicy' that is initially described as follows:

> I maintain that theodicy should not be understood as a series of disembodied arguments designed to defend God's love, goodness, and power. We require a different mode of understanding, a mode

---

[36] Camus, *The Myth of Sisyphus*, trans. Justin O'Brien (London: Penguin, 2000 [originally published in French in 1942]), 11.

[37] Camus, *The Myth of Sisyphus*, Preface. Even Schopenhauer did not see suicide as a valid response to our pessimistic predicament but instead advocated a 'denial of the will'. See Janaway, "Schopenhauer's Pessimism," 335–41.

[38] See N. N. Trakakis, "The Absurdity of Evil." In *Being Human: Groundwork for a Theological Anthropology for the 21st Century*. Ed. David Kirchhoffer, Robyn Horner and Patrick McArdle (Melbourne: Mosaic Press, 2013), 203–16.

[39] Swinton, *Raging with Compassion*, 3.

of theodicy that is embodied within the life and practices of the
Christian community. Such a mode of theodicy does not seek primarily to *explain* evil and suffering, but rather presents ways in
which evil and suffering can be *resisted* and *transformed* by the
Christian community and in so doing, can enable Christians to live
faithfully in the midst of unanswered questions as they await God's
redemption of the whole of creation.[40]

I will return shortly to Swinton's alternative proposal and how it
can meet the challenge of pessimism advanced by Shearn. But for now,
it is important to note that Swinton's position is not precisely an anti-
theodical one. Swinton does not reject the possibility that God has morally sufficient reasons for permitting evil; he only wishes to affirm that
at present (in this life) we do not have access to these reasons and that
the reasons (or theodicies) that have been proffered thus far are pastorally
dangerous. As he states,

> I am *not* suggesting that there is no explanation for the way the world
> is and why there is so much evil contained within it... Scripture tells
> us that ultimately we will know and understand. As the apostle Paul
> puts it in his first letter to the Corinthians: "Now we see but a poor
> reflection; then we shall see face to face. Now I know in part; then
> I shall know fully, even as I am fully known." (1 Cor. 13:12) All will
> be revealed in the fullness of the eschaton. The point of the preced-
> ing chapters [chs 1–2] is that, because of the limited nature of our
> present understanding and the inevitable boundaries of our intellect
> when it comes to fathoming the ways of God, we cannot reach a
> coherent understanding of the reasons for evil and suffering.[41]

Swinton thus positions himself as a 'skeptical theist' rather than an anti-
theodicist, where skeptical theism is the view that, given our cognitive
limitations, we are in no position to judge as improbable the statement
that there are goods beyond our ken secured by God's permission of the
evils we find in the world. As Alvin Plantinga expresses this view: "Why
suppose that if God *does* have a reason for permitting evil, the theist
would be the first to know?"[42] Since theists such as Plantinga respond to

---

[40]   Swinton, *Raging with Compassion*, 4, emphases in original.

[41]   Swinton, *Raging with Compassion*, 46, emphasis in original. Similarly, Swinton had
       earlier stated, "My point here is not that ultimately we won't understand [why God
       permits evil]. The point is that we cannot in the present reach a coherent understand-
       ing through human logic" (28, fn.36).

[42]   Alvin Plantinga, *The Nature of Necessity* (Oxford: Clarendon Press, 1974), 10, empha-
       sis in original.

the problem of evil by drawing attention to the limits of human knowledge, they have become known as *skeptical* theists. Such a position, however, has more in common with theodicy than with anti-theodicy. For, according to both skeptical theists and theodicists, there are morally sufficient reasons for God's permission of evil – it's just that skeptical theists think that these reasons are (presently) inscrutable to us, whereas theodicists are more confident about coming to know what these reasons are or might be.

Like Swinton, Karen Kilby defers to divine inscrutability. Kilby rejects the anti-theodicist response as an "overreaction," one which refuses to acknowledge the legitimacy of the problem of evil (as traditionally formulated) and thus seeks "essentially to 'change the subject'." Kilby's preferred response "is to accept the question [as to why God permits evil] and its legitimacy, but to acknowledge that Christian theology is utterly incapable of offering even an approximate answer."[43] On the basis of the unanswerability of the problem of evil, Kilby is led to doubt the possibility of a fully coherent theology: "There are points, then, at which systematic theology ought to be, if not systematically incoherent, then at least systematically dissonant."[44]

A central but neglected difficulty with these appeals to mystery is that they fail to recognize that they embody fundamentally the same structure as theodicies: in both cases there is a commitment to a 'teleology of suffering', the only difference being that the theodicist claims to presently have epistemic access to the workings and details of this teleological scheme, while the skeptical theist denies that any such access is available to us, at least in this lifetime. But if both responses can be considered 'theodicies', in the broad sense of the term, so that both say 'yes' to evil, deeming it to be (in an ultimate sense) good, meaningful, or valuable, then both are vulnerable to at least some of the principal objections brought against theodicy by the anti-theodicist – including the kinds of objections raised by Swinton and Kilby themselves.

---

[43] Kilby, "Evil and the Limits of Theology," 19. It's not clear whether, in Kilby's view, an answer is in principle unavailable or whether one could be revealed to us in the future. She appears to side with the former option in a footnote: "I am not advocating the assertion of *logically* incompatible propositions, but rather the holding of a set of beliefs which, somewhat more broadly, *we cannot make sense of.* There may be some other perspective in which they all make sense together, but if so this is something of which we cannot even begin to conceive" (29, n25, emphases in original).

[44] Kilby, "Evil and the Limits of Theology," 24. Kilby claims to find support for this view in classic (pre-Enlightenment) discussions of evil, such as those of Augustine and Aquinas, as well as in the work of Karl Barth (25 and 29, n24).

If not for this qualification, however, Swinton's case against (theoretical) theodicy could easily be read as a defence of anti-theodicy. Like many an anti-theodicist, Swinton identifies various pastoral dangers involved in theodicy-making, emphasizing three in particular. First, evil is justified and rationalized in such a way that its very reality is ultimately denied; theodicies such as Hick's, Swinton claims, "attempt to spiritualize away the pain of suffering" rather than acknowledging the reality, horror, and perplexing nature of suffering.[45] Second, global theodicies – which seek to account for broad kinds of evil, such as 'moral evil' and 'natural evil' in terms of some overarching good, such as free will – are highly problematic in that they overlook the particularities of concrete cases of individual suffering and do not allow the sufferer to give expression to 'reactive attitudes' such as anger, protest, and lament.[46] Third, theodicies may become evil in themselves insofar as they erect barriers between the victim and God rather than promoting a closer relationship with God: "If theodicy blocks people's access to the loving heart of God and the hope of experiencing God's redemptive power, goodness, and mercy as a living reality then it functions in a way that can only be described as evil."[47]

Having rejected theoretical theodicy, Swinton spends the remainder (and the bulk) of his book delineating and defending an alternative approach, which he calls 'practical theodicy':

> Practical theodicy is the process wherein the church community, in and through its practices, offers subversive modes of resistance to the evil and suffering experienced by the world. The goal of practical theodicy is, by practicing these gestures of redemption, to enable people to continue to love God in the face of evil and suffering and in so doing to prevent tragic suffering from becoming evil.[48]

This of course is not the traditional program of theodicy, in which the goal is to produce explanations for God's creation of a world containing evil; nevertheless, Swinton calls what he is offering a 'theodicy' in the

---

45 Swinton, *Raging with Compassion*, 20–1.
46 On the significance (within theistic traditions) of protest and dissent in the midst of great suffering, see Peter Admirand, "'My Children Have Defeated Me!': Finding and Nurturing Theological Dissent," *Irish Theological Quarterly* 77 (2012): 286–304.
47 Swinton, *Raging with Compassion*, 28.
48 Swinton, *Raging with Compassion*, 85. For similar accounts of 'practical theodicy', see Surin, *Theology and the Problem of Evil*, 59–60, and ch. 4; and Wendy Farley, "The Practice of Theodicy," in Margaret E. Mohrmann and Mark J. Hanson (eds), *Pain Seeking Understanding: Suffering, Medicine, and Faith*. (Cleveland, OH: The Pilgrim Press, 1999), 103–14.

attenuated sense that "it seeks to explore and respond to the problem of evil as it has been reframed."[49] The 'reframing' includes the replacement of theoretical explanation with practical resistance – specifically, "faithful practices of resistance that open up the possibility of transformation and redemption."[50] It is, indeed, by practising particular gestures of redemption that a (practical) solution or response to the problem of evil is attained. On this view, a successful solution to the problem of evil is one that helps people maintain their love of God despite their knowledge and experience of evil. In other words, a successful solution is one that *resists* evil, and in particular resists the capacity of evil to destroy faith, meaning, and hope. Importantly, these practices or gestures do not explain or justify evil, though they do "make a profound statement that evil does not need to have the final word."[51]

Swinton singles out for extended discussion four Christian practices that form the basis of his practical theodicy: lament, forgiveness, thoughtfulness, and hospitality.[52] By means of lament, for example, the victim gives voice to their anger and sorrow, in this way 'naming the silences' (as Hauerwas puts it) that suffering has created. But this takes place within the context of faith: the protest and rage against God are backgrounded by a broader horizon of faith and trust, where it is believed or hoped that God will overcome and redeem the evil. Thus, the endpoint of lament is not the mere expression of pain but reconciliation: the restoration of loving fellowship with God and others.

Even though Swinton is not, strictly speaking, an anti-theodicist, his 'gestures of redemption' can usefully be appropriated by the anti-theodicist to indicate how, *contra* Shearn, there are options available to the believer who wishes to dispense with theodicy but not with an essentially affirmative view of life. By responding to evil in the ways suggested by Swinton, the brokenness and hopelessness that result from evil and suffering may be overcome, making possible reconciliation with and a deeper love of God. In other words, healing and redemption are not ruled out by anti-theodicy and may in fact constitute the most crucial presuppositions of the anti-theodicy view. Here the idea of 'eschatology' becomes vital. John Hick liked to say, 'No theodicy without

---

49 Swinton, *Raging with Compassion*, 80.
50 Swinton, *Raging with Compassion*, 86.
51 Swinton, *Raging with Compassion*, 73.
52 See Swinton, *Raging with Compassion*, chs. 5–8. Swinton also briefly considers the response of silence (93–103) and acknowledges that a range of other redemptive responses are available, including eschatological hope, compassion, and perseverance (245).

eschatology'; following Hick, we may affirm: 'No anti-theodicy without eschatology'. Swinton, too, emphasizes the importance of developing an 'eschatological imagination' when responding to the problem of evil, where this demands an appreciation for the great difference between 'the way things are' and 'the way things ought to be, or will be'. Thus, an eschatological imagination is, according to Swinton,

> a way of perceiving the world that is not bounded by assumptions about the way that things seem to be according to our present understanding. Eschatological imagination is inspired and sustained by God's promises in scripture of how things will be... When we view the present in the light of the future, we begin to perceive both differently.[53]

It is largely by means of such an eschatological outlook that pessimism is circumvented. Once the anti-theodicist countenances the vast distance and tension between the world as it is and the world as it will or should be (and there is no reason why this cannot be countenanced by the anti-theodicist), then the possibility and indeed necessity of redemption arises. A Christian anti-theodicist, in particular, might say that in the person and work of Christ (and in our 'gestures of redemption' as modelled on Christ's salvific actions[54]) the world is being gently and lovingly redeemed and re-created, a process that will be fulfilled only in the eschaton, when "there will be no more death or mourning or crying or pain" (Rev. 21:4).[55]

---

[53]   Swinton, *Raging with Compassion*, 55.

[54]   Miroslav Volf writes: "Christian practices have what we may call an 'as-so' structure (or correspondence structure): *as* God has received us in Christ, *so* we too are to receive our fellow human beings" (quoted by Swinton, *Raging with Compassion*, 82).

[55]   The challenge, however, is to prevent any scheme of redemption from denying or trivializing the reality and horror of evil. It is easy, for instance, to think that evil that is redeemed is transformed in such a way that it is divested of its power and impact (Swinton himself becomes vulnerable to this criticism on p. 75 of *Raging with Compassion*). To avoid such consequences, it may be necessary to hold some such position as: nothing can make amends or compensate for some evils; or there is an inability to undo certain evils; or some evils are absolutely unforgivable (but see Swinton, *Raging with Compassion*, ch. 6, for a defence of the forgivability of any evil whatever) – though putting the matter in any of these ways may come dangerously close to admitting that some evils at least cannot be redeemed.

Work on this paper was supported by a William Paton Visiting Fellowship in Global Philosophy of Religion, at the John Hick Centre for Philosophy of Religion, University of Birmingham.

FURTHER READING

Burrell, David. (with A. H. Johns). *Deconstructing Theodicy: Why Job Has Nothing to Say to the Puzzle of Suffering*. Grand Rapids: Brazos Press, 2008.

Gleeson, Andrew. *A Frightening Love: Recasting the Problem of Evil*. Houndmills: Palgrave Macmillan, 2012.

Phillips, D. Z. *The Problem of Evil and the Problem of God*. London: SCM Press, 2004.

Pinnock, Sarah Katherine. *Beyond Theodicy: Jewish and Christian Continental Thinkers Respond to the Holocaust*. Albany: State University of New York Press, 2002.

Surin, Kenneth. *Theology and the Problem of Evil*. Oxford: Basil Blackwell, 1986.

Tilley, Terrence W. *The Evils of Theodicy*. Washington, DC: Georgetown University Press, 1991.

Part II

Interdisciplinary Issues

8 Cosmic Evolution and Evil

CHRISTOPHER SOUTHGATE

INTRODUCTION TO COSMIC THEODICY

This chapter will concern itself with what the sciences tell us about the structure and unfolding of the cosmos and the implications of those accounts of natural processes for the problem of evil. I shall be writing as a Christian theologian about the problems evil poses for a Christian understanding of the loving character of God, confessed as the creator and redeemer of the world.

I shall take the term 'evil' in its technical sense in this debate, as connoting the suffering of sentient beings (both human and non-human), and the infliction of such suffering by conscious, freely choosing agents. So wicked actions constitute only a proportion of what may be regarded as evil in this broader sense. Indeed, the most difficult areas of the problem of evil for the Christian theologian concern that suffering which cannot be attributed to the action of freely choosing agents and must therefore be attributed in some sense to the activity of God as creator.

Theodicy is the general term for efforts to reconcile the loving character of God with evils in the world. For the purposes of this chapter I shall refer to theodicy in respect of suffering caused by the natural processes of the universe as 'cosmic theodicy'. This will include suffering caused to human beings by natural disasters and by disease, be it inherited or caused by parasites or other pathogens, and also suffering caused to other sentient beings by predation, competition, and disease, leading at times to actual species extinction. In focusing on evil caused by natural processes, I recognize that this is often exacerbated by human cruelty or neglect. For example, the effects of the Indian Ocean tsunami of 2004 were made worse by the lack of an early-warning system, such as already existed in the Pacific, by the destruction of mangrove swamps on the coasts, and by the civil war in Banda-Ace. Yet there remains a very

148 Christopher Southgate

substantial amount of evil that must be assigned to the natural processes of the world.

Currently, the most interesting area of this subject concerns arguments that suggest that the suffering of sentient creatures is somehow a necessary element in the arising of values such as we see in this world. I shall evaluate these arguments and indicate where I think theology needs to supplement them.

But before embarking on such an analysis I need to acknowledge the power of what might be called 'anti-theodicy'. Some very important thinkers have rejected any sort of calculus by which God's action in allowing evils within creation can be justified. In their different ways such scholars as Kenneth Surin, Terrence Tilley, D. Z. Phillips, and John Swinton all make eloquent cases that such calculation is at best counterproductive and at worst downright evil in itself.[1] For Phillips, for example, it is simply an error to write of the divine as though God were a moral agent like human moral agents. For Tilley, theorizing about evil may itself prove to be a source of evil.

For Surin and Swinton, priority must rather be given to listening to the voices of the victims of evil, to the alleviation of their suffering, and to resisting those who cause it. In my own work I have focused on the sufferings of non-human creatures, caused by other such creatures, over the many millennia for which sentient creatures capable of suffering have been victims of aspects of the evolutionary process. These victims do not have 'voices' in any ordinary sense, nor can their suffering necessarily be alleviated, nor is it straightforward to think of resisting its causes. Nevertheless, this is a huge area of creaturely suffering that constitutes a charge against the goodness of God. So there are clearly aspects of this problem that escape at least some of the critique of the anti-theodicists.

The Scriptures, which are the natural starting point for the Christian theologian seeking to discern the ways of God with the world, offer curiously little help to the philosophical theodicist. They are certainly not interested in proving either the existence of God or the logical compatibility of belief in a loving God with the existence of profound suffering. They are not afraid to protest against God, as in the long central narrative of the Book of Job, or to cry out in the sort of lament that is full of protest, as in many of the Psalms. Indeed, it might be argued

---

[1] K. Surin, *Theology and the Problem of Evil* (Oxford: Basil Blackwell, 1986); T. Tilley, *The Evils of Theodicy* (Georgetown, VA: Georgetown University Press, 1991); D. Z. Phillips, *The Problem of Evil and the Problem of God* (London: SCM Press, 2004); J. Swinton, *Raging with Compassion: Pastoral Responses to the Problem of Evil* (Grand Rapids, MI, and Cambridge: Eerdmans, 2007).

(pursuing a line of thought from Terry Eagleton[2]) that the question 'why', which shrieks loud on the lips of sufferers and echoes long in the ears of Christian ministers after natural disasters, is not a philosophical request for a reason at all. It is rather something much more primal, a fusion of protest and lament.

Insofar as the Christian Scriptures do offer any hints as to the reason for suffering, these hints, disturbingly to the modern sensibility, suggest that suffering can be an instrument of the purposes of God. In the Old Testament, God sometimes sends suffering through the medium of what we would now see as natural processes, as punishment for sin, or as part of a divine plan. The story of the plagues of Egypt (and indeed the destruction of the Egyptian army at the Reed Sea) is the classic example. Even the New Testament is by no means free of the notion that suffering serves the purposes of God (Jn 9.1–3; 11.7–14; Rom. 5.2–5; Col. 1.24; 1. Pet. 3.17–18). At the centre of the Christian confession is the conviction, never explained though endlessly theorized over, that 'the Son of Man must suffer... and be killed' (Mk 8.31)[3] and that on that death rests the salvation of the world. So Jesus' innocent suffering, which came to be seen as the redemptive suffering of the divine Son, is understood to be instrumental in the purposes of God. I return to this point later.

The question raised by these initial reflections is: What should a Christian theodicist attempt? Some philosophical theologians, such as Richard Swinburne and Alvin Plantinga, have sought to provide logical demonstrations of the goodness of God in the face of evil, demonstrations that would convince someone of no faith.[4] Michael J. Murray has sought to consider what arguments might qualify as such demonstrations in respect of 'nature red in tooth and claw'.[5] I am not convinced that such arguments are very generative. It is not my experience that those whose preconceptions run counter to the compatibility of suffering and divine love are convinced by philosophical analyses. Rather, I prefer to think of theodicy as an exploration, from within the confessing community, of the ways of God with the world, given a belief in divine sovereignty and divine love. I make no distinction here between 'theodicies' and 'defences', since I am not convinced that these terms are clearly distinguished in the literature.

[2] T. Eagleton, *On Evil* (New Haven, CT: Yale University Press, 2010).
[3] All biblical quotations are from the New Revised Standard Version.
[4] R. Swinburne, *Providence and the Problem of Evil* (Oxford: Oxford University Press, 1998); A. Plantinga, *God, Freedom and Evil* (Grand Rapids, MI: Eerdmans, 1974).
[5] M. J. Murray, *Nature Red in Tooth and Claw: Theism and the Problem of Animal Suffering* (Oxford: Oxford University Press, 2008).

In 2007, Andrew Robinson and I published an analysis of different types of 'good-harm analysis' (GHA).[6] We pointed out that all attempts at rational theodicy tend to involve an aspect of balancing harms to creatures against goods that might arise in connection with those harms. This balancing will tend to be of one of three kinds.

> *Property-consequence GHAs*: a consequence of the existence of a good, as a property of a particular being or system, is the possibility that possession of this good leads to it causing harms.
>
> *Developmental GHAs*: the good is a goal that can only develop through a process which includes the possibility (or necessity) of harm.
>
> *Constitutive GHAs*: The existence of a good is inherently, constitutively inseparable from the experience of harm or suffering.

A familiar example of the first kind would be the free-will defence to moral evil. God is taken, in this defence, to have endowed humans with the property of freedom, the consequence of which is that humans often commit evil. Developmental arguments may be most pertinent to cosmic theodicy; it could for example be held that God instituted the process of evolution because it would give rise to certain goals, although harms were likely, or indeed certain, to arise. Constitutive arguments are the most subtle and elusive. One way to read the ever-problematic story of the sacrifice of Isaac in Gen. 22 would be that only in the crisis of Mount Moriah, sacrificial knife in his hand at God's command, does Abraham come to know the true character of the divine love.

THREE PROPOSALS IN COSMIC THEODICY

I now proceed to consider three moves in cosmic theodicy by important thinkers at the interface of science and theology. All three argue in different ways for a 'package deal' understanding, for a necessary connection between positive values arising within creation, such as beauty, creaturely ingenuity and diversity, and negatives or disvalues, in particular suffering and extinction. Robert J. Russell has been at pains to insist that the basic structure of the physical universe as God has created it, in particular the Second Law of Thermodynamics, is a source

---

[6]   C. Southgate and A. Robinson, "Varieties of Theodicy: An Exploration of Responses to the Problem of Evil based on a Typology of Good-Harm Analyses." In *Physics and Cosmology: Scientific Perspectives on the Problem of Evil*. Ed. N. Murphy, R. J. Russell, and W. R. Stoeger SJ (Vatican City and Berkeley, CA: Vatican Observatory and Center for Theology and the Natural Sciences, 2007), 67–90.

both of creaturely possibilities and of creaturely suffering.[7] (Put at its simplest, the Second Law states that the overall degree of disorder in a physical system will always tend to increase. This is the underlying reason why biological organisms, in general, continually need to take on nutrients and why they ultimately decay.) The nature of thermodynamics makes possible increases in complexity in the biological world, but it also makes inevitable decay and death and the life-strategies that follow from that.

John Polkinghorne has advanced what he has called the 'free-process' defence – 'all of created nature is allowed to be itself according to its kind, just as human beings are allowed to be according to their kind'.[8] At first sight this might be supposed to be a property-consequence argument by analogy with the free-will defence. The version of the argument recently offered (in other terms) by Elizabeth Johnson would indeed be of this form. It is a good – in her terms – that physical processes have their own autonomy and cause the cosmos to unfold according to their freedom. Perhaps surprisingly given her neo-Thomist framework, she wants to insist that these free processes are not instruments of the divine purpose.[9] But if this is the case, then it is not clear that this freedom is a good, certainly not a good that could be weighed against the harms that natural processes cause (for example through earthquakes, volcanoes, etc.).

Rather, the free-process defence is most helpfully seen as developmental – the freedom of physical processes is a good because it gives rise to the evolutionary development of certain values on Earth, values that, it may be presumed, God desired. So the tectonic processes that give rise to earthquakes have had an essential role in distributing and recycling nutrients to allow this to become and continue to be a planet fruitful for life. The asteroid impact that led to the extinction of the dinosaurs made possible the rise of the mammals and with that the possibility of intelligent life, culminating in modern human beings.

Holmes Rolston III has made a number of telling contributions to the debate. Particularly important are, first, his exposition of why disvalues in nature are closely bound up with values and why predation is necessary for complex life,[10] and second, his rejection of the notion that the

---

[7]   R. J. Russell, "Natural Theodicy in an Evolutionary Context: The Need for an Eschatology of New Creation." In *Cosmology: from Alpha to Omega* by R. J. Russell (Minneapolis, MN: Fortress Press, 2008), 249–72.
[8]   J. Polkinghorne, *Exploring Reality: The Intertwining of Science and Religion* (London: SPCK, 2005), 143.
[9]   E. Johnson, *Ask the Beasts: Darwin and the God of Love* (London: Bloomsbury, 2014).
[10]   H. Rolston, III, "Disvalues in Nature," *The Monist* 75 (1992): 250–78.

natural world stands in need of redemption. For Rolston, the processes by which the matter of a dead creature is recycled through other organisms does itself constitute redemption.[11] I return to the subject of redemption in what follows.

We are now beginning to have a sense of what has become a central issue in the contemporary debate in cosmic theodicy. Aspects of the natural processes of the world are profoundly ambiguous – they necessarily generate harms, be it the 230,000 human beings killed by the tectonic movement that caused the Indian Ocean tsunami or the myriad creatures torn apart by predators over the millennia of evolutionary history. At the same time they also generate values, a world fruitful for life, and a process (natural selection) that refines the characteristics of creatures, leading to the biosphere we know today. A number of scholars writing in this area want to suggest that certain types of natural law and process, be it the Second Law, plate tectonics, or natural selection, are necessary for the development of these values, in other words that God could not have created this sort of world without this extent of suffering. This was, even for God, *the only* way in which to give rise to the values we see in this world. Aside from Russell, Polkinghorne, and Rolston, others who have written along these lines include Robin Attfield, Nancey Murphy, and myself.[12] The notion of a package deal – the values cannot be had without the disvalues – is explicitly articulated by Niels Gregersen and Denis Alexander.[13]

---

[11]   H. Rolston, III, "Does Evolution need to be Redeemed?" *Zygon* 26 (1994): 205–29.

[12]   R. Attfield, *Creation, Evolution and Meaning* (Aldershot: Ashgate, 2006); N. Murphy, "Science and the Problem of Evil: Suffering as a By-Product of a Finely-Tuned Cosmos." In *Physics and Cosmology: Scientific Perspectives on the Problem of Evil*. Ed. N. Murphy, R. J. Russell, and W. R. Stoeger SJ (Vatican City and Berkeley, CA: Vatican Observatory and Center for Theology and the Natural Sciences), 131–51; C. Southgate, *The Groaning of Creation: God, Evolution and the Problem of Evil* (Louisville, KY: Westminster John Knox Press, 2008), ch. 3. Two articles criticizing the 'the only-way' argument have appeared since this chapter was drafted. They are N. W. O'Halloran SJ, "Cosmic Alienation and the Origin of Evil: Rejecting the 'Only Way' Option," *Theology and Science*, 13:1 (2015): 43–63; and M. Wahlberg, "Was Evolution the Only Possible Way for God to Make Autonomous Creatures? Examination of an Argument in Evolutionary Theodicy," *Int. J. Philos. Relig.* 77 (2015): 37–51. O'Halloran's advocacy of a primordial spiritual rebellion, 'a higher organizing principle of disorder and evil within the cosmos', is vulnerable to the same concerns indicated later in my chapter in respect of Lloyd's work. However, Wahlberg's article is very helpful in requiring 'only-way' theorists to clarify exactly what it was that God could not know or do that made evolution a necessary means of creating creaturely selves.

[13]   N. H. Gregersen, "The Cross of Christ in an Evolutionary World," *Dialog: A Journal of Theology*, 40.3 (2001): 192–207; D. Alexander, *Creation or Evolution – Do We Have to Choose?* (Oxford: Monarch, 2008).

Two questions then arise. First, what is this constraint on the power of God? Why was it not possible for God to create in some other, less suffering-filled way? Second, is this assertion – that this was the only or the best way that God could give rise to a world containing beauty, ingenuity, and diversity – sufficient to constitute a theodicy? I return to these questions after considering how what I am calling cosmic theodicy would have been tackled in the tradition.

TRADITIONAL THEODICIES BASED ON A FALL-EVENT

An enormous weight of Christian thought has rested on the notion that disvalues in the world, be they the toil of human life or the struggle of other creatures, are the product of the first human sin, as described in Genesis 3. This is still the reflex response of most Christians, and it is an urgent task for theological education to convey the inadequacy of this answer. The answer is problematic biblically, because even within the Genesis narrative itself the curse of Chapter 3 seems to be repented of at the end of Chapter 8.[14] And there is very little sign in the rest of the Hebrew Bible of the notion of a primordially corrupted world.[15] (Rather, the processes of the world, including predation, are affirmed in such important passages on the theology of creation as Ps. 104 and Job 38–41.) The notion of a 'cosmic fall' is also deeply problematic in the light of the scientific record. There is not the slightest evidence that humans ever lived harmoniously with all other creatures in a vegetarian paradise as depicted in Genesis 2. Moreover, predation and disease preceded human life by hundreds of millions of years.

The only refuge from these arguments from science is either to suppose that Eden was a special zone, insulated from the rest of the world, or that some sort of time reversal occurred. The first strategy can be found in Stephen Webb's *The Dome of Eden* and the second in William Dembski's *The End of Christianity*.[16] Webb's picture does not seem altogether consistent as to the extent of evil powers corrupting the creation and arrives at a fanciful picture for which there is no textual evidence. Dembski contrives a very elaborate argument about time but arrives at a

---

[14] The work of Bethany Sollereder (Ph.D. thesis, University of Exeter, 2014) brings this out particularly clearly.

[15] J. Bimson, "Reconsidering a "Cosmic Fall,'" *Science and Christian Belief* 18 (2006): 63–81.

[16] S. Webb, *The Dome of Eden: A New Solution to the Problem of Creation and Evolution* (Eugene, OR: Wipf and Stock, 2010); W. A. Dembski, *The End of Christianity: Finding a Good God in an Evil World* (Nashville, TN: Broadman and Holman, 2009).

position that is no theodicy at all. His God imposes suffering on myriad creatures because humans will one day sin.

Some scholars who accept the inadequacy of assigning disvalues in the creation to human sin nevertheless want to distance God from the violence and suffering of creation. Michael Lloyd is an example of a scholar who defends an angelic fall as the cause of suffering in creation.[17] This view is deeply difficult theologically, not only because of the lack of biblical evidence that the world is so corrupted, but also because it assigns to spiritual entities opposed to God more power than Christian theology has been willing to concede. God's sovereignty is severely compromised in schemes in which God set out to create straw-eating lions and was prevented from doing so. Furthermore, it is deeply difficult for theology in conversation with science to dissect out some elements of the physical world and assign those to malefic influences while attributing all beauty, order, and creativity to God. The whole essence of the scientific picture as it has emerged since the nineteenth century is that it is the same processes – tectonics, creaturely decay, mutation, natural selection, to name only a few – that generate the suffering as also generate the beauty, ingenuity and diversity of the world of creatures.

A more sophisticated version of a 'primordial fall' is found in the work of Neil Messer.[18] Messer's reading of Karl Barth encourages him to invoke a mysterious counter-force, *Das Nichtige* (nothingness), which prevents God from effecting the creation God desired. This formulation is subject to all the scientific and theological problems noted earlier and is in any case a contestable reading of Barth.[19] But it is important to note the theological motivation behind Messer's account (and Lloyd's). These authors cannot associate the God of Jesus Christ with the creation of processes that involve, indeed that seem to depend on, violence. This shows that this problem of cosmic theodicy cannot be treated in isolation from a whole range of other theological trajectories. And it must

[17]   M. Lloyd, "Are Animals Fallen?" In *Animals on the Agenda: Questions about Animals in Theology and Ethics.* Ed. A. Linzey and D. Yamamoto (London: SCM Press, 1998); "The Humanity of Fallenness." In *Grace and Truth in a Secular Age.* Ed. T. Bradshaw (Grand Rapids, MI: Eerdmans, 1998).

[18]   N. Messer, "Natural Evil after Darwin." In *Theology after Darwin.* Ed. M. S. Northcott and R. J. Berry (Milton Keynes: Paternoster, 2009), 139–54. This thinking is taken up in some important work on animal theology – see D. Clough, *On Animals: Volume I: Systematic Theology* (London: Continuum, 2012).

[19]   For further analysis, see C. Southgate, "Re-reading Genesis, John and Job: A Christian's Response to Darwinism," *Zygon* 46.2 (2011): 365–90; "God's Creation Wild and Violent, and Our Care of Other Animals," *Perspectives on Science and Christian Faith* 67 (2015): 245–53. For a different theological approach, see C. Southgate, "Divine Glory in a Darwinian World," *Zygon* 49.4 (2014): 784–807.

be acknowledged that Messer poses a hard question about 'only way' arguments such as the ones that I began to discuss earlier. Why must we picture God as constrained to act in a way that makes violence intrinsic to creation and necessitates a vast extent of creaturely suffering? The difficulty of that position persuades scholars such as Messer and Lloyd to seek alternatives that, as I have indicated, are themselves profoundly problematic. (A further, very problematic move currently being explored is to suppose that a whole range of other animals commit sin.[20])

Delving further into Messer's position leads one to ask whether this counter-force he postulates is a conscious agency (like Lloyd's fallen angels) or a part of the logical fabric of reality. If the former, then Messer's view seems to default to the sort of dualist position in which God cannot overcome the influence on creation of an evil counter-deity, a view that the Christian tradition has steadfastly resisted. If the latter, then his argument seems to acquire a congruence with only-way arguments in which the disvalues in creation become a necessary concomitant of the values. His *'Nichtige'* argument is a theological guess at a constraint on God, drawing its strength from Barth's not-wholly-clear language, and beyond that from the old tradition that evil has no real existence but is only a privation of the good. Only-way arguments, in contrast, are scientifically informed guesses at a constraint on God, drawing their strength from the contemplation of the world as science describes it and the inference that if God could have created without these suffering-filled natural processes, God would have done so.

There are other arguments analogous to Messer's postulate of a mysterious force or factor leading to an ambiguous creation. This type of argument may be deemed an appeal to 'mysterious fallenness'. Celia Deane-Drummond, likewise reluctant to accept that God might be implicated in the creation of violent processes, writes of 'Shadow Sophia', the underside of the wisdom in creation.[21] Yet it is never clarified what this influence is. Likewise, Nicola Hoggard Creegan has written of the disvalues in creation as being like the 'tares' in the parable of the wheat and the tares. However, in the parable, the tares are sown by an 'enemy' (Mt. 13.24–30), whereas Hoggard Creegan is reluctant to say what the origin of the disvalue is.[22]

20 Clough, *Animal Theology*; J. Moritz, "Animal Suffering, Evolution, and the Origins of Evil," *Zygon* 49.2 (2014): 348–80.
21 C. Deane-Drummond, *Christ and Evolution: Wonder and Wisdom* (Minneapolis, MN: Fortress Press, 2009), 185–91.
22 N. Hoggard Creegan, *Animal Suffering and the Problem of Evil* (New York: Oxford University Press, 2013).

It should be clear by now that cosmic processes that lead inevitably to creaturely suffering, as well as to all sorts of values, constitute a deep problem in the theology of creation. Delicate choices need to be made, none of which is problem-free. Messer himself contrasts theologies that privilege Christian doctrine, among which he would list his own cosmic theodicy, with those that in his view privilege science over doctrine.[23] While his taxonomy of interactions in the science–religion debate is useful as a rhetorical device, the interactions themselves are more complex. Scientific conclusions vary from those that are highly provisional to those (like evolution by natural selection) that are strongly supported by a range of robust data accumulated over a long period. Doctrinal positions often rest on scriptural passages that can be approached from very different strategies in biblical interpretation. For example, Messer's key passage, the account of the peaceable kingdom in Is. 11, can be understood in a range of ways, some cosmic and futuristic, some political and contemporary. For an account of the interpretative issues around the classic New Testament passages on the redemption of creation and of interpreters' strategies of privileging one type of text and using it to explicate others, see Horrell and colleagues (2010).[24] Also, predictions about the future (as for example regarding the ultimate fate of the universe) have a very different status in the debate from accounts of past events. There is an inherent uncertainty about the future that places it in a different category from the past or yet the present. In the case under discussion, the account of why there exist natural processes that have caused and do cause great suffering, robust science encounters theology at its most tentative, as theology must be in discussing the problem of evil. There is thus good reason for taking the main lines of the scientific conclusions with the utmost seriousness.

'ONLY WAY' ARGUMENTS

I return now to the argument we began to map at the beginning of this chapter, namely that suffering-causing natural processes are necessary to the realization of values within creation. I phrase this argument as follows: 'This was the only, or at least the best, process by which creaturely values of beauty, diversity and simplicity could arise'.[25]

[23]   N. Messer, *Selfish Genes and Christian Ethics: Theological and Ethical Reflections on Evolutionary Biology* (London: SCM Press, 2007), 48–62.

[24]   D. G. Horrell, C. Hunt, and C. Southgate, *Greening Paul: Re-Reading the Apostle in a Time of Ecological Crisis* (Waco, TX: Baylor University Press, 2010).

[25]   Southgate, *Groaning of Creation*, 48.

The key questions this argument raises are:

1. What is this constraint on God? and
2. Is such an argument enough of a theodicy?

First, I consider the nature of the constraint. According to usual Christian understandings of God's power, that power is only limited by logical constraint – God cannot make 2 + 2 equal 5 or the ratio of diameter to circumference of a circle to be other than 3.14159. It is not possible, at our current level of knowledge, to show that the constraint in the only-way argument is a logical constraint. Nevertheless, it makes common sense to a scientist. It is hard to imagine a universe not governed by the Second Law of Thermodynamics. It is hard to imagine (outside the script of *Star Trek*) a chemistry for life fundamentally different from the one we know on earth. It is hard to imagine an evolutionary process in which natural selection is not a very significant factor. But I am grateful to Dr Mark Ian Thomas Robson for pointing out that a Lamarckian universe, based on the inheritance of behaviours acquired during an organism's lifetime, *is* imaginable. The question would then be, is it plausible that such a universe would actually 'work' and have a better balance of goods and harms given what would need to change to neutralize the possibilities of natural selection?

Many hypothetical universes could be constructed, but it is not demonstrable that Attfield is wrong[26] and that there exists a type of universe that would give rise to a better balance of values against disvalues. It cannot be shown that this is a logical truth. The guess that God could no more dream into being a completely different sort of life-bearing universe than a square circle cannot be proven, but it is a reasonable hunch that it might be so. As we have seen, the theological alternatives to only-way arguments are not attractive. But only-way arguments leave the Christian theodicist in an uncomfortable position, having to assert that God, in the divine desire to create, was constrained to create processes to which suffering was intrinsic in pursuit of ends to which suffering was instrumental. I indicated in my opening comments on Scripture that instrumental suffering is not as foreign to the Christian imagination as some thinkers would like it to be. But it cannot be the end of the story, any more than Calvary was the end of Christ's story.

It seems to me that as Christians puzzle out the ways of God with the world, those who want to defend an orthodox faith that insists on the unity of creation and redemption must suppose not one but two

---

[26] Attfield, *Creation, Evolution and Meaning*, ch. 6.

constraints on God. The first is the one I introduced earlier, that God creates under some not-wholly-comprehensible constraint, such that a world evolving by natural selection, and therefore necessarily involving the suffering of sentient creatures, is the only sort of world in which the values represented by complex and diverse life could arise. The second constraint on God, amply familiar from Christian teaching, though still not clearly or univocally understood, is the necessity, oft-repeated in the New Testament, that Jesus should have to endure degrading execution to release, finally and fully, the redemptive purposes of God into the world.

The first of these constraints is unfamiliar to most Christians. The second is routinely confessed in various ways throughout the Church. But I would submit that they are comparable mysteries – indeed, if anything, the first is easier to understand than the second, since the first has the intuitions of the natural sciences to commend it, whereas the intuitions of a culture based on a sacrificial system are remote from us. Both carry that difficult sense that suffering might be instrumental to the divine purpose that I noted earlier.

To contemplate God in relation to the natural world is to contemplate both immense, staggering, unimaginable power and at the same time a powerlessness we cannot quite fathom either – the creation we so delight in and wonder at cannot arise all at once but only by an immensely long birthing, full, in Paul's word in Romans 8.20, of 'futility'. And the redemption of the world cannot be magicked either but only arises out of the sacrifice of the divine Son.

Having set the only-way argument in more of a philosophical and theological context, it remains to consider our second question: Is it enough to point to such a constraint in order to reconcile the loving character of God with the nature of this suffering-filled world? The difficulty with a theodicy that simply asserts that this is the best sort of system God could have created is that such theodicy describes a God who is the creator of systems but not a God who is in loving relationship with creatures. It is my view, therefore, that the best contemporary cosmic theodicies must start from a version of the only-way argument, but they must go on to make other moves that are more focused on God's relationship with the individual creature.

THE ROLE OF DIVINE REDEMPTION
IN COSMIC THEODICY

Russell has made a careful analysis of the options in what we are calling cosmic theodicy and concludes that none of them is satisfactory without a redemptive dimension.[27] We noted already that Rolston offers such a dimension in supposing that the cycles of nutrition constitute redemption of the dead creature. The impala calf torn apart by hyenas is for Rolston redeemed by the nourishment they and the bacteria in their guts extract from its corpse. But this, once again, is an argument at the level of the system and not the individual creature.

How then is the impala calf to experience the meaning of God's love? Only via a redemption beyond this present world, a redemption in the form of some sort of new life in the final 'new creation' at the eschaton. To include an eschatological dimension to cosmic theodicy is, as Russell shows, a necessary complement to only-way type arguments. If the love of God is shown in the re-creation of lives – at least those that have not known fullness of life – then the challenge to that love from suffering seems to retreat, and it once again becomes possible to stress God's love for the individual creature.[28]

However, the challenge returns in a different form. Because the possibility of such a new creation, in which (in the traditional visions we are offered in passages such as Is. 11; Rev. 21.1–4) there is no more pain, begs the question – why did God not just create in this way in the first instance? This is where a theodicy that is considering the suffering of all sentient creatures and not just mentally competent self-conscious humans must reject a straightforward appeal to 'Irenaean' argument, to the initial creation as a school in which individual creatures learn virtue.[29] So much of the suffering that concerns the cosmic theodicist is of creatures who are not in a position to learn from the experience, because they are physically torn apart or their lives are otherwise destroyed (e.g. by cataclysm, chronic disease, torture, or profound abuse).

The logic of the only-way argument is that particular sorts of values, embodied in creaturely selves, could only arise (or could best arise) through the operation of natural processes such as we see in this world. The challenge of the question, why did God not just create heaven? – posed for example by Wildman[30] – necessitates an extension of the argument, as follows:

[27] Russell, "*Natural theodicy.*"

[28] A particular concern in D. Edwards, "Every Sparrow that Falls to the Ground: The Cost of Evolution and the Christ-Event," *Ecotheology* 11.1 (2006): 103–23.

[29] J. Hick, *Evil and the God of Love* (London: Palgrave Macmillan, 2010 [1970]).

[30] W. J. Wildman, "Incongruous Goodness, Perilous Beauty, Disconcerting Truth: Ultimate Reality and Suffering in Nature." In *Physics and Cosmology: Scientific Perspectives on the Problem of Evil in Nature.* Ed. N. Murphy, R. J. Russell, and W. G. Stoeger, SJ (Vatican City and Berkeley, CA: Vatican Observatory and Center for Theology and the Natural Sciences, 2007), 267–94.

embodied[31] creaturely selves, which can only arise within an evolving world, are capable, once they have so arisen, of being transformed to a state in which they flourish without the possibility of suffering, but they cannot arise except within a world constrained by natural processes such as thermodynamics and natural selection.

Again, this can only be a guess, but it is the guess that fits best the scientific and theological constraints within which cosmic theodicy must operate.

Further questions arise about the nature and scope of the redeemed life of creatures. Will it be simply an 'objective immortality' in which all that is of value from individual lives is held within the loving memory of God, or will there be subjective experience? In 1987, Rolston introduced the example of the 'insurance' pelican chick, the second chick hatched by the white pelican, which is normally pushed out of the nest and starves. It is only 'needed' when the older chick fails to thrive. Rolston's comment that if God watches over the insurance chick, he does so from a vast distance, was rejected by Jay McDaniel, who propounded the notion of 'pelican heaven' as an expression of a subjective, redeemed experience for such victims of evolution.[32] Indeed, subjective immortality for creatures seems more in keeping with Christian visions of the eschaton. It is also more in keeping with the logic of Johnson's notion of 'deep resurrection'.[33] But it is extremely difficult to gain much traction in speculations as to whether only 'victims' or every sentient creature or indeed every creature receives redeemed life (or indeed how predators will be themselves in such a life).[34]

THE PROBLEM OF PROVIDENCE

A dimension of the problem of cosmic theodicy not yet touched on concerns God's providential action. Christian theologies picture God as immanently and lovingly present to all created entities and usually as acting selectively, providentially, in the physical world and the lives of certain creatures to bring about divine purposes. There is a very

[31]   As opposed to forms of spiritual being, such as angels.
[32]   H. Rolston, III, *Science and Religion: A Critical Survey* (Philadelphia and London: Templeton Foundation Press, 2006 [1987]); J. B. McDaniel, *Of God and Pelicans: A Theology of Reverence for Life* (Louisville, KY: Westminster John Knox Press, 1989).
[33]   This takes up Gregersen's notion of 'deep incarnation', which he introduced in "The Cross of Christ"; on deep resurrection, see Johnson, *Ask the Beasts*, 208–10.
[34]   For a set of speculations, see Southgate, *Groaning of Creation*, ch. 5.

extensive literature on such divine action.[35] What is striking is how the contemporary debate is focusing more and more on the interaction with theodicy; if God interacts with a single situation to benefit a single group of creatures, does this not place a moral responsibility on God to benefit similar creatures in other similar situations? Yet the world abounds with situations in which God seems not to have helped creatures. This question has been taken up with particular honesty by Wesley Wildman, whose conclusion is that it is wrong to regard the divine as benevolent.[36] Philip Clayton and Steven Knapp have concluded that God cannot, morally, act to change some physical situations but not others (their 'not even once' principle, which they apply tellingly to the case of the 2004 tsunami). Rather, they believe that God's action can be expressed in terms of encouragement and lure towards virtue.[37]

It is hard to reconcile this with the providential action within the human world described in Scripture and tradition, not least God's raising of Jesus from the dead.[38] But when one turns to the relationship between God and non-human creatures over the whole sweep of evolution, it may be that God's providential engagement is best understood in terms of loving, compassionate presence and lure rather than more overt intervention in the chain of physical causes. In William Rowe's famous example of the fawn suffering horribly through being trapped in a forest fire,[39] it is possible to accept that God companions each suffering fawn, but not necessary (and deeply problematic) to imagine God saving one specific fawn while letting others perish in agony.

It is also reasonable to go on to suppose that the divine presence expresses God's love for creatures and therefore also that God suffers

[35] K. Ward, *Divine Action: Examining God's Role in an Open and Emergent Universe* (West Conshohocken, PA: Templeton Foundation Press, 2007 [1990]); R. J. Russell, N. Murphy, and W. R. Stoeger, SJ (eds.), *Scientific Perspective on Divine Action: Twenty Years of Challenge and Progress* (Vatican City and Berkeley, CA: Vatican Observatory and the Center for Theology and the Natural Sciences, 2008); D. Edwards, *How God Acts: Creation, Redemption, and Special Divine Action* (Minneapolis, MN: Fortress Press, 2010); C. Southgate, "A Test Case – Divine Action." In *God, Humanity and the Cosmos: A Textbook in Science and Religion*. Ed. C. Southgate (London: Bloomsbury, 3rd edn, 2011), 274–312.

[36] Wildman, "Incongruous Goodness."

[37] P. Clayton and S. Knapp, *The Predicament of Belief: Science, Philosophy, Faith* (New York: Oxford University Press, 2011).

[38] Clayton and Knapp, *Predicament*, ch. 5.

[39] W. L. Rowe, "Friendly Atheism, Skeptical Theism, and the Problem of Evil," *Int. J. Philos. Relig.* 59 (2006): 79–92. Rowe's critique of theodicies is taken up in N. Trakakis, *The God beyond Belief: In Defence of William Rowe's Evidential Argument from Evil* (Dordrecht: Springer, 2007).

with the suffering of creatures that suffer. Since we have no idea what the inner experience of other creatures feels like to them, we can have no idea how the compassionate presence of God might make a difference. But it is a reasonable theological instinct that it does make a difference[40] and that no creature in this sense dies alone. It is also a reasonable instinct, though much contested, that this suffering makes a difference to God and that God suffers 'in, with and under'[41] the suffering of creatures.[42] This commitment of God to creatures' pain finds its epitome in the Passion of Christ, which in recent thinking must be seen as identification not only with human suffering but with all creatures.[43]

This sense of the role of the Cross and the Atonement may lead to a refinement of the only-way argument. I have given reasons to suppose that God was constrained in how to create a universe if it was to be fruitful for life, for intelligent life, for the extraordinary range and beauty of life as we know it. But it may be that an additional constraint existed, that the cosmos must be such as to give rise to a life form that could incarnate the life of God, as Christians believe that Jesus did, and inaugurate the era of redemption that will culminate in a state in which 'there will be no more crying' for 'God will be all in all' (Rev. 21.4; 1. Cor. 15.28).

To understand the full possibilities of such a cosmic theodicy, it is important to clarify the shape of the narrative that is being proposed. Scholars who insist of the necessity of a fall event sometimes argue as follows: for the Cross of Jesus to be required to transform the world, which originally was created 'very good' (Gen. 1.31), that world must have been subject to corruption. Fiddes refers to this as a 'U-shaped' narrative and points out that this is not the only possible narrative shape.[44] Rather, what an evolutionary view has to propose is that the world is not so much corrupted as intrinsically (and necessarily) *limited*, unable to transcend itself until the Incarnation, Passion, and Resurrection of the divine Son make that self-transcendence possible. A further step in the

40   Southgate, "Does God's Care Make Any Difference? Theological Reflection on the Suffering of God's Creatures." In *Christian Faith and the Earth: Current Paths and Emerging Horizons in Ecotheology*. Ed. E. M. Conradie, S. Bergmann, C. Deane-Drummond, and D. Edwards (London: Bloomsbury, 2014), 97–114.

41   A. Peacocke, "Kenotic Creation and Divine Action." In *The Work of Love: Creation as Kenosis*. Ed. J. Polkinghorne (London, Grand Rapids, MI, and Cambridge: SPCK and Eerdmans, 2001), 21–42.

42   For the debate about whether God can suffer, such a significant element in contemporary theodicy, see P. Fiddes, *Participating in God: A Pastoral Doctrine of the Trinity* (London: Darton, Longman and Todd, 2000).

43   Gregersen, "The Cross of Christ."

44   P. Fiddes, *Freedom and Limit: A Dialogue between Literature and Christian Doctrine* (Macon, GA: Mercer University Press, 1999), ch. 3.

argument is the one at which Paul the Apostle hints in that extraordinary passage about the cosmos, Rom. 8.19–22. Paul claims there that the whole creation awaits 'the freedom of the glory of the children of God' (8.21). This gives support to a narrative in which the final transformation of the cosmos awaits the free loving human response to the initiative of God in Christ. Only then will the world see that eschatological state from which pain and struggle has been eliminated.[45]

The further question of how this narrative of creation and salvation would interact with that of another planetary biosphere, if there were intelligent life elsewhere in the universe, is one that is attracting increasing attention from theologians.[46] It would certainly bear on the issue of cosmic theodicy in the following ways. First, it would shed light on whether indeed life could form out of a significantly different chemistry and whether less suffering would transpire in such a world. All I have said earlier sheds some doubt on the former possibility and major doubt on the latter. Second, it would lead to challenging questions for Christian theologians about the potential intersection of two narratives of salvation. Is it the work of Jesus of Nazareth that heals the whole cosmos, or would each civilization have its own incarnation?

CONCLUSION

This chapter has focused on the suffering that arises from the natural processes of the world. I have shown that Christian theology needs to part company with explanations of such suffering based on a fall event and have explored instead the very difficult territory of accepting that these were the only types of processes by which God could give rise to the values we see in this world. I suggested further that this theodicy at the level of systems must be complemented by an emphasis on eschatological redemption of creatures and on God's compassionate relating to them in their suffering.

FURTHER READING

Clayton, Philip and Steven Knapp. *The Predicament of Belief: Science, Philosophy, Faith.* New York: Oxford University Press, 2011.

---

[45] On this eschatological state, see J. Polkinghorne, *The God of Hope and the End of the World* (London: SPCK, 2002).

[46] E.g. D. Wilkinson, *Science, Religion and the Search for Extra-Terrestrial Intelligence* (Oxford: Oxford University Press, 2013).

Drees, William B. (ed.). *Is Nature Ever Evil?* London: Routledge, 2003 (especially article by Rolston).

Murphy, Nancey, Robert John Russell, and William R. Stoeger, SJ (eds.). *Physics and Cosmology: Scientific Perspectives on the Problem of Evil.* Vatican City and Berkeley, CA: Vatican Observatory and Center for Theology and the Natural Sciences, 2007.

Murray, Michael J. *Nature Red in Tooth and Claw: Theism and the Problem of Animal Suffering.* Oxford: Oxford University Press, 2008.

Russell, Robert John. "Natural Theodicy in an Evolutionary Context: The Need for an Eschatology of New Creation." In *Cosmology: from Alpha to Omega* by Robert John Russell. Minneapolis, MN: Fortress Press, 2008, 249–72.

Southgate, Christopher. *The Groaning of Creation: God, Evolution and the Problem of Evil.* Louisville, KY: Westminster John Knox Press, 2008.

Surin, Kenneth. *Theology and the Problem of Evil.* Oxford: Basil Blackwell, 1986.

9   Ancient Near Eastern Perspectives on Evil and Terror

MARGO KITTS

A few centuries ago, evil was dead. At the end of the nineteenth, Nietzsche exhorted ecstatic nihilism and famously rejected any absolute foundation for evil, good, or truth (via his *Zarathustra*). Earlier, during the Enlightenment, the specter of a demonic force lurking in history or in the human psyche might have appeared anachronistic, incompatible with a trust in human reason and distrust of seductive Church spectacle. Tougher to dispel, the theme of terror once seemed restricted to depth psychology and literature. Freud pursued our troubling sense of the uncanny and fear of annihilation, while before that, Gothic novels sought to cultivate terror's (and horror's) delicious chill. As intellectual history, all that seems almost quaint.

Today, both evil and terror have reemerged as rivets for popular and scholarly imagination, for at least two reasons: The obvious one is the renewed use of religious idioms to justify grotesque killings and mass-casualty violence. Not only do reports of these foster a pervasive sense of our utter contingency and of life's unpredictability – hence our "terror" – but they seem to have stimulated as well a search for exceptional categories of motive, as in "evil." So we ponder bewildering acts of "cosmic war[1]" and jubilant cruelty exalted by "sacred cause" and serviced by a "poetic-military complex."[2] The quest for motive is not restricted to this century, but has become particularly compelling in the last few decades, for philosophers, anthropologists, sociologists, art historians, and of course religious and literary theorists.

A second reason for the renewed interest in evil and terror is the explosion in researches into the literary and artistic foundations of Western cultures. Following the decipherment of ancient Near Eastern

---

[1]   Mark Juergensmeyer, "Religious Terrorism as Performance Violence." In *Oxford Handbook of Religion and Violence*. Ed. Mark Juergensmeyer, Margo Kitts, and Michael Jerryson (New York: Oxford University Press, 2013), 280–93.
[2]   Slavoj Žižek, "Notes on a Poetic-Military Complex," *Third Text* 23.5 (2009): 503–9.

cuneiform and hieroglyphic writing in the nineteenth and early twentieth centuries, a wealth of evidence for ancient imagination, stemming from as early as the third millennium BCE, has come into play. Reports of terrifying violence in the writings of some biblical prophets and psalmists (e.g., Amos 1:13; Psalm 137:9) can no longer be seen as exceptional. Rather, particularly in Assyrian royal art and annals of the first millennium BCE, we see and hear of beheadings, impalings, and a stream of mutilation and humiliation, often construed as expressions of divine power enacted by human vessels. Whether intended to terrorize challengers or actually to catalogue royal feats, the staggering cruelty in some of these depictions cannot be dismissed as only propagandistic. Rather, it seems to infer a relish for raw destruction, at least among the rulers, artists, and scribes. At the other end of the social spectrum, texts presumably reflecting popular interests support a widespread fear of the maleficent, as we see in numerous apotropaic ritual instructions and curses from Mesopotamia all the way west to Greece. From all this, it would appear that a profound awareness of our susceptibility to evil and terror, whether preternatural or eminently human in source, has been with us for a very long time.

This chapter will ponder the second of these. That is, it will sketch some ancient Near Eastern[3] artistic and literary representations of evil and, relatedly, terror. It will not attempt an encyclopedic compass, a semantic study of terms, or an exposé on ideological evolution. Rather, harnessing hermeneutics and some conceptualizations by, ultimately, Arendt and Agamben, it will attempt to show that reading selected ancient texts can open windows into our own intuitions. Such intuitions are not neutral, of course. As Gadamer saw, a contemporary grasp of an ancient work of art or poetry is based on a certain alienation from the conceivable religious force of the work and is situated in a preformed, aesthetic prejudice. Yet alienated or not, our encounter is not unimpassioned, nor is our anticipation of the work's meaning unengaged.[4] We may become "possessed" by a work, whereby our prejudices become "biases of our openness to the world .... conditions whereby ... what we encounter says something to us."[5] It is with these passions and prejudices in mind that we will explore ancient Near Eastern perspectives on evil and terror.

[3]   Spanning from Mesopotamia to the Greek colonies of Asia Minor, historically from the Bronze Age through the epics of Homer.

[4]   Hans-Georg Gadamer, *Philosophical Hermeneutics* (Berkeley: University of California Press, 1976), 8–9, 101.

[5]   Ibid., 9.

PROLEGOMENA ON THE NOTIONS

Evil

As portrayed in ancient literature, evil is a slippery notion. For instance, it is difficult to reconcile the evil fate (Il. 21:133) or evil deeds (23:176, 21:79, 23:176) that raging Achilles intends for his victims in the last books of the Iliad, with the insidious evil of Revelation's satanic dragon, who deceives the entire inhabited world (Rev. 12:9, cf. 2 Cor. 11:14). For the first, the poetic tradition provides a motive of despair, which makes Achilles' rampage signally human and easier to understand than the malice of an entity that delights in inhumanity and cruel deceit. This is because, despite its shrouding in hallowed terms for anger (*mēnis, cholos*, and the like), Achilles' pitiless turn of heart is not intrinsic to his character, as some of his victims grasp (e.g., at 21:97–119 – inferable too at 22:111–28, 22:252–9 and 22:335–54). In contrast, the wickedness of the dragon-like foe in Revelation is deemed primeval. From the victim's perspective, the end is the same – mortal terror and then death – but the triumph of the dragon insinuates a more profound end to life on earth, as iterated in numerous traditions of cosmic battle between chaos monsters and storm gods, from the earliest artistic and literary sources of the ancient Near East.

Of course, the distinction between injurious human evil and injurious supernatural evil is itself too facile. Accepting Bataille's description of evil as cognate with death,[6] we may designate as evil all the features of life that lead to its diminishment. As we shall see, ancient literature interlaces evil (e.g., Hittite *idalu*, Homeric *kaka*, Hebrew *ra*) with a vast web of such diminishments, ranging from tragic misfortune to human error and perfidy to the malicious powers of the monstrous and the destructive powers of the divine.

The last two notions, the malicious powers of the monstrous and destructive powers of the divine, require an imaginative leap for contemporary readers. After the massacres of the last century and the start of this one, most ethicists disdain notions of monstrous and divine evil in lieu of the pressing issues of war crimes and human indifference to suffering, that is, in lieu of "humanity's darkest side."[7] Striving to come to terms with Nazi evil, Hannah Arendt condemned monster-talk as glamorizing banal acts of killing and condemned as well the aggrandizing

---

[6]   Georges Bataille, *Literature and Evil* (New York: Marion Boyers Publishers, Inc., 1985 [1957]), 29.

[7]   Maria Pia Lara, Ed. *Rethinking Evil* (Berkeley: University of California Press, 2001), 2.

pageantry and rousing oratory of the Third Reich.[8] In the Balkan context, Slavoj Žižek challenged would-be bard Radovan Karadzic's Hades-like pretentions – "I am the cause of universal distress" – for poeticizing not Balkan roots, but self-deification and nihilistic cruelty.[9] For the philosophers, comparing cruel slaughter to supernatural evil is a platitude at best, or just bad taste.

And yet, as Arendt saw in totalitarian murderers and their seemingly superfluous, disposable masses of victims, nihilism compromises the very nature of humanity, for totalitarians and victims alike.[10] This nihilism is strangely, ironically, akin to the monster evil that Arendt disdained. Cruelty and the aggrandizement of it are unmistakable elements in ancient representations of evil, which display a fascination with evil's dehumanizing effects. This fascination can be seen not only in Assyrian wall reliefs of human carnage but in poetry and cylinder seals depicting threatening chaos dragons, sea serpents, and their antediluvian kin – abundant figures in art and literature from the third millennium through the biblical prophets. As will be shown, abundant too are representations of inimical gods. It would seem that the ancients recognized cruelty and vulnerability in many spheres of life.

Further, one cannot argue in good faith that intrigue with preternatural evil has dissipated entirely. Even today, a robust interest in witchcraft and "dark shamans" on the fringes of contemporary civilizations has led to a burgeoning scholarly literature on assault sorcerers and their calculated strategies for inflicting mystical harm on personal enemies and on representatives of hegemonic powers. What Neil Whitehead called a "poetics of violence"[11] – rumors and incantations wielded by numinous shamans – implies a mastery of sinister enchantments. Whether ancient, exotic, or here and now, specters of witches, monsters, and mystical evils are well within our conceptual grasp.

Terror

Terror is more than a political act on a global stage. It is first a personal experience of bodily (virtual) contingency in a world riddled

---

[8] Elizabeth Minnich, "The Evil of Banality: Arendt Revisited," *Arts and Humanities in Higher Education* 13.1–2 (2014): 163; Pia Lara 2001, 11.

[9] E.g., "I offer you inclemency and wine / The one who won't have bread will be fed by the light of my Sun / People nothing is forbidden in my faith / There is loving and drinking / and looking at the Sun for as long as you want / and this godhead forbids you nothing" (Karadzic's "For Izlet Sarajlić," in Žižek 2009).

[10] Hannah Arendt, *The Origins of Totalitarianism* (New York: Harcourt, Brace & World, Inc., 1966 [1951, 1958]), 459.

[11] Neil L. Whitehead. *Dark Shamans: Kanaima and the Poetics of Violent Death* (Durham, NC: Duke University Press, 2002), 191–94.

with unpredictability. One can imagine terror's immediate effects as extending from a sick dread of imminent annihilation all the way to Otto's *"mysterium und tremendum,"* which, of course, Otto saw as essential elements of religious experience. While few people today would deny that "evil" and our responses to it are at least in part socially constructed, our susceptibility to terror requires a glance beneath social constructions. We needn't invoke evolutionary fears of predators, startle reflexes, or "hyperactive agent detective devices" to explain this (cf. Teehan,[12] McCauley and Lawson[13]). It would be silly to deny any cognitive architecture to terror, but to offer that architecture as a sole explanation for it is to ignore a range of sensory and imaginative capabilities that elude the cognitive theorist's toolkit. The entire humanitarian lens offers perspectives which elude that toolkit,[14] but three such perspectives befit this discussion. The three overlap.

Let us begin with an existential perspective and the experience most likely to confuse moderns. That monster/divine evil can terrify reflects a sense of bodily vulnerability and an imaginative openness to unseen powers.[15] It indicates acute sensitivity to the hyperreal, to potential fissures in our everyday worlds of perception and hence to such figures as gods, ghosts, demons, and other unseen forces. This sensitivity surpasses artistic creativity. It evinces a world of sense perception that is not flat. While not usually concerned with the occult, the epistemology of depth perception has flourished during the last half century,[16] as have studies of the preverbal dimensions to trauma, pain, and terror.[17]

---

[12] John Teehan, "The Cognitive Basis for the Problem of Evil," *The Monist* 96.3 (2013): 325–48.

[13] Robert N. McCauley and Thomas E. Lawson *Bringing Ritual to Mind* (Port Chester: Cambridge University Press, 2002).

[14] James Laidlaw, "A Well-Disposed Social Anthropologist's Problems with the 'Cognitive Science of Religion.'" In *Religion, Anthropology, and Cognitive Science.* Ed. Harvey Whitehouse and James Laidlaw (Durham, NC: Carolina Academic Press, 2007), 211–46.

[15] I have argued elsewhere that ancient audiences must have been thrilled by tales of monster battles and that bards utilized all manner of poetic artifice, including onomatopoeia, to stir imaginations. Margo Kitts, "The Near Eastern *Chaoskampf* in the River-Battle of Iliad 21." *Journal of Ancient Near Eastern Religions* 13.1 (2013a): 86–112.

[16] E.g., Maurice Merleau-Ponty, *Phenomenology of Perception,* Colin Smith (trans.) (New York: Humanities Press, 1962); Gadamer 1976; Paul Ricoeur, "The Metaphorical Process as Cognition, Imagination, and Feeling." In *Philosophical Perspectives on Metaphor.* Ed. Mark Johnson (Minneapolis: University of Minnesota Press, 1981), 228–47. Z. Kövecses, *Metaphor and Emotion: Language, Culture and the Body in Human Feeling* (New York: Cambridge University Press, 2000).

[17] See, e.g., Vincent Crapanzano, *Imaginative Horizons: An Essay in Literary-Philosophical Anthropology* (Chicago: University of Chicago Press, 2003); Elaine Scarry, *The Body in Pain* (New York: Oxford University Press, 1994); Thomas J. Csordas, "Embodiment as a

These all acknowledge layers of experience that initially elude delineation into discursive categories. The recognition of prediscursive dimensions to human experience allows that, even if we no longer "believe" in supernaturals, we still may intuit unspeakable terror or evil intent.

From a literary perspective, a sense of terror may be elicited by poetic extension, whereby experiences that transcend straightforward exposition are insinuated instead through events, including preternatural events. In Iliad 21, for instance, riverbanks shriek, heavens rumble, the earth quakes, the gods fall together with a great shout, and a seemingly hallucinogenic turbulence (a confluence of river gods) almost swallows a terrified Achilles (21:125–390). Some Classicists have called this bad or comic art,[18] but others see, with Max Black[19] and with Aristotle,[20] that poetic extension renders comprehensible dimensions of experience that may elude other forms of discourse. Another illustration is in Iliad 20, where the battle frenzy is so extended into different spheres that the gulf between human and divine worlds seems to dissolve. Zeus unleashes the feuding gods, Eris arises, Athene and Ares scream across the plain, Zeus thunders from above, Poseidon shakes the earth and mountains, the streams and human cities tremble, and Hades leaps in fear lest the world break open and the houses of the dead be exposed – all this to describe how the Achaians and Trojans were roused to break out in heavy strife (20.48–56). At the hands of talented bards, these lurid figurations were

Paradigm for Anthropology," *Ethos* 18.1 (1990): 5–47; Bryan Turner, *Regulating Bodies: Essays in Medical Sociology* (London: Routledge, 1992).

[18] See, e.g., George M. Calhoun, "Homer's Gods-Myth and Marchen," *The American Journal of Philology* 60.1 (1939): 1–28; B. C. Dietrich, "Divine Epiphanies in Homer," *Numen* XXX/1 (July 1983): 53–79; Pietro Pucci, "Theology and Poetics in the Iliad," *Arethusa* 35 (2002): 17–34.; and Bruce Louden, *The Iliad: Structure, Myth, and Meaning* (Baltimore, MD: The Johns Hopkins University Press, 2006). But notice that when biblical supernatural forces collide, the effect is never presumed comic (Michael Fishbane, *Biblical Myth and Rabbinic Mythmaking* (New York: Oxford University Press, 2003); John Day, *God's Conflict with the Dragon and the Sea* (Cambridge: Cambridge University Press, 1985): 1–61; E. N. Ortlund, *Theophany and Chaoskampf* (Piscataway, NJ: Gorgias Press, 2010); Scott Noegel, "Dismemberment, Creation, and Ritual: Images of Divine Violence in the Ancient Near East." In *Belief and Bloodshed*. Ed. J.K. Wellman, Jr. (Lanham, Md: Rowman and Littlefield, 2007), 13–28; Nicholas Wyatt, *Mythic Mind: Essays on Cosmology and Religion in Ugaritic and Old Testament Literature* (London/Oakville: Equinox 2005); Kitts, 2013a, even when the biblical god scoffs would-be foes (Ps. 2:4–6), or when Leviathan does the same (Job 41).

[19] Max Black, "Metaphor," *Proceedings of the Aristotelian Society* (1954): 55, 280–81.

[20] Brook Holmes, "The Iliad's Economy of Pain," *Transactions of the American Philological Association* 137.1 (2007): 59. Hence Aristotle on metaphor: "But the greatest thing by far is to be a master of metaphor. It is the one thing that cannot be learnt from others; and it is also a sign of genius, since a good metaphor implies an intuitive perception of the similarity in dissimilars" (Poetics 22).

not dismissed by ancient audiences as laughable. As Aristotle saw, such figurations might elicit heightened and/or bent perceptions for audiences and bring subliminal discernments to consciousness. They were art.

Taking the larger perspective of whole societies, a sense of terror may be understood as rooted in the "violent imaginary." Charles Taylor defined an imaginary as "that largely unstructured and inarticulate understanding of our whole situation, within which particular features of our world become evident"[21] and crystallize often in marked images or behaviors. A recent example might be the U.S. imaginary in the decade post–9/11/2001, wherein extralinguistic sensations – agitation, dread, sense of the uncanny – combined with fear, panic, as well as rumors and assumptions about the political or even cosmological order, may be said to have precipitated for some an amorphous sense of social fragility and personal contingency.[22] A few striking images captured the mood, such as the crumbling world towers and the agglutinative bodily mass of Abu Ghraib's human pyramid – seemingly liminoid (Victor Turner's term) displays of cultural collapse and aberrant art. These speak to the iconic layer of violent imaginary as described by anthropologist Goran Aijmer. The iconic layer eludes ordinary discourse but features "symbolic displays of strong expressive force ... without referential meaning ... [that] make manifest people's intuitive cognizance as to what ultimately conditions social and personal experience."[23] Such displays may be more than unsettling; they can be instrumental in envisioning, building, and altering possible worlds. Émile Durkheim anticipated this conversation when he pointed out that, through its proffered world of representations, religion forms, condenses, and aestheticizes individual perceptions which are initially inchoate.[24] Arguably, the violent imaginary is anchored in an incipient rupture between those inchoate perceptions and the patterns of meaning offered by religious representations. There is no good reason to suppose that such ruptures and violent imaginaries are restricted to the aftereffects of contemporary global terror.

[21]   Charles Taylor, "Modern Social Imaginaries," *Public Culture* 14.1 (2002): 107.
[22]   Margo Kitts, "Religion and Violence from Literary Perspectives. In *Oxford Handbook of Religion and Violence*. Ed. Juergensmeyer, Kitts, and Jerryson (New York: Oxford University Press, 2013b), 410–423.
[23]   Goran Aijmer, "Introduction: The Idiom of Violence in Imagery and Discourse." In *Meanings of Violence: A Cross-Cultural Perspective*. Ed. Göran Aijmer and Jon Abbink (Oxford: Berg, 2000), 3.
[24]   Emile Durkheim, *The Elementary Forms of Religious Life*. Trans. Joseph Ward Swain (New York: Free Press, 1965 [1912]).

None of these perspectives is now a fringe perspective. Each is emergent in studies of the impact of global terror and also resonates into studies of ancient literature and art. The point of this prolegomena is to prepare us to see ancient representations of evil and terror as graspable, albeit within the constraints of our own imaginations.

ILLUSTRATIONS

Evil

Having attempted to narrow the gap between ancient and contemporary imaginations, we now foray into, first, preternatural evil, both the monster evil mentioned earlier and also divine evil. We follow with a look at human manipulations of these evils and at evil as human perfidy, punishable by gods and their representatives. In keeping with Bataille's identification of evil as cognate with death, we explore these various evils for their suspected ability to diminish life.

Chaos Demons and Inimical Gods

Monsters are abundant in the ancient Near Eastern artistic and literary repertoire and usually interpreted as representing an evil antiorder in need of vanquishing. For instance, a monster of the hydra variety, with seven heads, four legs, and flames shooting from its back, appears on an Old Babylonian cylinder seal; in front of the hydra, two gods are severing its heads.[25] Another seal, dated to the NeoAssyrian period, shows horned water serpent Tiamat being slain by god Marduk, while musicians drum on either side (indicating an apparent bardic tradition).[26] Hydras were popular all the way west to Greece, where we find vase paintings of, for instance, Zeus slaying Typhoeus[27] and Heracles slaying the Lernaean hydra[28] and wrestling with the River Acheloios, figured as a horned serpent.[29] Unvanquished monsters of the nonhydra variety are just as plentiful. An open-mouthed, winged dragon rampages on an Old Babylonian seal,[30] and on the edges of yet another seal, winged monsters devour the

---

[25]   No. 15618, from Tell Asmar (dated 2300–2200 BCE), Feared stolen. May be seen at http://oi.uchicago.edu/OI/IRAQ/dbfiles/objects/1065.htm.

[26]   British Museum 89589. May be seen at the Melammu Project, www.aakkl.helsinki.fi/melammu/database/gen_html/a0000495.php

[27]   Antikensammlungen, Munich, Germany Catalogue Number: Munich 596.

[28]   Getty Villa 83.AE.346.

[29]   British Museum, E437; Beazley Archive Number: 200437.

[30]   From Tell Agrab. Old Babylonian (ca. 1800–1700 BC). Feared stolen. See http://oi.uchicago.edu/OI/IRAQ/dbfiles/objects/1277.htm.

heads of bearded men.[31] It is difficult to draw conclusions about the effect of these images on their ancient proprietors or witnesses, but presumably the images reference some kind of struggle, whether heroic or divine.

Struggle is indeed a prominent theme in this very ancient art and literature. Divine combat is apparent not just on seals[32] but in literature from the Enuma Elish to the Hittite Kumarbi, Hedammu, and Ullikummi myths to the triumph of Ugaritic Baal over Yam and YHWH over the Leviathan, Lotan, Yam, and so forth. All herald the victory of celestial, usually storm-based, gods over opposing divinities or monsters, usually with aqueous characteristics. Scholars of the *Chaoskampf* argue that, along with various hybrid creatures (e.g., griffins, serpent-birds, lion-serpents, all on seals), sea monsters and disorderly waters represent a state of darkness, confusion, and lifelessness – says Day of West Semitic conceptions broadly[33] the power of chaos, rebellion, or evil – says Fishbane of biblical conceptions;[34] or the ever-emergent dangers of this life – says Wyatt of a variety of storm-god nemeses throughout the ancient Near East.[35] Such monsters are perceived as threats presumably because of their watery capacity to submerge terrestrials and their tendency for hybridity and discomfiting liminality (e.g., dragons rampage on land, in air, and in sea).[36]

Some, further, have riotous personalities: The Sea is furious when it invades the earth, floods the mountains, and reaches the sun, moon, and stars in the Hurro-Hittite Song of the Sea.[37] In biblical myth, waters writhe and convulse in fear of the god who once smashed Yam, crushed the heads of Leviathan, and made the rivers run dry (Ps. 77:16–19; cf. Hab. 3:8, 3:10, 3:15). In rabbinical myth, waters are sexualized: male waters once pursued and commingled with female over all the cosmos until "at His rebuke they fled" (e.g., Ps. 104:6–9; Is. 50:2) into their current channels on earth.[38] A Mesopotamian parallel is the longing of fresh

---

[31] From Ishchali (dated 1800–1700 BCE). Feared stolen. See http://oi.uchicago.edu/OI/ IRAQ/dbfiles/objects/1321.htm.

[32] E.g., Akkadian battle of the gods, seal from Kish, ca. 2220–2159 BCE. www.metmuseum .org/toah/works-of-art/L.1992.23.4; Akkadian Water God Facing Deity; God with a Mace and Lion-Headed Eagles Attacking Fallen God, dated ca. 2334–2154 BC, seal no. 201 at the Morgan, www.themorgan.org/collections/collectionsPaging.asp?page= 29&id=Seals.

[33] John Day, "God and Leviathan in Isaiah 27:1." *Biblotheca Sacra* 155 (1998): 423–36.

[34] Fishbane 2003: 14.

[35] Wyatt 2005: 32–3.

[36] Kitts 2013a.

[37] Alfonso Archi, "Orality, Direct Speech and the Kumarbi Cycle," *Altorientalische Forschungen.* Akademie Verlag, 36.2 (2009): 219.

[38] Fishbane, *Biblical Myth and Rabbinic Mythmaking,* (2003): 113–14.

water *apsû* to mingle with saltwater.[39] These images could not be so ably manipulated for mythopoeic effect if the scribes were not familiar with the notion of uncontrollable evils lurking in the cosmos, at least *in illo tempore*.

Numerous etiologies are proposed to explain the appeal of the *Chaoskampf*. Some see the use of the motif as cosmogonic, representing the agonistic model of world creation[40]; others see it as celebrating a tenuous triumph over persistent disorder[41] or as celebrating god-like feats accomplished by kings[42]. But Fishbane points out the fluid utility of the biblical trope. While it may be used to commemorate the triumph of YHWH as a storm god who once dried up primordial waters (Ps. 77:16–19; Ps. 89; Is. 50:2), it also may be used as a poetic artifice to convey the smashing of YHWH's enemies (Is. 30:27–33; Ps. 74:13–14; Ps. 89:9–10; Hab. 3; Nah. 1) or, strikingly, to allegorize the suffering of his chosen: "Am I Yam or Tannin [sea monster or dragon] that you have sent a guard upon me?" (Job 7:12; see too Ps. 89); "[Y]ou have pierced us instead of Tannin and covered us with the darkest gloom" (Ps. 44:19).[43]

The plaintive cry of Job and the Psalm speaks to the old problem of theodicy (explored elsewhere in this volume) and more broadly to a potentially inimical relationship between gods and humans. This extends beyond the multidimensional wrath of YHWH, itself celebrated and lamented in countless songs and prophetic texts. Woeful sufferings of a god's victims, not just monstrous but human, pervade ancient literature. The three Babylonian compositions known as the Poem of the Righteous Sufferer, the Theodicy, and the Dialogue of Pessimism treat divine abandonment in terms just as soulful as Job's,[44] as does Achilles in lamenting to Priam, "So the gods have spun it so that wretched

---

[39] Wyatt ties this to Ugaritic and also Homeric conceptions (ἀψορρόου Ὠκεανοῖο (Il. 18.399) (2005:200–204). See also Walter Burkert, *The Orientalizing Revolution* (Cambridge, MA: Harvard University Press, 1992), 88–127, and Jan Bremmer, *Greek Religion and Culture, the Bible and the Near East* (Leiden: Brill, 2008), 1–18. There are correlations too with second-generation Mesopotamian figures Lahmu and Lahamu, whose riotous concupiscence produced a chaotic profusion of noisy gods.

[40] George A. Barton, "Tiamat," *Journal of the American Oriental Society* 15 (1893): 1–27; Day, 1998; Fishbane, 2003.

[41] Mark Smith, "The Baal Cycle." In *Ugaritic Narrative Poetry*. Ed. S. Parker (Atlanta, GA: Society for Biblical Literature, 1997), 84.

[42] Wyatt 2005; Noegel 2007.

[43] Fishbane, *Biblical Myth and Rabbinic Mythmaking*, (2003): 38, 44–5, 52–4, 60, 70.

[44] For instance,

> "Just one word would I put before you.
> Those who neglect the god go the way of prosperity,
> While those who pray to the goddess are impoverished and dispossessed.

mortals live in grief, while they themselves are uncaring" (24.525–6). A developed Old Babylonian lamenting tradition broaches the same themes, bewailing divine abandonment of the city,[45] and numerous Hittite petitions – in both prayers and rituals – attempt to persuade the gods to rescind punishments on Hatti: "[What is] this, O Gods, [that you have d] one? [You have let in ...] a plague, and the land of Hatti is dying, so no one prepares the offerings of food and drink. The farmers who used to sow the sacred fields are dead, ... and you hold us guilty ... and from humankind your wisdom has departed;"[46] "Let Telepinu's evil wrath, anger and irrita- tion, sin, evil speech, and evil fetter go in. And let it not come out again. Let it perish in there!" (KUB 33.9 iii 10[47]). Although it has been argued that these show the literary–cultic motif of an absent god,[48] they more broadly illustrate the pervasive theme of divine indifference to mortal suffering. Without the attention of Telepinu, the natural world wilts and dies.

Of course the Hittite scribes would prefer that the gods look upon Hatti with eyes that bless[49] and cast evil upon her persecutors. This too is typical. While gods are said to "run in front" of their human favorites – from Assyrian kings to Hittite kings to biblical David and Barak to heroes on either side of the Trojan War[50] – they rain fire on,

> In my youth I sought the will of my god;
> With prostration and prayer I followed my goddess.
> But I was bearing a profitless corvée as a yoke.
> My god decreed instead of wealth destitution.
> A cripple is my superior, a lunatic outstrips me. The rogue has been
>   promoted, but I have been brought low."
>
> Babylonian Theodicy 69–77, translated by W. G. Lambert.
> www.etana.org/node/582

[45] See Mary Bachravova on the role of female figures (including female impersonators) in placating these angry gods: Bachravova, "Sumerian *Gala* Priests and Eastern Mediterranean Returning Gods." In *Lament: Studies in the Ancient Mediterranean and Beyond.* Ed. Ann Suter (Cary, NC: Oxford University Press, 2008), 18–52.

[46] O. R. Gurney, *Hittite Prayers of Mursili II* (Liverpool: The University Press of Liverpool, 1940), 25–9. Note the plague prayers to Telepinu and the Sungoddess of Arinna.

[47] Discussed in the *Oriental Institute Hittite Dictionary* (hereinafter CHD), 23, under *lala,* tongue.

[48] Paul Albertus Kruger, "A World Turned on Its Head in Ancient Near Eastern Prophetic Literature: A Powerful Strategy to Depict Chaotic Scenarios," *Vetus Testamentum* 62 (2012): 58–76.

[49] KUR ᵁᴿᵁHatti-ma-aš-ta an-[da aš-ša-u-i]t IGI.HI./a-it a-uš-te-en [Gurney 1940:28–29 (Section III: Plague Prayer C and D)].

[50] Poseidon runs in front of the Achaeans at Il. 13.345–55, 13.434–45, 13.554–56, 13.563– 64, 14.384–401; Athene reportedly of Achilles 20.94–98; Ares the Trojans at 5.590–95; Apollo the Trojans at 15.306-11; even Hector, resembling Zeus, runs in front at 11.61–64. For ancient Near Eastern matches, see Margo Kitts, *Sanctified Violence in Homeric Society* (New York: Cambridge University Press, 2005):188–195.

smash, and slit the throats of enemies, or at least do Assyrian Ishtar, Erra, and Ninurta, respectively.[51] Mursilis begs Telepinu to unleash plague, rebellion, famine, and evil (*idalun*) fever as retribution on Hatti's enemies, to send them evil pestilence[52] or even evil locusts.[53] The biblical god does much the same (Hab. 3:5–6; Ex. 10), and of course Apollo sends an evil plague on the Achaians (Il. 1:10), bewitches them (15.320–7), and strikes Patroklos with a stunning first blow (16.793). Divine activism pervades the Iliad. Thundering terribly all night long, Zeus devises evil for the Trojans and Achaians, instilling a green fear (7.478–89). Athene and Hera intend evil for the Trojans (8.458), and when Athene deceives Hector, he grasps that the gods are calling for his death (22.295). It is an "evil death" (22.300). Gods mixing it up in human affairs, with joy, tears, or viciousness, are seemingly ever-present realities in ancient literature. Gods bestow both *shalom* and *ra* (Is. 45:7).

Human Manipulations of Evil

If evil forces are felt to penetrate human life, life-loving humans naturally will attempt to harness or divert those forces. This harnessing and diverting extends beyond sorcerers, priests, extipicy experts, and the like to those who on behalf of the gods impose punishments on breakers of divinely sanctioned oaths and treaties to, finally, kings who, with acclaimed divine sanction, impose sovereign power over opponents.

As Tsvi Abusch has shown, Mesopotamian sorcerers and the exorcists assigned to combat them underwent a shift over the course of two millennia.[54] Initially the activities of the "witch" were confined probably to popular service, whereas the exorcist (āšipu) was called upon to combat

---

[51] Says Assurbanipal (Fishbane 2003:55, note 60). See too Fishbane's excursus on smashing enemies, from Tiamat to Lotan (2003:39–40). Sennacharib reports about the Elamites, that he "cut their throats like lambs" (John David Luckenbill, *Ancient Records of Assyria and Babylonia, Vol. I and II* (New York: Greenwood Press, 1968), section 254).

[52] Gurney 1940:19. This prayer is a composite of three texts in KUB XXIV. The pertinent ones read: nu-za-kán DINGIR.MEŠ saraa Ú-UL iaanzi. na-aš-ta NI-EŠ šarriir. ...É.HI.A DINGER-MEŠ-ma lauaarruna šaanhiiškanzi. na-at A-NA DINGIR.MEŠ-aš kat-taaatar nam-ma kisaru. nu-uš-ša-kán hiinkan kuruur gaaštaan idaaluun tapaaššan A-NA^KUR.URU miittani Ù A-NA^KUR.URU ar-za-u-a. tarnaatten ("They do not extol (sara ianzi) the gods. They violate the oath of the gods. ... They keep despoiling the houses of the gods. Let them become a cause for vengeance again. Allow in plague, evil enmity, and fever to Kizzuwatna (Mittani) and Arzawa).

[53] Discussed in CHD.

[54] Tsvi Abusch, "Considerations When Killing a Witch: Developments on Exorcistic Attitudes to Witchcraft in Mesopotamia. In *The Dynamics of Changing Rituals*. Ed. Jens Kreinath, Constance Hartung, Annette Deschner (New York: Peter Lang. 2003), 193.

demons. As the exorcist's activities became increasingly important to the civil order, an evil–good and female–male dichotomy set in, which affected the understanding of the supernatural and transformed how sorcerers trafficking in evil were to be combatted. One solution, burning a witch (or her effigy), came to be accompanied by petitions to Nergal that she not be allowed to commingle with the dead in the underworld and to Shamash that she melt or dissipate in the desert. Later, interestingly, she was to be confined to the underworld among the dead and away from the living. An increasingly complex science of exorcism developed, which included enlisting the unhappy spirits of improperly treated corpses to mingle with free-floating evils and, after receiving proper corpse treatments, to capture and guide those evils to the underworld. As cities developed, strategies for capturing felt evils apparently grew more creative.

Although no history of this scope has been identified for other cultural regions in the Near East, we are not lacking in ritual recipes for repelling evils, including evil gods. The Hittite milieu is instructive because of its vast array of expellable evils, such as evil tongue (HUL-lu-un EME-an), evil impurity (idalu papratar), sin (wastul), sorcery (alawazatar), curse (hurtais), and the "tongue of the multitude" (pangauwa EME-an), which presumably refers to rumor.[55] We have already mentioned expelling Telepinu's evil wrath.[56] Evil as an abstract is also richly attested,[57] not to mention evil wood, evil beam, and evil floorboard, presumably referring to faulty constructions.[58] Then there are specific evils associated with impurity, namely blood (eshar), oaths or bindings (linkais), illness (inan), curse (hurtais), and again sin (wastul).[59] Hittite ritualists were adept at exorcism: "From this sacrificer [EN.SISKUR] withdraw in the same way evil impurity (idalu papratar), sorcery (alawazatar) ... the anger of the gods, the oath of the god, the tongue of the multitude and the short year."[60] Many of these evil harms were harnessed and dispelled through ritualization.

[55] CHD. *The Hittite Dictionary of Oriental Institute of the University of Chicago*
      http://oi.uchicago.edu/research/publications/hittite-dictionary-oriental-institute-
      university-chicago-chd, 23–24.
[56] Ibid., 23.
[57] Ibid., 294.
[58] Ibid., 331.
[59] Ibid., 24.
[60] kēdaniyakan ANA EN.SISKUR idalu papratar alwazatar āštayaratar DINGER.
      MEŠ-aš NIŠ DINGER-*LIM* pangauwaš ...huittiya. Discussed in CHD 173, under
      manninkuwant- (to shorten).

Persuasive arguments have been made by Noegel,[61] Faraone,[62] Bottéro,[63] and others that ancient strategies to destroy some realities and to create others were enhanced by punnings, onomatopoeia, special dialects, inscriptions, and destructions of inscriptions across the ancient Near East and Greece. Rituals of inscribing and smashing texts rely on what Noegel has called "an ontology of words,"[64] whereby inscribed or effaced words are felt to sensuously manipulate the objects they name. Etching fate into a cosmic text was made to occur through inscription on clay, wood, wax, or other surfaces,[65] just as that fate was effaced or destroyed through the effacement or destruction of those surfaces (Ex. 34:32:19–33; Job 19:23:24; Isa. 30:8; Jer. 36:22–23).[66] Needless to say, these strategies give humans a presumed power to control not just any fate but evil fate. Such performative illocutions, enhanced by special media and ritual expertise, are found all over the world and are not essentially different from the aforementioned assault sorceries, which attempt to manipulate realities through the sinister use of utterances. All of these show acute awareness of the power of the spoken or engraved word to elicit evil or good.

A similar awareness has been argued to motivate the engraving of ancient images. Some Assyrian palace reliefs ostensibly were performative in that they effected change through representation.[67] That is, rather than simply reflecting events, the complex wall reliefs indicate a presupposed connection between the rendering of images and the realities represented, ostensibly effecting indexical changes in those realities. In fact, to the learned eye, the wall reliefs not only strive to effect indexical changes but also, through thematic repetition, to instigate a relentless movement toward those changes, a movement that may be felt. Toward this end, they also harness mythical prototypes of divine figures who are to have imposed order on evil antiorder; human rulers are made to mimic these.[68]

---

[61]   Noegel, 2010.
[62]   Christopher Faraone, "Molten Wax, Spilt Wine and Mutilated Animals: Sympathetic Magic in Near Eastern and Early Greek Oath Ceremonies," *Journal of Hellenic Studies* cxiii (1993): 60–80.
[63]   Jean Bottéro, *Religion in Mesopotamia*. Trans. Teresa Lavender Fagan (Chicago: University of Chicago Press, 2001).
[64]   Noegel, 2010: 34–38.
[65]   Bottéro, 2001: 178.
[66]   Noegel, 2010: 33–46.
[67]   Zainab Bahrani, *Rituals of War* (New York: Zone Books, 2008), 52–55; Zainab Bahrani, "The King's Head," *Iraq* LXVI (2004), 115–18.
[68]   Noegel 2010.

One example is the Til Tuba relief, whereon masses of supplicating, slain, and mutilated bodies portray the dominating of the Elamites by Assurbanipal. The relief depicts a veritable banquet of carnage with repeating themes – the Elamite king's severed head is one – that index the increasing sovereignty of Assurbanipal, who finally is shown in victory feast with his wife near a tree from which hangs that severed head.[69] Assurbanipal and queen imitate a god and his consort celebrating victory over evil. In the textual description of the battle, the conquered king Teumman is said to have planned evil, but the moon god Sin planned evil for him in return (and there were other telltale omens, as well), so this beheading was his destiny. As Bahrani would see it, Teumman's humiliation and destruction occurred not only in the flesh but in the supernatural reality rendered in art.

This is because, according to Bahrani, the practice of engraving and destroying images, just like the engraving and destroying of texts, was deemed to have eternal repercussions. This is supported by the practice of engraving protective curses on statues of kings, by the burial and installation of apotropaic statues at building foundations and entrances, and by the ancient practice of destroying or stealing monuments – including statues of divinities, thereby removing protection from and disheartening populations. A related phenomenon is the wall-embedding of cylinder prisms recording the exploits of kings.[70] The prisms were apparently for cosmic readers (or at least future builders), as they were out of view for the public. All of these engravings and destructions support the notion of artistically manipulating realities, including evil realities.

If we continue to hold evil as, in Bataille's terms, "cognate with death" and thereby as encompassing diminishments to life, we can find no more striking invocation of evil fate than in the ritualized killing of oath-victims. Commensal killings of animals are complicated enough; as Walter Burkert points out, we are the only creature to make a ritual out of killing the animals we eat, the only carnivore who prepares meat on sacred altars.[71] But in oath-sacrifice, there is no dining on animals, because oath-victims are never eaten. Rather, they are killed to make a dramatic point: the cost of perjury and treaty violation:

> This shoulder is not the shoulder of a spring lamb, it is the shoulder of Mati'ilu, it is the shoulder of his sons, his magnates, and the

---

[69] Bahrani, 2008: 35–42; 2004: 115–18.

[70] Bahrani, 2008, 41–2.

[71] Walter Burkert, "Sacrificial Violence: A Problem in Ancient Religions." In *Oxford Handbook of Religion and Violence*. Ed. Juergensmeyer, et al., 2013: 437–54.

people of his land. If Mati'ilu should sin against this treaty, so may, just as the shoulder of this spring lamb is torn out ... the shoulder of Mati'ilu, of his sons, [his magnates] and the people of his land be torn out.[72]

[J]ust as [thi]s ewe has been cut open and the flesh of [her] young has been placed in her mouth, may they make you eat in your hunger the flesh of your brothers, your sons and your daughters.[73]

Just as young sheep and ewes and male and female spring lambs are slit open and their entrails rolled down over their feet, so may (your entrails and) the entrails of your sons and your daughters roll down over your feet.[74]

The quality of shock and awe to these oath-making rituals (or envisioning of the same, based on textual descriptions) supports the observation of Roy Rappaport that spoken words are often felt as too fluffy and ephemeral to signify commitment so must be made heavy by acts.[75] What acts could wield more gravitas than these ritualized cruelties?

The divine role in this is ambiguous. Oath-gods may or may not be invoked to implement punishments for perjury,[76] but when they are, inscriptions or other dramatic acts still may be felt necessary to compel the gods to perform these punishments, as we see by the presumably binding inscription on this ostensibly inviolable kudurru stone of Assurbanipal:

But whoever blots out my written name, destroys my royal image, or changes its location, and does not set it up beside his (own) image, – may Nabu, the mighty lord, look upon him in anger, may he overthrow his royal throne, may he make his rule gloomy (or "eclipse" his rule), may he destroy his name and his seed in the lands, and have no mercy upon him.[77]

[72]   Bill Arnold and Bryan Breyer, *Readings from the Ancient Near East* (Grand Rapids, MI: Baker Academic Press, 2002), 101.

[73]   Luckenbill 1968, section 69.

[74]   Simo Parpola and Watanbe, Kazuko, Eds. *State Archives of Assyria, Vol. II, Neo-Assyrian Treaties and Loyalty Oaths* (Helsinki, Finland: The Neo-Assyrian Text Corpus Project and the Helsinki Press, 1988), 52, section 70.

[75]   Roy A. Rappaport, *Ritual and Religion in the Making of Humanity* (Cambridge: Cambridge University Press, 1999), 141.

[76]   E.g., "Behold to you these words under oath I put: If you ... do not protect them, these sacred oaths of yours, your lives, together with your wives, your children, your brothers, your sisters, your families, your houses, your fields, your cities, your vineyards, your threshing floors, together with your possessions, let them be destroyed! May the oath-gods seize you from the dark earth!" (Hittite king Mursilis to Haggana; Kbo V3 IV 36–40). Kitts 2005.

[77]   Luckenbill, *Ancient Records of Assyria and Babylonia*, 1968, section 977.

Gods presumably are invoked when the anticipated punishments are so dire as to transcend human capability. Divinely imposed punishments for perjurers from Mesopotamia to Asia Minor include not just annihilation of one's name and seed but famine, cannibalism of kin, being devoured by wild beasts, and being rendered as "dung on the ground."[78] There are

---

[78]   A few examples:

"Just as the *Cursers* sinned against Bel and he cut off their hands and feet and blinded their eyes, so may they annihilate you, and make you sway like reeds in water; may your enemy pull you out like reeds from a bundle"

(Parpola and Watanabe, 1988:57, sec 95).

"May [the gods] [slaughter] you, your women, your brothers, your sons, and your daughters like a spring lamb and a kid"

(Parpola and Watanabe, 1988:57, sec. 96A)

In no way barren is the oath and the blood of lambs,
the unmixed libations and the right hands in which we trusted.
For if the Olympian does not fulfill it at once,
he will fulfill it later, and with might he will avenge (*apeteisan*) it
with their heads and their wives and also their children.
For well I know this in my mind and my heart:
There shall come a day when sacred Ilion will be destroyed
and also Priam and the host of Priam of the ashen lance

(Iliad 4, 158–65 [translation by author])

"In this place I will shatter the plains of Judah and Jerusalem as a jar is shattered; I will make the people fall by the sword before their enemies at the hands of those who would kill them, and I will give their corpses to the birds and beasts to devour. I will make this city a scene of horror and contempt, so that every passer-by will be horror-struck and jeer in contempt at the sight of its wounds. I will compel men to eat the flesh of their sons and their daughters, they shall devour one another's flesh in the dire straits to which their enemies and those who would kill them will reduce them in the siege"

(Jer. 19:7–9; cf. Jer. 7:30–34; Jer. 8:1–3; Jer.9:22; Jer.15:3–4; Jer. 16:4).

"Uaite', together with his armies, who had not kept the oath (sworn) to me, who had fled before the weapons of Assur, my lord, and had escaped before them, – the warrior Irra (the pest god) brought them low. Famine broke out among them. To (satisfy) their hunger they ate the flesh of their children. Every curse, written down in the oath which they took, was instantly visited (lit. fated) upon them by Assur, Sin, Shamash, Adad, Bel, Nabu, Ishtar of Nineveh, the queen of Kidmuri, Ishtar of Arbela, Urta, Nergal (and Nusku). The young of camels, assess, cattle and sheep, sucked at seven udders (lit. suckling mothers) and could not satisfy their bellies with the milk. The people of Arabia asked questions, the one of the other, saying: "Why is it that such evil has befallen Arabia?" (And answered), saying: "Because we did not keep the solemn (lit. great) oaths sworn to Assur; (because) we have sinned against the kindness (shown us by) Assurbanipal, the king beloved of Enlil's heart"

(Luckenbill, 1968, sec. 828).

For discussions, see, e.g., Kitts (2005); E. J. Bickerman, "Couper une alliance." In *Studies in Jewish and Christian History*, Vol. I. (Leiden: E. J. Brill, 1976), 1–32;

few other areas of ancient thinking that reveal as grisly an imagination as the punishment for oath breaking. Presumably the extraordinary penalties are felt proportional to the crime.[79] Agamben[80] and, for that matter, Cicero (De officiis 3.29.10) have pointed to the historical problem of how to confirm affirmations made without sacred sanction. The seemingly cruel ritualizations of Near Eastern antiquity attempt to address just this problem of securing affirmational gravitas.

Replicating the force of the gods against oath violators is the royal human exercise of the right to impose death on disobedient vassals who have committed the evil of oath violation. In this, kings mimic the gods. As Ponchia showed decades ago,[81] it is common for Assyrian kings to be reported as performing battle feats in language identical to that reported for divinities, a mimicry we see in art and prose over the rest of the Near East and Egypt too.[82] Kings mimic gods by, among other things, suppressing representatives of cosmic chaos, radiating divine attributes (e.g., *melammu*[83]), and wielding weapons bestowed as divine gifts.[84] But,

---

Dominique Charpin, "Manger un serment." In *Jurer et Maudire: practiques politiques et usages juridiques du serment dans le Proche-Orient ancient* (Paris: L'Harmattan Mediterranees 10–11, 1996), 85–96; Giogieri (2001:421–40), Delbert Hillers, *Treaty-Curses and the Old Testament Prophets* (Rome: Pontifical Biblical Institute, 1964), Parpola and Watanabe (1988).

[79]   In the Homeric context equivalent in gravity to the severing of blood bonds and punished by the same forces. See Kitts (2005).

[80]   Giorgio Agamben, *The Sacrament of Language* (Stanford, CA: Stanford University Press, 2011), 1–23.

[81]   Simonetta Ponchia, "Analogie, Metafore, e Similitudini nelle iscrizioni reali assire: Semantica e Ideologia," *Or.Ant.* XXVI:3–4 (1987): 223–55.

[82]   Noegel 2007: 3–28.

[83]   Noegel 2007; A. L. Oppenheim, "Akkadian *pul(u)ḫ(t)u* and *melammu*," *Journal of the American Oriental Society* 63/1 (1943): 31–34; Kitts 2013a.

[84]   E.g., "At the word of Aššur, the great lord, my lord, on flank and front I pressed upon the enemy like the onset of a raging storm. With the weapons of Aššur, my lord, and the terrible onset of my attack, I stopped their advance, I succeeded in surrounding them" (Luckenbill, 1968, Sec 284; Annals of Sennacharib); "The king, who wears on his head a golden tiara from the inside of the temple, ... while they carry him and go to the palace, is Ninurta, who avenged his father. The gods, his fathers, gave him the scepter, throne and the staff" (KAR 307 (VAT 8917. I 20 23 Fishbane, 2003:43, note 17). A Mari king boasts of receiving from the storm god the very weapons "with which I smote Ti'amat" (*ša itti temtim antaḫsu* (Fishbane, 2003:33, note 12). Hittite Hattusilis prays to the Sun Goddess of Arinna that he is truer to Nerik than the kings before, "to whom the Storm-god had given the weapon" (Itamar Singer, *Hittite Prayers* (Atlanta: Society for Biblical Literature, 2002) 99–100). "[This is] the image of Assur as he advances to battle into the midst of Tiamat, the image of Sennacherib, king of Assyria, of Shar-ur, Shar-gaz, Gag, Nusku, Daianu, Tishpak, Mash of the Wall, Kubu, Hani, Sibitti–these gods who were advancing in front of Assur; Ninlil, Sheru'a, Sin,

most strikingly, kings claim divine sanction by imposing punishments on those who violate loyalty oaths. Hence,

> Adad, the violent, the powerful son of Anu, let loose his fierce tempest against them and, with bursting cloud and thunderbolt (lit. Stone of heaven), totally annihilated them. Ursa, their prince, who had transgressed against Shamash and Marduk, and had not kept sacred the oath (sworn by) Assur, king of the gods, became alarmed at the roar of my mighty weapons, his heart palpitating (being torn) like (that of) an owl (or bat; lit. bird of the cave), fleeing before an eagle. Like a man whose blood is pouring from him, he left Turushpa, his royal city; like (an animal) fleeing before the hunter, he trod the slope of his mountain; like a woman in travail he lay stretched on his bed, his mouth refusing food and drink (water), a fatal injury (lit. Disease without escape) he inflicted upon himself. I established the might of Assur, my lord, upon Urartu for all time to come, leaving there for future days his never-to-be-forgotten fear. The surpassing power of my might and the fury (lit. Onset) of my all-powerful weapons, which are without rival in the four regions (of the earth) and cannot be turned back, I let loose (lit. Made bitter) against Urartu in a bitter fight. The people of Zikirtu and Andia I bespattered with the venom of death.[85]

Notice the substitutions of king Sargon II's mighty weapons for those of Adad, Sargon's ostensible defense of divinely backed oaths, and the calamitous terror imposed on reputed oath violators. Although the Assyrians surely were the masters of this rhetoric, many other Near Eastern examples might be cited. Backed by the gods, these reported behaviors of kings show what, in today's discourse, might be deemed "sovereign power over bare life."[86]

Terror
The notion of sovereign power over bare life brings us to the theme of ancient terror. We've described terror as a sense of virtual contingency before the prospect of utter annihilation. As argued in the prolegomena, terror may be understood as a fundamentally prediscursive experience,

---

Ningal, Shamash, Aia, Gamlat, Anu, Antum, Adad, Shala, Ea, Damkina, the mistress of the gods, Mash,–these gods who are behind Assur. I am the one who conquers, stationed in Assur's chariot" (Luckenbill 1968, sec. 447). For discussion, see Kitts (2013a).

[85] Luckenbill, *Ancient Records of Assyria and Babylonia*, 1968, section 155.

[86] Giorgio Agamben, *Homo Sacer: Sovereign Power and Bare Life* (Stanford, CA: Stanford University Press, 1998).

yet certain artistic and literary constructions manage to elicit recognition of it. We will treat first literary depictions of the terror inspired by gods and then depictions of terror instigated by humans.

Divine Terror

Battlefield terror is one of the defining features of ancient holy war. We have already seen it in some Assyrian rhetoric, but perhaps the crowning examples are biblical. As von Rad has shown,[87] once the wrath of YHWH is aroused, Israel's enemies are thrown into confusion, panic, fear, and trembling.

> [T]he Lord thundered loud and long over the Philistines and threw them into confusion. They fled in panic before the Israelites
>
> (1 Sam. 7:10).

> Terror spread through the army in the field and through the whole people; the men at the post and the raiding parties were terrified; the very earth quaked, and there was panic
>
> (1 Sam. 14.15).

> Nations heard and trembled,
> agony seized the dwellers in Philistia.
> Then the chieftains of Edom were dismayed,
> trembling seized the leaders of Moab,
> all the inhabitants of Canaan were in turmoil;
> terror and dread fell upon them:
> through the might of thy arm they stayed still as stone
>
> (Ex. 15:14–16).

> Wail, for the day of the Lord is near;
> it will come like destruction from the Almighty.
> Because of this, all hands will go limp,
> every man's heart will melt.
> Terror will seize them,
> pain and anguish will grip them;
> they will writhe like a woman in labor.
> They will look aghast at each other,
> their faces aflame
>
> (Is. 13:6–8).

---

[87] Gerhard Von Rad, *Holy War in Ancient Israel*. Trans. Marva J. Dawn (Grand Rapids, MI: William B. Eerdmans Publishing Co., 1991 [1958]).

Disobedient Israelites too may experience divinely inspired panic and terror.

> And I will make those of you who are left in the lands of your ene-
> mies so ridden with fear that, when a leaf flutters behind them in
> the wind, they shall run as if it were a sword behind them; they shall
> fall with no one in pursuit. Though no one pursues them, they shall
> stumble over one another, as if the sword were behind them, and
> there shall be no stand made against the enemy.
>
> (Lev. 26:36–8)

These remarkable passages attest to our earlier point that ancient narratives of terror can elicit our own sense of terror, at least to the extent
that we may conjoin our own discourses to those of our sources.[88]

Let us demonstrate the point by scrutinizing the last example,
wherein the fluttering of the leaf is made to manufacture the terrifying
specter of a sword-wielding enemy whose pursuit causes one to stumble
over one's neighbor and to fall, by implication prone for stabbing (Lev.
26:36–8). All three of the perspectives outlined in the prolegomena under
terror are implicit in our grasp of this passage. First, in the simile of the
person pursued by a sword, there is an existential dimension rooted in
the bodily experience of running, sensory confusion, presumably loss of
balance (falling), and spatial orientation (stumbling over one another)
before a shadowy enemy in pursuit. The simile evokes physical and emotional disarray and conceivably too foreboding and the uncanny. Second,
comprehending the simile relies on a collapse of semantic domains, as
would a metaphor. So the figure of the leaf is not just substituted for
but overlaid with the figure of a sword – by poetic connotation shaking
or menacing just as the leaf is fluttering. As Ricoeur taught us,[89] figurative language is effective not just because of the paradoxical substitution of words (sword for leaf) but because of the rapprochement that
occurs when the figure of the rustling leaf merges with a brandishing
sword in our imaginations. The rapprochement insinuates sword-like
characteristics in the leaf. This rapprochement is supported also by tension among elements in the whole sentence. In this case, the rustling
leaf-sword, stumbling victims, panic, and flight precipitate a startling
visceral awareness of the danger in the natural world, here thick with
menace. Finally, all of the examples given may be said to elicit a violent

---

[88] Paul Ricoeur, 1981: 158.
[89] Ibid.

imaginary, wherein the safety and comfort presumed in our domestic lives are potentially ruptured by the sudden emergence of unpredictable and nonhuman forces. Hence the usual patterns of meaning are violated, and we are thrown back on unnamed, inchoate fears.

Other ancient poetry, but particularly the Iliad, also captures dimensions of this experience of terror. We have already mentioned the theomachy of Iliad 21, with its extraordinary poetic extension depicting the terror experienced by Achilles fleeing the river gods. But there are other examples wherein figurative language insinuates collapsed semantic domains and blurred sensory divides. On the first day of battle, distressing animus is figured as Ares rousing the Trojans, Athene the Achaians, while Terror, Fear, and insatiably desirous Strife – planting her head in the sky and striding over the earth – increase the groaning of men (4.439–45). Another example is Ares' impending *cholos* and *mēnis* (anger and fury) figured as his horses Terror and Panic, about to descend into battle along with the god, who yearns to avenge the death of his mortal son (15.119–22). Both passages portend imminent terror and carnage, extended poetically into the disturbed cosmos. Again, some would call this "bad art," but from the perspective of oral literature, it is better understood as creative use of poetic metonyms to lure the listener into an expanded world of sensory perceptions. The effect is predicated on the audience's suspension of disbelief and was effected, ostensibly, by clever muses and their human counterparts.[90]

An awareness of the conjuring capacity of poetic artifice is evident too from an ominous scene on Achilles' divinely manufactured shield. Here the metonyms are visual. Eris/Strife and Kudoimos/Din of Battle are pictured as consorting together, while destructive Ker/Death, holding a newly wounded man and an unwounded man, drags a dead man through the melee by the foot, all the while wearing around her shoulders a garment stained with human blood (18.535–8). Achilles' Myrmidons cannot actually bear to look upon this shield (19.14–17), but our eyes and ears are spared none of it. The same is inferred for the aegis of Athene (5.738–42), for Agamemnon's shield (11.36–7), and for Hector's eyes (8.349–50), all said to be flashing with/like the face of the Gorgon, with her instantly disintegrating stare.[91] Such adroit figuration is intended to capture and elicit terrifying imagination.

[90]   Od.8.491, 499, Od.1.337. See Kitts, "What's Religious about the Iliad?" *Religion Compass* 7.7 (2013): 225-244.
[91]   Thalia Feldman, "Gorgo and the Origins of Fear," *Arion* IV:3 (1965): 486-7.

Last, as in the reference to god Hades at the start of the theomachy, referred to earlier, we have a few rare depictions of gods who are terrified. Two of these are cryptic Hittite illustrations. In one, Ishtar of Nineveh initially is so paralyzed with fear about the monster Hedammu that she cannot bring herself to accept an offered throne, food-table, and cup (Kbo XIX 112 5a and 5b). Based on other examples of gods who refuse offerings (e.g., Telepinu), this inability to eat indicates a failure to thrive. The second occurs just before Teššup's vanquishing of Ullikummi, wherein Ea descends to the underworld to acquire a primordial weapon for Teššub. The trip is horrifying: "Go away from in front of me, my son. Do not stand up in front of me. My mind within me has become sad/angry, for with my eyes I have seen the dead, seeing the dead in the Dark Earth, and they are standing like dusty and .... Ones" (CTH 345 3 A iv 9–12).[92] There are surely stories behind these (the first possibly amusing, as the goddess will try to seduce Hedammu). Note that these are a far cry from the terrifying splendor of Sargon II's avenging gods or the spectacle of gods running in front of their human favorites on the battlefield. What they have in common is presumably their radiating effect into the experience of mortals.

Humanly Imposed Terror

As already suggested, there is a thin line between the terrifying splendor of gods and of their mortal counterparts on the battlefield. A striking element in the human displays is an apparent relish for destruction, particularly in the famous first-millennium BCE Assyrian reports. Consider this by Assurbanipal:

> As for those men (and) their vulgar mouths, who uttered vulgarity against Assur, my god, and plotted evil against me, the prince who fears him, – I slit their mouths (v. Tongues) and brought them low. The rest of the people, alive, by the colossi, between which they had cut down Sennacherib, the father of the father who begot me, ... at that time I cut down those people there, as an offering to his shade. Their dismembered bodies (lit. flesh) I fed to the dogs, swine, wolves, and eagles, to the birds of heaven and the fish of the deep.[93]

---

[92] Harry Hoffner, *Hittite Myths*, Atlanta: Scholars Press, 1990: 59–60.
[93] Luckenbill, *Ancient Records of Assyria and Babylonia*, section 795.

Also this by Sargon II:

> ... I plunged into his midst like a swift (lit. frightful) javelin, I defeated him. I turned back his advance; I killed large numbers of his (troops), the bodies of his warriors I cut down like millet (?), filling the mountain valleys (with them). I made their blood run down the ravines and precipices like a river, dyeing plain, countryside and highlands red like a royal robe (?). His warriors, the mainstay of his army, bearers of bow and lance, I slaughtered about his feet like lambs, I cut off their heads.[94]

And this by Esarhaddon:

> Before me, in the land of Hanigalbat, all of their mighty warriors blocked my path, offering battle. The terror of the great gods, my lords, overwhelmed them. They saw the fierce onset of my battle (-array) and became as insane (men). Ishtar, queen of war and battle, lover of my priesthood, stood at my side, broke their bows, shattered their battle line. ... Following [after me like lambs] they employed my majesty's (favor). The people of Assyria, who had sworn allegiance before me by the great gods, came into my presence and kissed my feet.[95]

These reports of human sacrifice, slaughter, and terror surely served not just to catalogue royal feats but to aggrandize the might of the sovereign.

The last example ends with a successful petition for pity. The custom is well developed in Homeric literature, where the mandate to respect suppliants is exemplified by the gods themselves, with some notable exceptions (n.b. Athene to the Trojan women in Iliad 6). On the other hand, most human-to-human supplications in the Iliad fail, which, by inversion, arouses our expectation that they should not. Presumably the same applies to the Assyrian materials, where, with a few exceptions, the sovereign claims to have remained pitiless in the face of beseeching subjects. The Homeric poems and Hittite laws and prayers are probably not distinctive in offering an array of divinely supported customs (e.g., supplication and hospitality among humans and between humans and gods), which are supposed to soften impulses to cruelty and to ensure compassion. But Assyrian sovereigns, at least in their boasts, rarely claim to have accepted similar supplications from subjected populations.[96] It

---

94   Ibid., section 154.
95   Ibid., section 504.
96   The exceptions are famous. See, e.g., the palace reliefs from Nimrud depicting the surrender of Jehu.

is perhaps strange that ancient Near Eastern gods are known to have accepted supplications for pity by human sovereigns whose cities were under siege,[97] when human sovereigns do not accept such supplications for pity. Broadly speaking, it is against the expectation for mercy that these refusals take on terrorizing force.

In addition to literary depictions of pitilessness, we have some startling artistic depictions, especially from art-rich Mesopotamia. We have already mentioned the Til Tuba relief. Here we touch on another artifact, the late-third-millennium victory stele of Naramsin. The semiotics of Mesopotamian power may be seen in the configuration of images on this famous artwork. Below the solar disc representing celestial gods stands the king, helmeted, horned, armed, a giant among underlings. He stands with his right foot on the necks of two puny and naked victims, he faces one man falling backward with a spear in his neck and another standing with hands uplifted as if in supplication. Below the king are ascending rows of his soldiers marching over the bodies of the slain. The whole effect is of momentum toward the top, where stands the aggrandized king, and it is all supported by trampled bodies of the slain.[98] Our lasting impression is of the terrorizing specter of sheer might.

CONCLUDING THOUGHTS

Relying on Bataille's notion of evil as cognate to death and extending the term to encompass diminishments to life, this chapter has attempted a selective sketch of evil in ancient literature from the Mesopotamian milieu to the Homeric. Terror has been shown continuously associated with the specter of imminent annihilation. Of course these findings are circular, in that we found what we set out to find. However relative, though, the findings do invite questions about human nature as envisioned in this ancient evidence. One of those questions concerns a seeming enthrallment with evil and terror and another a fascination with pitilessness. For this context, these interrelate and force us to, as Ricoeur put it, conjoin our discourses to the discourses of our sources.

---

[97] Israel Eph'al, *Culture and History of the Ancient Near East, Volume 36: The City Besieged: Siege and Its Manifestations in the Ancient Near East* (Boston: Brill, 2009), 159–62.

[98] Bahrani, 2008: 110–14.

Considering enthrallment with evil and terror, at least some of what we have found calls to mind the ponderings of Arendt. To the totalitarian force that dehumanizes both itself and its victims, Arendt attributed the name "radical evil,"[99] which she measured by its transcendence of our powers of understanding. This is cruelty beyond self-interest, greed, resentment, lust for power, and the like – these being human drives that most people can grasp. Some of the illustrations of evil herein befit that totalitarian force, from monsters devouring humans to gods and kings mangling whole populations. The slaughter reliefs of Til Tuba are a provocative illustration. Some panels bear a striking thematic resemblance to spectacles of torture in the well-known photos from Abu Ghraib, such as the pyramid of bodies or the electrified, robed figure teetering on a black box. Such spectacles might be argued to transcend simple sadism to infer a captivation with the power of sheer might, conceived as the capacity to configure bodies or body parts into aberrant art. If, as Noegel, Ponchia, and others point out, kings are imagined to mimic the force of the gods, what does the Til Tuba relief tell us about the gods, or at least conceptions of them? It is arguable that such spectacles of bodily degradation gauge the might of the sovereign and, by mimicry, also of his gods. The irony in this sovereign creative destruction is, as Arendt put it for Fascism, "the totalitarian belief that everything is possible seems to have proved only that everything can be destroyed."[100] In these ancient examples, godlike power would seem proportional to its capacity to destroy.

As for pitilessness and subjection to terror, an apt figure for pondering might be the Roman *homo sacer*, as politically conceptualized by Agamben. This is the extraordinary figure of the "sacred man" who could not be immolated as a human sacrifice but was immune to protections from murder. That is, *homo sacer* was outside of both sacred law, wherein he might enjoy elevated status as a sacrificial victim, and of profane law, wherein he might enjoy protection from harm. Despite his name, then, he was neither sacred nor quite accursed, and he was not an emblem of sacred ambivalence, as often supposed. Rather, as Agamben carefully lays out, the *homo sacer* is viewed as the measure of the sovereign's exceptional power to destroy life, a power proportional to *homo sacer*'s susceptibility to being destroyed.[101] So *homo sacer* is not sacred

[99]   1966: 458–9.
[100]   1966: 459.
[101]   "The sovereign sphere is the sphere in which it is permitted to kill without committing homicide and without celebrating a sacrifice, and sacred life – that is, life that may be killed but not sacrificed – is the life that has been captured in this sphere" (1998:83).

life (an ironic misnomer), but bare life. The Roman establishment of this figure reveals a profound realization that the foundation of political life rests on "the life that can be taken, can be killed, [and] is politicized through its very capacity to be killed."[102] Political life thus is established in the sovereign's power to destroy bare life.

To add to the Roman conundrum, bare life is *homo sacer* only in that he is an implied mystical double for the sovereign.[103] Both he and the sovereign occupy a zone of exception, as can be seen in funeral ceremonies in which the *homo sacer*, essentially a living dead man, is the cipher for the sovereign before he dies, even in some contexts a kind of pacified ghost whose presence paves the way for the death of the sovereign. Curiously, his susceptibility to being killed insinuates also the sovereign's susceptibility. Ritual surrogacy is not unknown in the ancient world, of course (e.g., Nagy,[104] van Brock[105]), but the dire plight of *homo sacer* arouses an implicit specter of common suffering, not just reverse empowerment, between himself and the sovereign.

The complexity of the figure of *homo sacer* in Roman context exceeds what we might say with confidence about the ancient Near Eastern evidence. Yet because of the vivid nature of the art and poetry examined here and the striking carnage in some of it, it is hard to deny the persuasiveness of Agamben's construction that sovereignty may have been gauged by power over bare life and by the dehumanizing totalitarian force recognized by Arendt. By these perspectives, terror reflects the experience of unpitied victims and is anchored in the unprotected fragility of life, which gods, monsters, and sovereigns may deign to destroy.

FURTHER READING

Bahrani, Zainab. *The Graven Image*. Philadelphia: University of Pennsylvania Press, 2003.

Frankfurter, David. *Evil Incarnate: Rumors of Demonic Conspiracy and Satanic Abuse in History*. Princeton, NJ: Princeton University Press, 2006.

Juergensmeyer, Mark. *Terror in the Mind of God*. Berkeley, CA: University of California Press, 2000, 2003.

Juergensmeyer, Mark, Margo Kitts, and Michael Jerryson, Eds. *The Oxford Handbook of Religion and Violence*. New York: Oxford University Press, 2013.

---

[102]   Agamben 1998:89.
[103]   Ibid., 87–103.
[104]   Gregory Nagy, *The Best of the Achaeans* (Baltimore, MD: Johns Hopkins University Press, 1979).
[105]   Nadia Van Brock, "Substitution Rituelle," *Revue Hittite et Asianique* 65 (1959): 117–46.

Juergensmeyer, Mark, and Margo Kitts, Eds. *Princeton Readings in Religion and Violence*. Princeton, NJ: Princeton University Press, 2011.

Siebers, Tobin. "The Return to Ritual: Violence and Art in the Media Age." *Journal for Cultural and Religious Theory* 5.1 (2003): 9–33.

Sontag, Susan. *Regarding the Pain of Others*. New York: Farrar, Straus, and Giroux, 2003.

Stewart, Pamela, and Andrew Strathern. *Violence: Theory and Ethnography*. New York: Continuum International Publishing Group, 2002.

10 Judaism and the Problem of Evil

LENN E. GOODMAN

THE SUFFERING OF INNOCENTS

The problem of evil in Jewish contexts typically means the suffering of innocents and, correlatively, the prosperity of the wicked. Rarely is it made a dialectical lever to challenge God's goodness or rule. Normally, even normatively, the question is laid, humbly, if insistently, before God rather than before presumed hearers eager to throw off what the Rabbis call heaven's yoke.

Discovery of the tension between God's justice and human suffering does not await the drama of the book of Job. Abraham, learning of the impending destruction of Sodom and Gomorrah, did not retire resigned but *remained standing before the Lord* – almost confrontationally: *Abraham neared Him, saying, "Wilt Thou indeed sweep away the righteous with the wicked?... Far be it from Thee to do such a thing, to slay guilty and innocent together, letting the righteous and the wicked fare alike! Far be it from Thee! Will not the Judge of all the earth do justice!...* And then, his voice growing less urgent, he moves from denial to negotiation: *I am dust and ashes...*, he pleads, will God not spare a city if fifty honest men are found there? As soon as God has agreed, Abraham is not embarrassed to haggle: will forty-five do? – *wilt Thou destroy the whole city for lack of five?* (Genesis 18:22–28). Human lives are at stake.

The reasoning that gives backbone to Abraham's wheedling rests on the premise of God's justice. Glossing the word "neared," Rashi, the great medieval exegete (1040–1105), writes, "Abraham advanced ready to say hard things – and to plead and pray." The prayers and pleas and the hard words were all elements of his brief for the Cities of the Plain. But the case rested on Abraham's grasp of the logic of God: universal sovereignty demands universal justice. God underscored that premise by adding mercy to the bargain: He would spare the cities, condemned by their own decadence, should He find there even ten honest men. God's justice is implacable and His judgment secure (18:22–21, 32). But mercy will spare the wicked for the sake of the righteous.

It is not always so. The Psalms' lyrical celebrations of God's rule over nature and destiny repeatedly yield to querulous rephrasings of Abraham's question, probing the tender joint between experience and the divine ideal. God's rule, bodied forth in the imagery of the Psalms, rests on His justice:

> The Lord reigns, clothed in majesty, girded with strength.
> But the earth stands firm, unmoved.
> Right from of old is Thy throne –
> Thou being eternal.
> The floods rise, Lord. The floods raise their clamor.
> But above the roar of surging waters, mightier than the
>   breakers of the sea,
> The Lord holds sway on high –
> Thy promises, most faithful,
> Thy house, Lord, worthy of its holiness forever!
>
> (Psalms 93)

That core idea, that God rules in and by righteousness, that justice tempered only by mercy is the true warrant of holiness,[1] makes unmerited suffering all the more unbearable:

> Like a deer panting for freshets,
> So doth my soul pant for Thee, God.
> My soul thirsteth for the living God.
> When will I arrive and see God's face?
> My tears were my bread day and night,
> As they asked me, "Where is thy God?"
> All this I recall, as I pour out my soul –
> How I marched with the crowd to God's house,
> Amid voices of joy, song, and thanks,
> As I moved with the holiday throng…
> Now I say to my God and my Rock,
> Why hast Thou forgotten me?
> Why do I go grieving, oppressed by the foe?
> Mine enemies taunt me as my bones are crushed,
> Asking all through the day, "Where is thy God?"
>
> (Psalms 42:2–5, 10–12)

---

[1]   Lenn E. Goodman, *Judaism: A Contemporary Philosophical Investigation* (London: Routledge, 2017), 70–77.

The poet comforts himself with thoughts of past joys and hopes of future grace (42:6–7, 9), but the visions only intensify his questioning:

> Deep calleth to deep.
> At the sound of the cataracts,
> All Thy breakers and billows
> > Overwhelm me (42:8).

Natural and human evil are linked by the premise that God ordains all events, or at least permits them. So the marauders who steal Job's livestock and slay his servants are one with the storm wind that takes his offspring. The book of Job universalizes the problematic that was poignantly personal in the Psalms, making Job an everyman, a non-Israelite like Adam or Noah; and it sharpens its questioning by making Job a figure of fiction, sinless and god-fearing by hypothesis (Job 1:1). So it cannot matter when Resh Lakish in the Talmud holds that Job never existed.[2] Everyone knows of undeserved suffering and death.

The Torah constrains the parameters in which Jewish thinkers meet the problem of evil. To begin with, there is no original sin.[3] The burden of inherited guilt that makes a default of suffering in this world and damnation in the next, to be answered only by vicarious atonement, is as foreign to the Torah as the notion of karma if that means a moral load carried from previous lives. The Judaic ethos rejects the idea that suffering, per se, is deserved; and the otherworldliness that might have assuaged the doubts raised by God's seeming silence is antithetical to the Mosaic canon. It is true that intimations of immortality touch the fringes of Judaic scripture – in marginal books like Maccabees, invited by faith in the triumph of life over death.[4] So Hosea can hear God exulting, even mocking death, as He promises Israel's revival:

> From the grave would I redeem them,
> Rescue them from death itself –
> Death, where are thy plagues?
> Where is thy sting, Sheol!
> > (Hosea 13:14)

---

[2] See B. Bava Batra 16a; cf. Genesis Rabbah 57.4.

[3] Each morning, an Orthodox Jew recites lines from the Talmud that begin, "My God, the soul Thou gavest me is pure. Thou didst create it, Thou didst form it, Thou didst breathe it into me" (B. Berakhot 60b).

[4] See Jon Levenson, *Resurrection and the Restoration of Israel: The Ultimate Victory of the God of Life* (New Haven, CT: Yale University Press, 2006). My phrase "the triumph of life" comes from Shelley.

The lines re-echo in the New Testament:

> Death, where is thy victory?
> Death, where is thy sting?
>
> (1 Corinthians 15:55)

The mocking turns earnest long before Donne ends his tenth Holy Sonnet with the challenge, "death, thou shalt die!" But the Torah pursues other themes. Rejecting an Egyptian fixation, it has little to say about death and almost nothing about immortality[5] – a fact sometimes troubling to those who presume the pair to be the universal cynosure of religion.

Job, confronting evil personally and emblematically, denies any reprieve from mortality: *A cloud fades and is gone, so one who descends to the grave does not return* (7:9; cf. 14:10). The Talmudic Sages may castigate Job: "dust in his mouth," they say, for "trying to upset the plate." Only the fact that he spoke out of pain mitigates their censure (B. Bava Batra 16a). But the Psalms agree with Job:

> Thou returnest man to dust,
> Saying, "Go back, ye children of Adam!"
> For a thousand years in Thy sight
> Are like yesterday when it's gone,
> Like a watch in the night.
> You sweep over them and they sleep.
> Just as the grass is fresh in the morning,
> Frolicking in the dawn's light,
> Only to wither and fade before nightfall,
> So are we, at the touch of Thy wrath,
> Overcome by Thy hot anger.
>
> (Psalms 90:5–7; cf. Isaiah 40:7–8)

God knows well that we are *but flesh, a breath that passeth and doth not return* (Psalms 78:9).

The Pentateuch, notoriously, regulates every aspect of life, but its few laws regarding death center on the linked realms of physical and spiritual purity. They invoke ritual to affirm communal responsibility for unaccounted, unrequited bloodshed (Deuteronomy 21:1–9) and guard the human image, even in an executed criminal (21:22–23). But they include no funeral laws or obsequies. Moses' grave is unknown (34:6),

---

5   See Lenn E. Goodman, *On Justice* (Oxford: Littman Library, 2008), 195–211.

and the Hebrew liturgy, taking the hint, offers praises of God where prayers "for" (or to, or against) the dead might have been expected.

The Kaddish, said by mourners in Aramaic, is the same prayer that punctuates each phase of worship or the study of sacred texts. It opens by inviting the assembled congregation to bless God's name: "Magnified and sanctified be His great name in the world He created as He designed. His rule prevail in your lifetime – in your days and the lives of the whole house Israel. And let us say, Amen." The congregation then blesses God in words drawn from the book of Daniel (2:20): "Infinitely and ever blessed be His great name!" The reader takes up that theme: "Blessed, praised, extolled, exalted, glorified, held beautiful and splendid, celebrated and uplifted, be the name of the Holy, beyond all blessings, songs, lauds, and comforts spoken in the world. And let us say, Amen." The prayer concludes, "Abundant peace from Heaven, and life for us and all Israel. And we say, Amen. May He who maketh peace in His celestial heights grant peace for us and all Israel. And let us say, Amen."

Death is not mentioned. Life is the focus in the penultimate line. The first reference to a mourner's reciting this prayer comes in the prayerbook known as Mahzor Vitry (1208). The custom of mourners leading the Kaddish at key points in a worship service probably reflects an ancient hope that no one should die without a survivor to offer God's praises. But the themes of the Kaddish, beyond the transcendent grace of creation, are cosmic and worldly peace (*shalom*, referring broadly to well-being) and the deep concern that God's splendor be recognized in the world – hence the focus on His name. The sole reference to suffering in the prayer is the word *neḥemata*, Thy comforts, alluding to God's consolation of Israel for the destruction of His Temple in Jerusalem, chiefly in the seven passages from Isaiah read annually in the aftermath of Tisha b'Av, the Ninth day of the Hebrew month of Av, which commemorates the destruction of both the first and second Temples.[6] So even here the theme is grace. For the Torah is a law of life (cf. Leviticus 18:5). Its aim is to guide its recipients in sanctifying their lives (Leviticus 19:2, 26; Exodus 19:6) by following God's precepts (Numbers 15:40; Deuteronomy 26:18, 28:9),[7] not to extricate them from the world they love or from their cherished hopes.

---

[6]   The comforting passages: Isaiah 40:1–26, 49:14–51:3, 54:11–55:5, 51:12–52:12, 54:1–10, 60, and 61:10–63:9.

[7]   The specific blessing recited at the performance of each divine commandment blesses God, "who sanctified us with His commandments" – since the performance of God's

SAADIAH GAON AND THE SUFFERINGS OF LOVE

The affirmations of immortality that do penetrate Jewish hearts and postbiblical texts are more clearly moved by love and admiration for individuals and communities too precious to be lost than by eagerness to explain away death and suffering as acts of God. For Jewish sources do not hold God's sovereignty incompatible with human finitude – not if creation is an act of grace.

Saadiah Gaon, the first systematic Jewish philosopher (882–942), did argue that God's justice demands an afterlife to reward merit and requite innocent suffering – since evils prevail in this world. Saadiah steadfastly affirmed that some sufferings are undeserved, despite Job's companions and the midrashic rationalizations that assume Job must have harbored some hidden guilt. Saadiah urges all who suffer to examine their ways to see where they may have done wrong. But he is confident that honesty with oneself can reveal whether sufferings are deserved. Yet to preserve God's justice, he turns to the rabbinic doctrine of the sufferings of love – the idea that God lays unmerited sufferings on those He especially loves to justify enhancing their reward in the hereafter.

In his commentary on Job, the book of the Bible that he assigned the title *The Book of Theodicy*, in keeping with his practice of giving thematic titles to biblical books when he translated them into Arabic, Saadiah sees Job's sufferings as a trial. That, he argues, is the reason for God's silence before Job's desperate pleas to know why he has been made to suffer:

> Job had tried to understand why God tormented him and had entreated God to make the reason known to him ... But God did not make this known to him. Sifting through many of the accounts of the ancients, we find that whenever one of them was afflicted by God in some way, and then asked his Lord to make known to him why that misfortune had been loosed upon him, we find a division: if the victim had suffered deservedly, God made it clear to him and told him, "This was for your wrong doing." ... But if the sufferer was being tested and had committed no offense to begin with, God did not explain his sufferings, so as not to undermine his forbearance in people's eyes ... This is the pattern with those who are undergoing a trial. God does not directly inform them that they will be recompensed. Rather they must persevere on the basis of their reason alone.[8]

commandments, the biblical mitzvot, and those rabbinically constructed in elaboration of their themes allow us to bring God's holiness into our lives.

[8] See Saadiah ben Joseph al-Fayyumi, *The Book of Theodicy*, tr. with commentary, L. E. Goodman (New Haven, CT: Yale University Press, 1988) 382–83; for Elihu's human

Trials, on Saadiah's view, are an expression of God's grace, warranting an enhanced otherworldly reward. Why does God not simply extend the blessings His favor intends? Blessings, Saadiah answers, must be earned, not simply given. Life is authentic, not a mere game. So doubt and dismay are inherent in the human condition, just as suffering and pain are.

Saadiah tempers his commitment to the rabbinic view by ascribing the doctrine of recompense to Elihu, making it, in effect, a human response, as distinguished from what Job will hear when God speaks from the storm wind, affirming, with many an illustration, that nature must follow its course, since providence is comprehensive. But human as the idea may be, Saadiah stands by the sufferings of love.

MAIMONIDES ON THE PRIMACY OF GOOD OVER EVIL

Maimonides (1138–1204), by far the more cogent and coherent thinker, saw a more promising avenue of response in Saadiah's more authentically biblical contention that the act of creation portends infinite grace, since the gift of being answers to no prior desert.[9] And Saadiah's turn to general providence is compelling. After all, even Elihu knows that rain falls on the sea, where, as Saadiah says, no human use can be derived from it.[10] But Maimonides denounces Saadiah's admission that evils outweigh goods in this life, calling it an Epicurean notion, grounded in the false assumption that pleasure and pain are the true measures of value.[11] And he categorically rejects the sufferings of love as unbiblical and untrue.[12]

Sufferings, Maimonides argues, are real enough evils, and pleasures clearly can be (instrumental) goods.[13] But neither pain nor pleasure denominates the true coin of God's realm. Health and well-being predominate in this world. Disruption is the exception. But no bodily good affords the ultimate standard against which God's acts must be gauged. The true good that vindicates our vulnerability is the possibility afforded by the very embodiment that grounds our vulnerability, of

---

response, esp. 358, 367–70; cf. Goodman, "Saadiah Gaon on the Problem of Evil," in Andrew Pinsent, ed. (forthcoming).

[9]   Saadiah, *The Book of Theodicy*, 123–24.

[10] Saadiah, *The Book of Theodicy*, 372, glossing Job 36:30.

[11] See Maimonides, *Guide* III 12. Maimonides refrains from naming Saadiah here but responds to the Gaon's Muslim contemporary, Muhammad ibn Zakariya al-Razi (a great physician and freethinking philosopher, d. ca. 925), who had argued that evil must outweigh goods, on the Epicurean grounds that living beings are aggregates of atoms inevitably dispersed.

[12] Maimonides, *Guide* III 24.

[13] See Maimonides, "Eight Chapters," chapter 5.

rising intellectually and spiritually – as Job did in the end – to knowledge
of God. It is here that we realize the inner affinity for which we are said
to be created in God's image.

Maimonides pulls rank on the rabbinic authorities by calling their
doctrine of the sufferings of love unbiblical. He does not share Saadiah's
deference to the ancient sages. He often weaves brilliant tapestries of
argument from their aggadic tropes, but he does not share Saadiah's commitment to culling truths from every midrash. Citing a favorite piece of
rabbinic anti-anthropomorphism, he freely writes, "I wish all their words
were like it!"[14] But what enables him to brand the sufferings of love not
just unbiblical but untrue? Empirically, he can judge that human evils
are the exception rather than the rule: "nowhere in the world is there a
city dominated by such evils ... Only in major wars is such violence generalized over a sizeable number of people, and even then it rarely engulfs
the greater part of the earth."[15]

Maimonides has suffered persecution and has lived close to war.
So this is no mere whitewash. He can call on his medical experience to
affirm the rarity of birth defects – although clinical practice today may
see (and save) greater numbers than lived to be noted in his day. But what
clinches the argument philosophically is the ontic priority of good over
evil. The sufferings that challenge the very idea of divine justice are real
evils. But what makes them evils is the injury they do to real goods. There
would be no evils unless there were sound claims to be harmed – health
undermined, wisdom scorned or addled, beauty desecrated or destroyed.

Maimonides takes to task the philosophers of his day who defended
a hybrid of neoplatonic and Aristotelian themes for failing fully to
exploit the opportunity their own system gave them to lay evil at the
door of matter. The adversary (*ha-saṭan*) in the book of Job, he argues,
who tempts God to wager on Job's steadfast integrity, even with the loss
of all he has – save only his life and sanity – is in fact matter. Hence
scripture's periphrasis in introducing the adversary: he is not one of
the "sons of God" but "came along with them."[16] What this means to
Maimonides is that the "adversary" is nothing real in himself, not a
fallen angel (a notion that Saadiah had vigorously refuted[17]) – thus, not
a form by which reality is imparted by emanation[18] but an inevitable

14   Maimonides, *Guide* I 59, citing Babylonian Talmud 33b.
15   Maimonides, *Guide* III 12.
16   Maimonides, *Guide* III 22, citing Job 1:6.
17   Saadiah, *The Book of Theodicy*, 154–59.
18   See Maimonides, *Guide* II 6; Goodman, "Maimonidean Naturalism," in Goodman,
       ed., *Neoplatonism and Jewish Thought* (Albany: SUNY Press, 1992), 139–72.

concomitant of creation. Matter here, as in Plato, represents otherness. It is necessary in the sense that God cannot in the nature of the case "create His like" – another infinite being. The absolute remains absolute. Evil is privation. But that privation, that very otherness, is being's receptivity – the condition of God's generosity, of His not withholding, as Plato put it, the gift of being.[19]

Job, Maimonides writes, was a good man but not wise or discerning. Had he been wise, the source of his sufferings would not have been obscure to him.[20] It was no hidden sin, as the text itself announces. To take that line undermines not only the book's premise and problematic but the testimony of God Himself, who confirms Job's integrity and rebukes his companions for what Job rightly called their bad faith.[21] Galen pinioned the issue, as Maimonides sees it:

> Galen says well in *De Usu Partium* III (10), "Do not delude yourself with the false hope that from semen and menstrual blood an animal will develop that will not die or feel pain, or that will shine like the sun, or be capable of perpetual motion."[22] Galen's words call attention to a special case of the general proposition that whatever arises from matter develops as perfectly as it can from the matter proper to its species. The deficiencies affecting members of a species reflect the limitations of its matter. The most that can develop from blood and semen is humanity as we know it, living, rational, and mortal.[23]

Moderns might have spoken of energy and entropy rather than matter to clinch the case. But the brunt of the argument remains: Much human suffering reflects the structure of nature: natural evils, as Maimonides concludes, are inevitable. He is not above adding a bit of abuse aimed at those who complain that nature is not ordered to their wants and needs:

> All necessities have a definite measure, but there is no limit to superfluities. If you want silver dishes, gold would be still better. Others have crystal. Why not emerald or diamond if you could get it! Every foul minded boor is forever pining and miserable over failing to attain the luxuries others have. Often he exposes himself to

[19]   Plato, *Timaeus* 29e–30a.
[20]   Maimonides, *Guide* III 22.
[21]   See Job 42:7 with 13:8, 16, 21:34 and Saadiah ad loc.
[22]   The full passage in May's translation, p. 189, "Consider well the material of which a thing is made, and cherish no idle hope that you could put together from the catamenia and semen an animal that would be deathless, exempt from pain, endowed with never-ending motion, and as radiantly beautiful as the sun."
[23]   Maimonides, *Guide* III 12.

grave dangers like sea travel or royal service to acquire things utterly unnecessary. But when stricken by any misfortune in the course he's taken he bemoans God's judgment and decree, blames fate, and rails at the fickleness of fortune for denying him wealth enough to buy wine to keep him drunk forever, and girls decked out in gold and gems to keep him excited beyond his capacities – as though the whole object of existence were the pleasure of such scum! This delusion of the vulgar leads them even to believe God powerless if He gave being to a world naturally subject to what they imagine are such dreadful evils, since nature does not cater to the pleasure of every base profligate or gratify his vice to his wicked heart's content – seeking to fill an unbounded demand, as I've indicated.[24]

Maimonides' anger may seem excessive, but some of it may target himself. It was his brother who was lost on the Indian Ocean, traveling as a merchant of jewels, his death leaving Maimonides prostrate for a year, profoundly changing his fortunes and those of his family and setting Maimonides himself on a course of royal service as a court physician and a spokesman for his community in Egypt.[25] That course had gone well, but as a client of al-Qadi al-Fadil, the éminence grise behind Saladin's rise and the overthrow of the Fatimid dynasty, Maimonides knew well the risks of court life.

The heart of his argument is that matter sets limits. Our embodiment limits our potential. It is in that sense that matter is "the adversary." Yet matter for Maimonides is not a sump of evil any more than it is a positive principle of evil – as though that were possible. It is the condition of creation. That is why the neoplatonists had made it the first yield of emanation, stemming straight from the One. Nor are our bodies evil, Maimonides argues, as though God hated them.[26] They should be preserved and their needs met in the interest of good health, physical and emotional, since the body is the base from which we seek our highest goal, knowledge of God.[27]

Rather than argue geometrically, as Proclus does, to situate matter and thus privation in the pleroma,[28] Maimonides turns to scripture,

[24] Loc. cit.
[25] See Joel Kraemer, *Maimonides: The Life and World of One of Civilization's Greatest Minds* (New York: Doubleday, 2008), 244–58.
[26] Maimonides, "Eight Chapters," chapter 4.
[27] Maimonides, "Eight Chapters," chapter 5.
[28] See Proclus, *Elements of Theology*, Proposition 57, ed. and tr. E. R. Dodds (Oxford: Clarendon Press, 1964): "even privation of Form is from the Good, since it is the source of all things; but Intelligence, being Form, cannot give rise to privation" (pp. 55–56).

finding two allegories of matter in what superficially might read as advice about two kinds of woman. Proverbs 7 (6–23), Maimonides argues, likens matter to the seat of our appetites and passions, comparing it "to a whore who is married." For matter constantly changes "partners," the forms that give it definition and render it effectual. Our embodiment is a problem, not least for the wants and needs to which it gives rise. It is the source not only of the vulnerability Galen addressed but also of our moral weaknesses and the passions like anger and grief that may cloud our insight.[29] "For all that impedes one's ultimate fulfillment – all that is unruly or lacking in us – comes strictly from the physical side."[30]

But this negativity is hardly the whole story. For, as Maimonides remarks, Solomon, the traditional author of the book of Proverbs, "closes this book of his with praises of a woman who is no harlot but devotes herself wholeheartedly to her family's welfare and her husband's interests." That passage in Proverbs, again read as an allegory, is an acrostic poem praising the *good wife* (*eshet ḥayyil*, often mistranslated the "woman of valor"): *A good wife*, it begins, *is a precious find, rarer than rubies* (31:10). Strikingly, its first comparison is to matter in a precious form. The good wife, as Maimonides reads Proverbs 31, represents our embodiment's positive potential. "For if one is fortunate enough to have apt and good matter that does not dominate him or corrupt his constitution, that is a divine gift. Matter in general, if tractable, is easy to guide… But even if intractable it is not impossible for a disciplined person to control it."[31]

What we see here, under the flag of theodicy, is not an indictment of womankind but a portrayal of the human condition, taking finitude as a given and matter as its condition, embracing matter not for the sufferings to which it renders us vulnerable nor for the passions by which it allows us to misrule ourselves but for the opportunities it opens us as human agents and knowing subjects.

When moderns pronounce life meaningless, as Maimonides suggests in his little diatribe, they're referring to the fact that too often human hopes are dashed, worthwhile aims thwarted, worthy plans derailed. But the evils, we note, are parasitic on goods too easily taken for granted or

---

What Proclus "is anxious to vindicate," Dodds explains, "is the direct presence of the divine everywhere, even in Matter." This expedient, "bold as it is, was the only possible view," for "there are no Forms of negations" (p. 231) – a nice counterpart to Maimonides' making the adversary no son of God but an inevitable concomitant of *any* act of creation.

29   See Maimonides, "Eight Chapters," chapter 7.
30   *Guide*, Introduction, ed. S. Munk (Paris, 1856–66) 8ab.
31   Maimonides, *Guide* III 8.

brushed aside once they've served their dialectical role in the argument. It's easy to preen oneself on one's sensitivity to human suffering, as Voltaire did in his poem on the earthquake in Lisbon. The case is not weaker since the Holocaust or the killing fields or the Boxing Day tsunami.[32] But the idea of evil is parasitic on that of the good in the same way that evils themselves prey on the goods they disrupt or destroy. It is in this sense that the categorical dismissal of the goodness of being is incoherent: To find a tragic irony in the bestowal of a gift that cannot last is at once to affirm and deny the worth of the gift, to decry a loss in the same breath affirming and overlooking the preciousness of what was lost.

THE BIBLICAL GOOD AND PURSUIT OF PERFECTION

If we want to find the heart of biblical metaphysics (which is rarely conducted in abstract terms), we need to consider God's first appraisal of His work – light and life in particular: *God saw that it was good* (Genesis 1:4,

---

[32] Theodicy gets (or is given) a bad name by the pretense (or pretension) that its task is one of denial. But that is not its task. Explanation is not aided by elimination of what it seeks to understand. Still less is encounter. Marilyn McCord Adams offers what she calls "horrendous evils" as a sort of trump card in arguments about theodicy, "defining the category," as she puts it, by reference to "'evils the participation in (the doing or suffering of) which gives one reason prima facie to doubt whether one's life could (given their inclusion in it) be a great good to one on the whole." See her "Horrendous Evils and the Goodness of God." In *The Problem of Evil*. Ed. Adams and Robert M. Adams (Oxford: Oxford University Press, 1990), 211; her essay first appeared in the *Proceedings of the Aristotelian Society*, 1989. Her aim, like Saadiah's when he appeals to mass murder to warrant his arguments for an afterlife, is to set the beatific vision promised in the hereafter as the counterbalance to the evils she addresses. My friend Tim Jackson offers what might count as a paradigm case: "Pace Socrates, a good person can be harmed. It is empirically undeniable that some lives are undone either by the malevolence of others or by sheer bad luck. Some infants are so stunted by abuse early in life, for instance, as never to be able to love or even to achieve the threshold of personal agency. Others, like my imagined Job, are victimized as adults to the point of despair, 'spiritual toxicosis.' Even though ethical innocence cannot be taken from without, happiness and functionality can." Paper presented at the Shalem Institute for Advanced Study, Jerusalem, July, 2013. The case is not unique, of course. I would argue that not even the survivors of the Holocaust or the killing feels or the gulag (and no perpetrator either) escaped unscathed. The modern capability of setting science and technology, and not least the mass media and other means of manipulating public attitudes, in service to a mythology of violence does not create a new category but only lifts the skirts or ups the ante on schemes and programatics of mass murder, torture, and oppression that have threatened the human project from its inception. It remains dubious whether an afterworldly recompense can warrant our exposure to such evils. I would argue that life, if it is to be justified, must be justified in its own terms: What is pled to justify our exposure to these or any other evils must be values inherent in our condition, not predicated on escape from its parameters.

1:12, 1:18). This, before we humans existed to draw our own (typically interested) judgments. And, once the world was complete and housed the paradigmatic first human pair: *lo it was very good* (1:31). Biblically, being is good. Light and life are goods – life, intrinsically; light, intrinsically but also emblematically, symbolizing understanding. Light and life raise being to higher powers. God is the giver able and willing to impart such gifts:

> O Lord, thy love is in the heavens,
> Thy faithfulness reacheth the clouds –
> Thy justice, like God's mountains,
> Thy fairness, right as the vast deep.
> Man and beast dost Thou preserve, Lord.
> How precious, God, is Thy love!
> Adam's children shelter in the shadow of Thy wings,
> Sated by the bounty of Thy house,
> Their thirst slaked by Thy river of delights.
> For with Thee is the fountain of life.
> By Thy light do we see light.
>
> (Psalms 36:6–10)

Being, I repeat, is a good. Life is the stage on which being makes its higher claims. Evil is what violates such goods. That is why life must be respected – why fruit trees must not be destroyed, even in war (Deuteronomy 20:19), why the newly married are exempt from the call of battle (Deuteronomy 24:5), why man and beast enjoy the Sabbath (Exodus 23:12), and even the land must have its rest (Leviticus 25:1–7), why strangers and the helpless must be cared for (Deuteronomy 10:19, 24:19–21, Leviticus 19:9–10, 34, 23:22)[33] and lost goods returned (Deuteronomy 22:1–3), why hazards must be prevented (Deuteronomy 22:8),[34] why the ox and ass may not be yoked together (Deuteronomy 22;10), why creditors may not enter debtors' homes (Deuteronomy 24:10–11), why day workers must be paid by sundown (Deuteronomy 24:14–15), why a widow's cloak (Deuteronomy 24:17; cf. Exodus 22:25–26) and a millstone may not be taken in pledge (Deuteronomy 24:6), why lies and fraud are forbidden (Exodus 23:7, Leviticus 19:11),[35] why murder and kidnaping are capital crimes

---

33 The Talmud (Bava Metzia 59b) counts in the Pentateuch thirty-six special provisions protecting the rights and deserts of the stranger, a more frequently mentioned concern than love of God or observance of the Sabbath.

34 For Talmudic generalization of the principle found here and in Exodus 21:28–36, 22:4–5, see Bava Kamma 21b, 52ab, 55b, 99b, etc.

35 The biblical prooftext for the prohibition of lying is in the passage in Leviticus: *thou shalt not steal or commit fraud, or lie to one another* (Leviticus 19:11). The Exodus

(Genesis 9:6, Exodus 21:12–16, Leviticus 24:17), and why charity (Deuteronomy 15:7–8) and love of others (Leviticus 18:19) are divinely mandated obligations. The entire fabric of biblical law is spun out from recognition of the good of being. Not that these laws are deducible from that sheer unity, but the worth of being shines forth clearly through and throughout the Torah's legislative program.

It is the goodness of being that disarms any claim to the primacy of evil. The question for theodicy is not the dominance of evil, since the very claim to that effect is self-refuting, given the prior presumption of the value of being in any complaint against the evils that assail it. The only question is whether the light is worth the candle: Is the prospect and promise of suffering sufficiently counterbalanced by the gift? In the human case, that question receives a rabbinic answer in terms of the opportunity life gives us for the exercise of kindness (*ḥesed*), by which a human being can emulate God's holiness.

Thus, when the Torah urges all who hear its message, *walk in the Lord's ways, revere Him, keep His commandments, heed His voice, and worship Him alone* (Deuteronomy 13:5), the Talmudic Sage Hama ben Hanina (third century), asks how mere flesh and blood can possibly be commanded to *walk in God's ways*. He answers by citing acts of kindness as ways of emulating God's grace: As God clothed the naked, so should we clothe the naked; as He visited the sick, so should we visit the sick; as He comforted the bereaved, so should we comfort the bereaved; as He buried the dead, so should we bury the dead.[36] In the artful Talmudic manner, Hama found prooftexts to warrant each of these modeling acts: God clothed Eve and Adam when they were expelled from Eden (Genesis 3:21), visited Abraham as he recovered from his circumcision (Genesis 18:1), blessed Isaac after Abraham's death (Genesis 25:11), and buried Moses (Deuteronomy 34:6). *Imitatio Dei* begins in acts of kindness.[37]

---

passage, *keep far from falsehood* (23:7), seems in context to refer to false charges, especially in a capital case. Maimonides, in the book of his legal code devoted to the Ethical Laws, characteristically generalizes, treating truth telling as a moral ideal, not remote but manageable and calling for the exercise of good judgment and tact: "A disciple of the wise... in speaking will not deviate from the truth, neither adding nor omitting anything except to make peace." *Mishneh Torah*, Hilkhot De'ot 5.7. The model here, suggested by the tradition that Aaron was a supreme peacemaker, is Aaron's legendary making peace by telling each of two people who had quarreled that the other was regretful.

36   B. Sotah 14a; cf. Genesis Rabbah 8.13, Sifre to Deuteronomy 11:22, piska 49.
37   See Warren Zev Harvey, "Grace or Loving-Kindness." In *Twentieth Century Jewish Religious Thought*. Ed. A. A. Cohen and Paul Mendes-Flohr (Philadelphia: Jewish Publication Society, 2009), 299–302.

But to emulate God's acts of kindness in our human way does not suffice as our means of pursuing the holiness that can make life worthwhile. For the biblical commandments include spiritual *mitzvot* like the imperative to love God, ritual *mitzvot* that express and intensify that devotion, and hybrid *mitzvot* like Sabbath observance, in which moral concerns fuse with spiritual interests and constructively interact with them. Thus Deuteronomy (10:12–13) links the admonition to walk in God's ways with the command to revere and serve God with all our hearts. So Maimonides supplements the Talmudic answer by pointing to the opportunity life opens to the possibility of knowing God.[38] For this too, as both Plato and Aristotle argued,[39] is a way of emulating God, realizing our affinity to God on an intellectual or spiritual plane.[40]

There are problems, of course, in both the moral and the intellectual pursuit of God's perfection. On the moral side, God's infinite goodness seems to render emulation an impossible goal. Not less difficult is the challenge of seeking to know an infinitely transcendent being. But the moral problem is allayed in Maimonidean terms by the rabbinic recognition, rooted in the Torah, that benevolence and grace mark the pathway to God. God's is not the boundlessness of the indefinite. We emulate divine perfection not by pursuing God's infinitude – or even immortality, I might add! Our task is not to become gods but to become, as Maimonides echoes Plato's prescription, as like to God as humanly possible. We pursue perfection by seeking to perfect humanity in ourselves.

Intellectually, too, our task is scaled to our skills. For even Moses was denied a vision of God's face – by the very fact of his finitude. But he was shown God's "back parts," by which Maimonides understands all that follows, as it were, in God's wake: Nature gives us access to God's ways of governance (what Moses, at that moment, needed to know). God's work reveals His attributes. Following the lead of the Muslim theologian al-Ghazali (1058–1111), Maimonides argues that monotheism reaches its peak in those who see God in all things. But that idea, for

[38] Maimonides, *Guide* I 54, ad fin.; cf. III 33, 47.

[39] Aristotle, in Book X of the *Nicomachaean Ethics*, finds knowledge the freest, most self-sufficient, and thus the most divine mode of action, as well as that which is the most distinctively human, and God the highest object of knowledge; Plato sets the precedent in *Theaetetus* 176b. For, as the first *Alcibiades* argues, we attain likeness to God by knowing God.

[40] Maimonides, characteristically, merges Plato's prescription of *homoiosis theoi* with the Biblical command (Leviticus 19:2) to emulate God's holiness. See also Goodman, "Happiness: Jewish, Christian, and Muslim Perspectives." In *Cambridge History of Medieval Philosophy*. Ed. Robert Pasnau (Cambridge: Cambridge University Press, 2010). 457–71.

him, is more than a doorway to mystical monism. It is an invitation to close study of nature.

That proposal sets a particular challenge for contemporaries, who often imagine science as a rival to spiritual sensibilities and take scientific explanations as precluding their presumed alternatives in religious understanding. It might refresh the scientific enterprise and give heart to those who have imagined that religion must dwell in the cloud of unknowing, a realm of feeling devoid of insight, or faith stripped bare of logic, to realize that the constancy and intelligibility presumed in the work of scientists and confirmed by their discoveries are hallmarks of God's handiwork.

The trend in the natural sciences, with some notable exceptions, has been reductive, often in search of ever more elemental foundations within nature and ever more basic principles of explanation in the mind. But the love of analysis and abstraction, which are great strengths in science, should not blind us to the fact that synthesis is inseparable from analysis and that explanation often needs to study wholes and complexes, not just their parts, if it is to make sense of natural phenomena – or, better phrased, to find the sense in those phenomena that scientists presume is there to be discovered.

Reason and order, as Genesis proposes, are deep themes in nature's construction. But they are not the only themes of axiological moment. Beauty goes hand in hand with order in the cosmos, as Einstein and Newton before him clearly understood. And grace is the great theme most visible in nature, silent in the flow of light that leaves the psalmist awestruck (19:4), but ever more vocal and explicit as creatures advance, to the shores of life, as Lucretius put it, affirming and taking charge of their own purposes, as autonomy renders itself a theme, allowing the rise of persons.

To see God's hand in nature is a blessing made possible by the emergence of intelligence, a vision open to the scientist who manages to curb the hubris that discovery and invention may prompt or tempt – to the scientist, that is, who succeeds in conquering his inclination. We can see here the enduring intellectual relevance of the quest for moral perfection, which in Maimonides' view is the object of the Torah's moral precepts and admonitions, the goal intended by the practices it prescribes, and the stepping stone to spiritual/intellectual perfection. For our intellectual quest is ungrounded and unguided without the moral virtues of calm and discipline and the hybrid virtues of intellectual honesty and courage to keep us clear of self-deception and open to the beauties of nature, ready and able to dispel the fashionable illusion that science must be value free and indeed must acknowledge no values in nature. Alongside human kindness, with its service of God through love and care for all His creatures, natural science in its intellectual engagement with the world, and even mathematics in its purity, pursuing truths that owe no debt to circumstance, can aid us in opening pathways to knowing and emulating God. It can help us in that way to see the primacy of goodness and beauty that stand up against the ravages to which our very being exposes us.

FURTHER READING

Berkovits, Eliezer. *Faith after the Holocaust*. Brooklyn, NY: Ktav, 1973.

Fackenheim, Emil. *The Human Condition after Auschwitz*. Syracuse, NY: Syracuse University Press, 1971.

Katz, Steven T. *Post-Holocaust Dialogues*. New York: New York University Press, 1983.

Kraemer, David. *Responses to Suffering in Classical Rabbinic Literature*. Oxford: Oxford University Press, 1995.

Lamentations Rabbah, trans. A. Cohen, in *The Midrash*, volume 7. UK: Soncino, 1939.

Leaman, Oliver. *Evil and Suffering in Jewish Philosophy*. Cambridge: Cambridge University Press, 1995.

Rubenstein, Richard L. *After Auschwitz: History, Theology, and Contemporary Judaism*, second edition. Baltimore, MD: Johns Hopkins University Press, 1992.

Usque, Samuel. *Consolation for the Tribulations of Israel*, trans. Martin A. Cohen. Philadelphia, PA: Jewish Publication Society, 1977.

11 Christianity, Atonement and Evil

PAUL S. FIDDES

TWO PERSPECTIVES ON ATONEMENT

Christianity was born from Judaism, just as Jesus Christ himself was born into a Jewish family, and so into a profound Jewish heritage which becomes visible in the various accounts of his life and ministry in the Gospels. Christianity thus inherited an approach to the phenomenon of evil which was characteristic of the Judaism of its time: as a strongly monotheistic religion, the Jewish faith could tolerate no form of dualism. There was no question of eternal forces of good and evil locked in conflict; Yahweh, the God of Israel, was the sole creator and ultimate ruler of all things. Evil, in some way, had to occupy a place within the realm of absolute divine sovereignty. So one prophet of Ancient Israel declares on behalf of God, 'I make health and I make woe', and another ponders, 'does evil befall a city unless the Lord has done it?'[1] At the same time, the prophets made it clear that evil was the enemy of God and were eloquent about God's attack on injustice, greed and violence within the nation. How the thinkers whose reflections we have in the Hebrew Bible treated this paradox is not directly my concern here. Rather, I want to consider the way that the Christian faith, through its central doctrine of atonement, has addressed the same tension between ultimate divine responsibility for evil, sin and suffering and a conviction that God does everything possible to exterminate evil, remove sin and alleviate suffering.

This question may be handled from two perspectives. First and most obviously, the Christian faith from its beginning has been concerned to declare that, as a matter of fact, evil *has* been finally overcome through the life, death and resurrection of a particular person, Jesus Christ. The theme of Christ victorious over evil (*Christus Victor*) was one of the earliest images by which the early church attempted to interpret what seemed at first sight to be a shocking end to a promising ministry of Jesus.

[1]   Isaiah 45:7; Amos 3:6.

Since then, theology has occupied itself over the years with exploring *the way* that evil has been defeated, though no doctrine of atonement has ever been defined as normative by the church. Second, however, there has been an undercurrent of theodicy. Woven together with doctrinal explanation has been the concern to show – however implicitly – that the atonement in Christ at least begins to tackle the problem of God's justice and goodness in a world where evil seems endemic and suffering remorseless.

Up to the twentieth century, the first approach was the most prominent in Christian theology, while since then, the question of theodicy has become predominant, perhaps prompted by the tragedy of two world wars and the Jewish Holocaust. Few theologians have attempted a 'theodicy' in the literal sense of the word, as a rational 'justification of God' in the face of suffering. But there has been increasing interest in thinking in one focus about a loving God and the hard facts of evil and suffering, and atonement has been a key place for doing this. In German scholarship in particular, the end of the last century saw the emergence of a 'theology of the cross' newly understood as a 'theology *from* the cross', seeking to explore the nature of the triune God from the very event of the cross of Jesus.[2]

Inevitably, this has involved a reconsideration of the question of divine passibility. Jürgen Moltmann, for example, has urged that 'the material principle of the doctrine of the Trinity is the cross of Jesus', in that this is an event that happens between the persons of the Trinity, revealing both the unity and distinction between Father, Son and Holy Spirit; here the suffering and dying of the Son is different from 'the suffering of the Father in the death of the Son'.[3] The significance for theodicy is that 'the Father delivers up his Son on the cross in order to be the Father of all those who are delivered up' – that is, the Father of all those experiencing the forsakenness of suffering.

My own intention here is to show how these two strands of thought – overcoming evil and meeting the problem of human suffering – have always been interwoven to a certain extent and how they will need to intersect even more, both for a satisfactory doctrine of atonement and for a Christian account of the existence of evil.

---

[2] See, for example, Eberhard Jüngel, *God as the Mystery of the World*, trans. D. Guder (Edinburgh: T. & T. Clark, 1983), 12–14, 92–5, 362–73; Paul S. Fiddes, *The Creative Suffering of God* (Oxford: Oxford University Press, 1988), 12–15.

[3] Jürgen Moltmann, *The Crucified God*, trans. R. A. Wilson and J. Bowden (London: SCM Press, 1974), 243.

EVIL AND HUMAN SIN

Strictly speaking, the term 'atonement' refers to a particular model of salvation. In English translations of the Hebrew Bible, it is widely used for the Hebrew word (*kipper*) which expresses the reconciling effect of an act of sacrifice when relations are broken between God and God's people, Israel. Sacrifice was in fact one metaphor by which the early church tried to understand the transformative effect that the death of Jesus had made in their experience. However, 'atonement' is usually employed in wider senses of reconciliation in any situation in which relationships between human beings and God, and so also intra-human relations, have been disturbed and people are experiencing alienation and estrangement. In his early English version of the New Testament (1526), William Tyndale was the first to apply it to the Greek word meaning 'reconciliation'. The original context of the term implies that relationships can be repaired only through a specific act or event; in Ancient Israel, the critical act was the ritual of sacrifice, and for Christian believers, atonement happens universally because of a scandalous historical particularity – the death of Jesus Christ in a Roman execution in a remote Jewish province one Friday afternoon.

If we ask what has caused the estrangement that calls for reconciliation, we need to attend to a Christian understanding of both evil and 'sin'. The Hebrew and Christian scriptures concentrate on 'sin' as the reason for alienation, a term identifying human responsibility and guilt for human failures. 'Sin' has been understood in two major ways. First, it is an attitude and action towards God marked by rejection, rebellion and a breaking of agreement (or the 'covenant' bond). As Karl Barth puts it, sin is the human 'arrogant attempt to be [one's] own master, provider and comforter'.[4] Second, it is a failure to grasp the potential given by God to human beings, a lack of trust in gifts (or 'grace') that God is freely offering in the face of the human predicament to enable human beings to go beyond themselves. As Paul Tillich puts it, sin is 'unbelief', which 'turns away from the infinite ground of being'.[5] 'Sin' in these senses describes not only individual actions but corporate structures. Estrangement might be experienced because of personal failings or (as Karl Marx perceived it) because of the appropriation of resources by a privileged group in society.

---

[4]   Karl Barth, *Church Dogmatics*, trans. & ed. G. W. Bromiley and T. F. Torrance (Edinburgh: T. & T. Clark, 1936–77), III/3, 305.

[5]   Paul Tillich, *Systematic Theology*. Combined Volume (London: Nisbet & Co., 1968), Vol. 2, 54–5.

Yet behind this diagnosis of 'sin' in the Bible, there lurks a wider cosmic context, a situation of universal estrangement and opposition to the Good in which sin somehow participates but which is larger than human actions. There is something 'transcendent' about evil, 'going beyond' human control, eluding rationalization. The Hebrew Bible pictures hostile forces of chaos from which the creator God delivers the world in creation, setting it free from the oppression of disorder into a life of order and harmony (Gen. 1:1–3). This disorder is always likely to break out again, symbolized in the image of unruly waters which constantly threaten to overflow the earth and spread havoc and which can be personalized in a 'sea-monster' or great 'dragon'.[6] Another powerful image is that of the 'wilderness' which continually presses in on the cultivated land, undoing human work, and to which people might find themselves banished.

This universal hostility to God's purposes is implied, though rarely so named, to be evil. It was Christian theologians, and pre-eminently Augustine, who gave conceptual definition to this phenomenon. Evil, according to this account, is merely absence of good, *privatio boni*. Evil has no positive ontological standing, no reality of its own; it is strictly nothing or non-being, a turning away from being. It is always parasitic upon the good.[7] Drawing upon an already existing tradition of thought in Neo-Platonism,[8] Augustine was thus able to answer his critics who asked him whether God had created evil; this was a nonsense question, he replied, as evil was not a created thing at all, but simply a turning away from the created good through the free will of the creature.

Thus Augustine distinguishes between an 'absolute' or neutral non-being from which God creates and an aggressive non-being which is hostile to the Good (not unlike the Platonic distinction between *ouk on* and *me on*) and which emerges when created beings release their grasp on the Good and so slip back towards the nothingness from which they came.[9] While the primordial nothingness is not evil (which would be an eternal principle), the slipping back towards it is. This account depends upon the mystery of free will, and in Christian tradition, rational beings, whether conceived as fallen angels or fallen humans, have thereby been made responsible for evil in general. Later I want to suggest that fallenness might be extended more thoroughly into the whole of created reality.

---

6 See Job 26:12–13, 38:8–11; Pss. 18:16, 74:12–7, 89:9–10; Isa. 51:9–11.
7 Augustine, The City of God, 11.9; Enchiridion, 4.13.
8 See Plotinus, *Enneads*, 1.8.3–5.
9 Augustine, *On Free Will*, 3.1, 2, 18.

The human situation of sin and the wider context of evil overlap and interact. In the Hebrew Bible, there is a sense that if human beings had been obedient to God, chaos might have been overcome, the wilderness cultivated and the sea tamed, or at least coped with better. Another way of conceiving this overlap is visible in the New Testament, in the concept of 'principalities and powers'.[10] Under this title, the Apostle Paul and others include spiritual powers in the cosmos, together with the human powers that rule and organize the state, and which they conceive as being in some way the visible face of the invisible cosmic forces. All these powers have a legitimate place in the divine economy but have usurped their proper authority; they have become rebellious powers, perverted and distorted as they are treated as idols, becoming objects of 'worship' and demanding absolute loyalty.

Modern theologians such as Tillich and Walter Wink have re-used this Pauline concept, at least partly de-mythologizing it.[11] They urge that we can recognize the earthly face of the powers in all systems and institutions that lay a claim to ultimate authority and demand complete allegiance, whether these are religious, political or economic. The best structures can become 'demonic', a diagnosis that is also prominent in liberation theology. Thus, structural and social sin merges into a sense of evil that exceeds either individual or society. We shall return to this image of 'the powers' in exploring the *Christus Victor* model of atonement, since as early as the New Testament, it is affirmed that Christ has broken the hold of the 'principalities and powers' over human beings through the cross (Col. 2:13–15).

Another way of conceiving of the overlap between sin and evil is to be found in modern times in Karl Barth's re-use of Augustine's thinking in his own account of 'nothingness' or *das Nichtige*. Barth does not want to say that *das Nichtige* exists by the will of God, since this would seem to question God's goodness. On the other hand, he does not want to attribute its emergence entirely to the exercise of creaturely freedom, as this would seem to question the sovereignty of God. His solution is to declare that *das Nichtige* exists as that which God does not will; God's very rejection of it gives it reality, as 'his own enemy'. Destructive, hostile nothingness came to be as an 'impossible possibility', as that which God rejected when God elected a good creation. According to Barth, by saying 'no' to it, God gave it objective reality as an 'alien work'

---

[10] I Cor. 2:6–8; Eph. 6:12; Col. 2:14–15; cf. 2 Thess. 2:6–7.
[11] Tillich, *Systematic Theology*, vol. 1, 55, 149–50; vol. 2, 30, 197–8; vol. 3, 108–13; Walter Wink, *Naming the Powers* (Philadelphia: Fortress Press, 1984), 104–31.

(*opus alienum*).[12] Later I will comment on the adequacy of this scheme as a theodicy, but for the moment, I simply want to observe that for Barth, this 'opposition and resistance to God's world-dominion' is manifested in human sin: 'the concrete form in which nothingness is active and revealed is the sin of man as his personal act and guilt'.[13] For Barth, this actualizing of nothingness in sin has implications for a doctrine of atonement, which expiates sin by confronting nothingness.

In Christian tradition, suffering is the consequence of both evil and sin, and atonement must deal with both realities. There is then a three-sided relation in atonement between evil, sin and theodicy.

SIN AND THE PROBLEM OF EVIL AS ISSUES IN ATONEMENT

Attending to the way that atonement overcomes evil and sin, we notice that among the variety of images by which theologians have tried to understand atonement, some metaphors focus on sin and others on evil originating outside human life. 'Sin', I have suggested, has been envisaged either as an offence or failure of human potential. If sin is conceived in the first manner as rebellion against God or the breaking of the covenant relation with God, images become prominent that express a legal transaction and a payment of debt. With Anselm, humankind is considered to have sinned against God by not giving the honor which is due to a supreme lord within a law of vassal-allegiance.[14] If sufficient honor cannot be given, punishment must follow. Through his obedient death, Christ alone, as God as well as man, can give infinite honor to God; this act wipes out the human debt of honor and so cancels punishment. While this is not strictly a concept of propitiating a wrathful God, such an idea does appear in Calvin. For him, because human beings have broken the divine law, there is a debt to the law which has to be paid through punishment, without alternative. Christ pays the debt by making himself a substitute victim.[15] Human sin as offence against God is also to the fore in the model of sacrifice, where sins of individuals lay a stain upon the whole community, which can only be purified by a sacrificial offering, supremely that of Christ himself.

---

[12] Barth, *Church Dogmatics*, III/3, 289–302, 349–56.
[13] Barth, *Church Dogmatics*, III/3, 305.
[14] Anselm, *Cur Deus Homo* I. 10–14. In *Anselm of Canterbury. The Major Works*. Trans. and ed. Brian Davies and G. R. Evans (Oxford: Oxford University Press, 1998), 281–7.
[15] Calvin, *Institutio* II. 16.2–5. In *Calvin: Institutes of the Christian Religion*, 2 Volumes. Trans. Ford Lewis Battles, ed. John T. McNeill (London: SCM Press, 1961), vol. 1, 504–11.

This is not the place to make a critical examination of these theories which have developed in Christian tradition. Suffice it to say that while the *language* of sacrifice and the law-court derives from attempts in the New Testament to grasp the atoning significance of the death of Christ,[16] there these images are not associated with concepts of propiti- ation and satisfaction of an angry God. Rather, sacrifice is understood as 'expiation', or a wiping out of sin performed by God's own self through the death of Christ. In the law-court imagery used, while Christ is por- trayed as identifying himself with the human predicament of being under the rightful judgement of God, he shares in our death not to pay a debt but so that we can share in his resurrection. Thus we are put into a 'right relation' with God and the human community ('justified'). It is a changing cultural environment, largely in the West, that has made the language of sacrifice and law more transactional.[17]

If sin is conceived in a second way as failure to reach the poten- tial offered by God, then other models of atonement become prominent. Early eastern Christian thought developed the conviction that through the death of Christ, the likeness of God in human beings could be restored and human life be 'divinized' (*theosis*).[18] Peter Abelard in the West later developed the view that the love of God revealed in the cross had power to create love that was lacking in the human heart and so achieve human transformation (as we shall see later). Modern ideas of atonement that replace penalty inflicted on Christ with penitence awo- ken in people who behold the cross belong to the same kind of thinking[19] and fit into perceptions about the need for the healing of fragmented per- sonalities and broken social relationships.

When the focus of atonement is on dealing with evil rather than sin, estrangement and alienation are envisaged as originating outside the human self, and they must be dealt with beyond the self. Hostile powers in the cosmos or in an invisible world need to be defeated, and atone- ment means that Christ achieves this in the victory of the cross. The model of sacrifice can also take on a more cosmic dimension, as a sac- rificial offering is understood as renewing the life not only of a human

---

[16]   For sacrifice, see, e.g., Rom. 3:25, 1 Jn. 4:10, Heb. 2:17. For forensic imagery, see, e.g., Rom. 8:3–4, 2 Cor. 5:21, 1 Pet. 2:22–4.

[17]   See Paul S. Fiddes, *Past Event and Present Salvation. The Christian Idea of Atonement* (London: Darton, Longman and Todd, 1989), 68–75, 96–104.

[18]   E.g., Athanasius, *De Incarnatione*, 20.

[19]   See Walter Moberly, *Atonement and Personality* (London: John Murray, 1924), 39–46, 111–33; P. T. Forsyth, *The Work of Christ* (London: Independent Press, 1938), 150–64.

community but of the whole universe.[20] The whole of creation is purified, chaos is brought to order and the cycle of life can begin again.

Interwoven with the overcoming of sin and evil in the atonement, I have suggested, is the issue of theodicy. How can we reconcile belief in a good and loving God with the surplus of evil and suffering in the world? The 'free-will defence' is often advanced, arguing that for human beings to be truly free persons rather than automata or puppets, they must have the possibility of choosing evil as well as good. They must, it is said, have the possibility of refusing God's purposes for a flourishing life.[21] Leaving on one side for the moment whether this argument covers what is often called 'natural evil' outside human life, the scenario still leaves God responsible for creating a situation in which evil is not only possible but likely. While human beings are responsible for their life within the created world, God is ultimately responsible for the existence of that creaturely world with all that it implies.

Throughout his classic book *Evil and the God of Love*, John Hick argues that for this kind of ultimate responsibility to be consistent with a God of love, it must be the case that the good attained through suffering – that is, the creation of 'souls' or persons in relation with God and others – could not be reached by any other means than by the risks of evil and suffering. Given that the process of making personalities is often frustrated in this life, he also urges that theodicy requires that evil play a part in a divine aim that is working towards a fulfilment beyond human time, in a future 'Kingdom of God' where all evil will be overcome.[22] But even if this criterion can be shown to be satisfied, I suggest that it still does not answer the question posed by Dostoevsky's character Ivan Karamazov, 'Is the whole universe worth the tears of one tortured child?'[23] Even if persons can be created only through suffering, and all persons will be fully formed in eternity, the question remains: is it *worth* it? There can thus never be a complete theodicy, since this question calls for evaluation and so for a leap of faith. Yet careful thinking can build a platform from which the leap can reasonably be made, and

[20]   See F. W. Dillistone, *The Christian Understanding of Atonement* (London: James Nisbet, 1968), 29–59.
[21]   John Hick, *Evil and the God of Love*. New Edition (Basingstoke: Palgrave Macmillan, 2010), 265–6; Richard Swinburne, *Providence and the Problem of Evil* (Oxford: Oxford University Press, 1998), 126–31.
[22]   John Hick, *Evil and the God of Love*, 260–1, 277–83, 374–7.
[23]   F. Dostoyevsky, *The Brothers Karamazov*, transl. D. Magarshack (Harmondsworth: Penguin Books, 1982), 287.

this requires, I suggest, another criterion. With many other theologians today, I judge that a God of love must participate in the risk that created beings endure. Only if God suffers in God's own self is it credible to trace suffering to the free will of the creation. A loving God who commits created beings to the hazards and contingencies of freedom will accompany them on the way with the deepest solidarity and empathy, and this must mean a co-suffering with them.[24] So we return to issues of atonement, which are usually missing in discussions of evil in the work of philosophers of religion.

Accounts of atonement today increasingly offer a 'practical theodicy'. This is neither proof nor vindication of God in the face of evil and suffering but a means of coping with suffering through affirming that God suffers in solidarity with a suffering creation, offering fellowship, consolation and the assurance that sufferers are not abandoned. As Jürgen Moltmann insists, 'Only if all disaster, forsakenness by God, absolute death, the infinite curse of damnation and sinking into nothingness is in God himself, is community with this God eternal salvation ...'[25] Human beings find wholeness when they 'recognize rejection, curse and final nothingness' in the history of God. Through the cross of Jesus, God is the God of all the forsaken and shares in their protest against suffering as an alien presence in creation.[26]

There is a tendency to classify this kind of thinking as a 'subjective' view of atonement, over against supposedly 'objective' views such as a penal transaction. In fact, however, all theories of atonement blend objective and subjective elements; they differ in the relative stress laid on each. The 'objective' aspects of atonement are that salvation depends on a past event, that it involves an act of God and that it implies some kind of change in God. The 'subjective' aspects are that salvation happens in the present, that it includes a human response and that it involves a change of human attitudes. A rounded theory of atonement includes all these elements.[27]

Some theories envisage objective 'change' in God in the sense of God's being satisfied or propitiated or moving from an attitude of wrath to acceptance. But change may be of a different kind: it might mean a

[24] See Fiddes, *Participating in God*, 164–70; Christopher Southgate, *The Groaning of Creation. God, Evolution and the Problem of Evil* (Louisville, KY: Westminster John Knox Press, 2008), 50–4; Ruth Page, *God and the Web of Creation* (London: SCM Press, 2006), 40–3.

[25] Moltmann, *The Crucified God*, 246.

[26] Moltmann, *The Crucified God*, 252–3; Fiddes, *Creative Suffering of God*, 221–9.

[27] See Fiddes, *Past Event and Present Salvation*, 26–34.

movement in divine experience such as the enduring of suffering or the gaining of new joy. The fact that suffering must involve a change of state is, of course, why much traditional theology has denied passibility in God and attempted to define divine compassion without pain. Both suffering and mutability are compatible, I suggest, with the sovereignty of God if God chooses freely to be so limited for the sake of created beings.

The 'subjective' dimension in which salvation is a present event is essential if we understand atonement as 'reconciliation', or the re-making of broken relations. This must involve the engagement of both God and human beings here and now. Older theories of atonement (with the exception of Abelard) tended to begin at the objective end and add on a subjective application. Some of these views, such as the penal substitution model developed by Calvin, seem to overbalance in the direction of the objective. Alienated and estranged persons cannot be won back into fellowship with God by an event which is purely in the past and outside their experience. Salvation cannot be a transaction which is simply 'applied' to lives in the present; it must happen to them and in them.[28] On the other hand, modern theories of atonement tend to begin at the subjective end with human response to God in the present and then affirm an objective focus for this response, making it possible. In some way, the past event is envisaged as having a decisive, creative effect on reconciliation here and now.

OVERCOMING EVIL: AN OBJECTIVE EMPHASIS

One model of atonement, that of *Christus Victor*, makes its main image a victory over evil, and so by exploring it, we can test out the key issues of atonement I outlined earlier. First, the model might take the form of an objective event with a subjective appendix.

In the Fathers of the Early Church, the victory of Christ was objectively decisive because it was the defeat of the Devil.[29] The figure of the 'Satan', beginning his career in Hebrew religion as God's chief prosecutor, remorselessly exposing human sin,[30] had evolved over the years into being the symbol and quintessence of evil. Evil, difficult to grasp in the abstract, was made concrete in an individual.[31] Atonement was thus

---

[28]   See Vincent Brümmer, *Atonement, Christology and the Trinity* (Aldershot: Ashgate, 2005), 70–1.
[29]   See, e.g., Irenaeus, *Against Heresies*, 5.1.1; Gregory of Nyssa, *Great Catechism*, 24.
[30]   See Job 1:9–12, Zech. 3:1–12.
[31]   See Walter Wink, *Unmasking the Powers. The Invisible Forces that Determine Human Existence* (Philadelphia: Fortress Press, 1986), 9–30.

understood as a final battle between two cosmic champions. Evil was overcome in the struggle between the Christ and the Satan.

Theological problems immediately arise with this account. If the Satan symbolizes *absolute* evil, he cannot be a person who could be defeated in a battle. Persons always exist in relationships and make others more personal (and pre-eminently this is true of a personal God), whereas evil de-personalizes. There is certainly a mystery to evil, transcending human persons, but by its very nature as a 'nothingness' which is hostile to personhood, it cannot be personalized. Further, the model tips towards the over-objective. The victory is a drama happening 'above our heads',[32] not involving actual human sinfulness 'on the ground' and failing to deal with the brokenness of human lives.

The model in its 'classical' form also fails as an adequate theodicy. The presence of evil in the world requires God to do everything possible to overcome it, and the model proposes that God has indeed defeated the prime mover of evil. But this implies a weakening of the objective power of evil in the world, and in the face of such events in recent history as the Armenian genocide, the Jewish Holocaust and recent massacres in Iraq and Syria, together with the potential for nuclear and ecological catastrophe, there is little evidence of this. Resorting to an image from human conflict, that a key battle may have been won while the war itself still continues,[33] reduces to a human scale what is meant to be a cosmic event.

Within an account of a victory over 'the Satan', attempts have been made to get the issue of human sin (and so a properly subjective element) back on the scene. Following Luther, Gustav Aulen in his study of *Christus Victor* understands the victory over Satan as God's removal of God's own wrath against sin.[34] This approach effectively leans upon the ambiguity of the figure of the Satan, recalling his earlier legitimate role in Hebrew religion as advocate of God's law and executant of his wrathful judgement, as well as his later manifestation as the prince of darkness. Triumph over the devil is thus the quenching of divine wrath. According to Aulen, the 'classic' view resolves a perceived conflict between love and anger in God in a 'dramatic' rather than a theoretical or doctrinal way.[35] God's love overcomes his wrath in a drama which, urges Aulen, escapes final conceptualization.

---

[32]   So Tillich, *Systematic Theology*, vol. 2, 198.
[33]   Gustav Aulen, *The Faith of the Christian Church* (London: SCM Press, 1961), 226.
[34]   Gustav Aulen, *Christus Victor*, trans. A. G. Herbert (London: SPCK, 1937, repr. 1970), 55–60, 111–16.
[35]   Aulen, *Christus Victor*, 119–22, 154–8.

But there are no fewer theological problems with this version of *Christus Victor* than with the patristic accounts. A drama of conflict is no more metaphorical or less theoretical than other images for the atonement[36] and cannot escape critique on the grounds of genre. There is no *necessary* conflict between love and wrath in God to be overcome. In love, God passionately desires to bring all humankind into fellowship with God's self. We may then understand the wrathful justice of God as God's confirming the self-inflicted consequences of sin, though – as the Old Testament prophets make clear – God does so in a kind of divine agony.[37] When sin is wiped out, then judgement is lifted and the accusing voice of law is silenced. The issue is how to make cogent a removal of sin and evil (to which we will return), and once again Aulen's account presents this as a drama happening outside the existential realities of human life. Neither is Aulen's model a satisfactory theodicy. Evil continues unabated, and the need to quench God's righteous anger – which Aulen identifies as 'reconciling' God – implies a theodicy in which God is excused from any final responsibility for evil.

A further modern attempt to employ the *Christus Victor* model is presented by Karl Barth. For Barth, in the cross, Christ comes into conflict neither with a personalized Satan nor with divine wrath but with the 'nothingness' that human beings have brought upon themselves through their sin. Here Barth relies on the overlap between evil and sin in his concept of *Das Nichtige*. He affirms, with Paul and Luther, that Christ in becoming a human son comes under the shadow of divine judgement against human sin. This is a passion story in which 'the Judge himself was the judged'. He treads the dark path to its end to meet the death that sinners have inflicted upon themselves and to which God consents, in so far as 'my turning from God is followed by God's annihilating turning from me'. The sting of this death is the 'nothingness' whose power and aggressive vitality sinners themselves have fostered and 'towards which they relentlessly hasten'.[38] The nothingness that lurks in death takes its rightful prey by engulfing the sinner, and sin together with him. Thus God employs the enemy of nothingness or 'eternal death' in God's own service, wiping out the sin which is the obstacle between God and humankind: 'this worst becomes an instrument in the hand of the merciful and omnipotent God for the creation of the best'.[39]

---

[36] See Colin E. Gunton, *The Actuality of Atonement* (Edinburgh: T. & T. Clark, 1988), 61–4.

[37] For example, Hos. 11:8–9; Jer. 31:20.

[38] Barth, *Church Dogmatics* IV/1, 253.

[39] Barth, *Church Dogmatics* IV/1, 254.

There is much to be appreciated in this account. Barth rejects any idea that Christ atones for our sin by satisfying the wrath of God. Rather, the point of identifying himself with humankind in a representative way as 'the one great sinner' is for Christ to 'cause sin to be taken and killed on the cross in his own person'. But we are bound to ask how *our* actual sin can be 'killed' in another person (Christ). The account tips too much towards the objective end of the spectrum. Then, from the point of view of theodicy, despite this theological objectivity, the threat of nothingness still appears to be present in the world. Barth's argument that, following the cross, God allows nothingness to 'appear' real to our blinded eyes as a reminder of what evil used to be like is too close to the kind of unsatisfactory theodicy Leibnitz produced: that if we could but *see* it, this is the best of all possible worlds.[40]

While an objective stress in the *Christus Victor* model thus rightly affirms the decisiveness of the past event of the cross, this cannot be convincingly explained as the 'slaying' of sin or the dealing of a fatal blow to Satan or the quenching of divine wrath. In these accounts, our own engagement in the crucial event can only be by way of passive acceptance, in a kind of subjective appendix.

THE TRANSFORMING VICTORY OVER SIN: A SUBJECTIVE STRESS

If we start at the subjective end of the spectrum, within present human existence, the *Christus Victor* model takes on a different form. God, we may say, is always offering created beings the possibility of victory over the hostile forces that spoil life, while the problem is gaining cooperation with the divine purpose.[41] Christ's victory over the powers is thus seen as an event in the past that creates and enables a victory in lived experience here and now. Atonement is objective in that the self-offering of Christ on the cross moves our will to respond in harmony with God's and empowers us to enter upon God's victory over evil in the present.

This dynamic fits in with the emphasis on sin as 'idolatry' in modern theological thinking, exemplified by Paul Tillich and John Macquarrie and anticipated by Reinhold Niebuhr.[42] In an analysis indebted to existentialist

---

40   Barth, *Church Dogmatics* III/3, 367; G. W. Leibniz, *Theodicy. Essays on the Goodness of God, the Freedom of Man and the Origin of Evil*, trans. E. M. Huggard (Chicago: Open Court, 1990), 99, 130–2, 281–3.

41   Brümmer, *Atonement, Christology and the Trinity*, 53–60, emphasizes the difficulty of eliciting a change of heart.

42   Tillich, Systematic Theology, vol. 1, 239–40; vol. 2, 378–9; John Macquarrie, *The Principles of Christian Theology*. Revised Edition (London: SCM, 1977), 259–61, 318–21;

thinking, and behind this to Kierkegaard, they all diagnose human beings as caught in a tension between their freedom and the limitations that condition them. The result is anxiety, a sense of being threatened by 'non-being' (akin to Barth's 'nothingness'), which we try to alleviate in an inauthentic way. From a Christian perspective, these thinkers urge, anxiety can be met by trust in 'grace' – a conviction that God will give the courage to live authentically and affirm the possibilities of life within the tensions of existence that can never be resolved before death. But the tragedy is that we try to overcome anxiety by 'idolatry', or making something limited and finite (whether possessions, nations or economic theories) into our 'ultimate concern' as a security within the tensions we feel so acutely.

Good things of the world that ought to be our tools thus become our masters; since we must have them, they control us, and the idol becomes 'demonic'. Ideologies, structures and systems become demonic like this and appear as the hostile 'principalities and powers' we have already considered. The Gospel story of Jesus shows us someone who 'breaks all the idols', refusing to give ultimate value to any religious or political system but living in openness of trust to God and to God's future. Finally, in his death, we see that Jesus offers himself, refusing to make an idol even of himself. This version of *Christus Victor* affirms that Jesus's actions enable us to break our own idols and confront the 'demonic', both personally and in life together in society. Personal sin and structural evil are thus overcome in an ongoing process of resistance and transformation. 'Sin' is not an object that can be removed or killed; as we have seen, it is an attitude of rebellion and lack of trust which is overcome by transforming the person that *has* this attitude.

The key question then is how a particular event in the past (the cross of Jesus) has this effect of enabling cooperation with God's saving actions in the present. Imitation of Christ, while a powerful dynamic for ongoing Christian life, seems insufficient to overcome the momentum of sin in the first place and achieve a complete reorientation of existence. John Macquarrie suggests two ways in which the victory of Christ over the idols creates victory in human life in the present. First, he appeals to the power of revelation. Once a new possibility in existence has been disclosed, once some new path has been pioneered in human endeavor, other people can make it their own; the event is 'eschatological' in the sense of being open to being repeated in the future. 'Empowered by ...

Reinhold Niebuhr, *The Nature and Destiny of Man*, 2 Volumes (London: Nisbet, 1941), vol. 1, 175–8, 222–5.

the Holy Spirit operating through the revelatory event of the cross, the disciple ... rejects the temptations of idolatry'.[43]

We may add here that an event in which some really new possibility is disclosed is objective in the sense that it actually *provokes* repetition of itself; it is not only capable of repetition but *elicits* re-enactment. This must be even more true of the event in human history in which God is present to a unique depth of involvement, identified totally with Jesus Christ. The writer of the Letter to the Colossians expresses this power of revelation: in the cross, Christ has made a public exhibition of 'the powers', exposing them for the tyrants and usurpers they are. The unveiling of the divine glory in the weakness of death has de-glorified the powers, showing them up as mere weak and beggarly elements, so that human beings need no longer tremble before them.[44]

Second, Macquarrie finds a creative power in the community of the crucified. The absolute self-giving of Christ has created a community in which his victory goes on being repeated. A new situation has been created by the coming of the church into existence, which 'began with Christ's victory over the powers of sin and evil [and] is the ever-expanding centre in which Christ's reconciling work continues'.[45] At the center of this community are the sacraments, providing focal moments in which its members can share the movement of Christ himself from death to life, overcoming the effects of evil.

To these ways in which we can conceive of the cross of Jesus as having a unique degree of power to evoke and create a human response to the transforming love of God, we can add two more. First, God is actually present to unveil God's own self, both in the revelatory event of the past and in the experience of salvation in the present. The past event is creative because the triune God is *there* in it to enable our response. God is revealed in the cross as living in relationships of suffering love, like a father losing a beloved son and a son being separated from a father in a spirit of self-surrender and hope. This same God in whose experience is the cross is present to human persons now, so that God draws them into the divine fellowship and enables new victories over evil to be won. Nothing less than God is finally the link between past event and salvation in the present.

Second, we should notice the power of story. Here we enter most clearly the area of theodicy. The story of the suffering of God in the costly

---

Macquarrie, *Principles*, 324–5.
44   Col. 2:15, cf. Gal. 4:9.
45   Macquarrie, *Principles*, 326.

victory of Christ can enable us to find some meaning in the story of our own lives and our own suffering.[46] Much of human suffering appears meaningless. It is not heroic, not part of a great crusade, not the death of a martyr giving himself or herself for a glorious cause. It usually does not mean that evil is being overcome. Suffering just befalls us, and because we cannot see the sense of it, we are driven into silence. We are numbed by suffering, paralyzed in our will and our emotions. We may be helped to cope with suffering and find some hope there for coping with evil if we place alongside our story a greater story, a story of suffering which does have that meaning. God's story of suffering has an aim in view, to bring resurrection life out of the worst kind of death. But if we follow this line of thought, we must be very careful to stress that we are talking about each person *finding* a meaning for himself or herself, not having some meaning thrust upon them. Suffering can *acquire* a meaning. We can put the story of God's suffering alongside our apparently senseless suffering and see what meaning emerges.

The idea that the victory of Christ enables an overcoming of evil in the present is a shift of emphasis from objective to subjective, though with an objective focus. This is essentially the shift being made in the twelfth century by Peter Abelard in his theology of atoning love. In an often-quoted passage from his commentary on the Epistle to the Romans, he writes, '[God's] Son has taken upon himself our nature and persevered therein in teaching us by word and example even unto death – he has more fully bound us to himself by love, with the result that our hearts should be enkindled by such a gift of divine grace'.[47] According to Abelard, the love of God manifested in the life and death of Christ 'enkindles' or 'ignites' love in our hearts: elsewhere, he uses the expressions that the cross 'incites' love and 'inclines' us to love.

Abelard intends to say that the love of God revealed in the cross has the power to *move* human hearts in a way which is more than an emotional prompting of observers to their own efforts of love. Objectively, the divine love has power to create or *generate* love within human beings. He writes that 'Christ died for the wicked so that love might be *poured out* in our hearts'.[48] Since it is humankind that needs to be reconciled

---

[46]   J. Denny Weaver, *Non-Violent Atonement* (Grand Rapids, MI: Eerdmans, 2001) reflects on 'Narrative Christus Victor' throughout his argument.

[47]   Peter Abelard, *Commentary on the Epistle to the Romans*, 2.3.26. In *A Scholastic Miscellany: Anselm to Ockham*. Trans. and ed. E. R. Fairweather (London: SCM Press, 1956), 283.

[48]   Abelard, *Romans* 2.5.7–8, in *Corpus Christianum Continuatio Mediaevalis* 11 (1961), 155.

to God rather than God to the world, the need is for human beings to be changed: 'everyone is *made* more righteous, that is more loving towards God, after the passion of Christ'.⁴⁹ Abelard perceives that this infusion of love must have an impact on the situation of evil in the world. Having dismissed the idea that a cosmic battle releases us from 'rights' that the Satan holds over us, he asserts that it is love that 'frees us from slavery' and 'acquires liberty' for us.⁵⁰ Significantly, Abelard gives special attention to the power of the story, urging his former lover Heloise to enter the story of the passion of Christ in her imagination.⁵¹

THE TRANSFORMING VICTORY OVER EVIL

Abelard's account, however, leaves him with a problem that he never properly solves: why must this transforming love be shown in the death of Christ and not simply in his life? Why a death at all? An answer which is coherent with my account so far is this: the atoning love that achieves reconciliation and overcomes evil must involve the death of Christ because such a love has to undergo the most bitter depths of human experience. Only this extreme of empathetic participation in the human predicament, to the point of alienating death, will have the power to move a fixed attitude of hostility to God and create response. This is also a matter of theodicy. On the one hand, the presence of evil and suffering requires that a God of love will do everything possible to overcome evil, at whatever cost. On the other hand, this immersion of God into suffering offers a 'practical theodicy' of the sympathetic presence of God in our suffering.

Abelard cannot give this answer, as he is working with the classical presupposition of the impassibility of God. Exploiting, as do other theologians, the two-nature Christology of Chalcedon, Abelard believes that God suffers only in the human nature of Jesus and not in divinity. Thus he restricts the freedom of God to love. By contrast, Karl Barth affirms that

> According to the biblical testimony, God has the prerogative to be free without being limited by His freedom from external conditioning, free also with regard to His freedom.... God must not only be unconditioned but, in the absoluteness in which He sets up this fellowship [with humankind], *He can and will also be conditioned.*⁵²

⁴⁹   Abelard, *Romans* 2.3.26, in *Scholastic Miscellany*, 284.
⁵⁰   Ibid.
⁵¹   Abelard, *The Letters of Abelard and Héloïse*, trans. Betty Radice (Harmondsworth: Penguin, 1974), 151 (Letter 4).
⁵²   Barth, *Church Dogmatics* II/1, 303. My italics.

Such an understanding of the free sovereignty of God makes it quite coherent to say that God is affected, conditioned and changed through suffering with the world, and also that this experience contributes to the glory and completeness of God's own being.[53] As Keith Ward urges, while affirming the 'aseity' (self-existence) of God, we should not confuse self-existence with self-sufficiency.[54]

But can this theory of transforming love work for the wider manifestations of evil beyond its appearance in human life? The question may seem redundant if we think that talk of 'natural evil' is simply a reference to the harsh environment which is a necessary 'educational' situation for human beings to mature and develop moral responsibility. If there were no storms at sea, there would be no possibility of developing skills of navigation; if there were no earthquakes, viruses and genetic malfunctions, we could not develop altruism and skills of prevention of damage.[55] Some have even suggested that 'natural evil' is a category error, that it would be better to speak of 'chance' and 'randomness' in the physical world, and that the term 'evil' can only meaningfully refer to human, moral evil. I take the theological view that God has indeed created a universe in which randomness plays a significant part alongside order and that a certain amount of 'educational' suffering is necessary for human development and evolution generally. But suffering on the wider scale is excessive, beyond any educational need, and other sentient beings than humans are badly harmed by it. It does seem appropriate to address the problem of 'natural evil'.

We can at least work towards a theodicy, I suggest, if we extend the 'free-will defence' of God's goodness into the whole range of nature. I mean holding a vision of a universe in which there is a capacity for response or resistance to the creative Spirit of God at every level of existence, analogous to a free human response. This is not to suggest that there is a universal mentality in the universe but that there is some 'family likeness' to human consciousness for which as yet we have no adequate language except poetry, such as the biblical imagery of a 'covenant' between God and every living thing and the 'groaning' of the universe in frustration.[56]

Attempts have nevertheless been made at a quasi-scientific description of this reality. One notable example is process philosophy, according

---

[53] For detail, see Fiddes, *Creative Suffering of God*, chs. 3–4.
[54] Keith Ward, *Rational Theology and the Creativity of God* (Oxford: Blackwell, 1982), 138.
[55] See Hick, *Evil and the God of Love*, 324–6, 369; Richard Swinburne, *Providence*, 161–8.
[56] Gen. 9:16–17; Hos. 2:18; Rom. 8:19–22.

to which the basic building blocks of the physical world are microscopic entities which have objective and subjective poles, analogous to the body and mind with which we are familiar. In the process vision, these dipolar entities occupy a vast network of mutual influences in which they relate and grasp ('prehend') each other, forming the large-scale objects we perceive. God is immersed into this process as 'the great companion – the fellow-sufferer who understands',[57] being affected by the whole and moving it through the 'lure' of persuasive love towards fullness of value and beauty. Because there is an aspect of 'feeling' in every entity, all can accept, modify or even reject the divine aims that are offered.[58]

Even if we regard this scheme as more metaphorical than metaphysical, I suggest that it does express the truth that all created things have shared in a similar slipping away from the Good as is attributed to human beings and from which evil as non-being emerges. Another way of thinking of the divine 'lure' that may be embraced or resisted is as an invitation to each living thing to transcend itself, exploring new behaviors in its environment as well as growing to maturity within its own species.[59] Even 'inanimate' objects belong in webs of relationship and consist, at the quantum level, of fundamental particles in movement; we can begin to conceive how these might be influenced by being held within the dynamic life of a triune God which consists in movement and relationship.[60] Though we do not as yet have the language to express it, all created being in its own way has failed to respond fully to the persuasive urging of God towards fullness of life and the phenomena of both natural and moral evil witness to this tragedy.

Now, if fallenness can be extended into the whole of nature, then so can atonement as a transforming act. Human beings have the greatest potential for response to the lure of God towards a flourishing life; in them, 'expiating' of sin is the removal of an attitude of rejection and lack of trust. But the presence of a suffering God will have an effect on the way all things in the universe 'hold together' (Col. 1:17), and response to this creative offer at all levels of life will also mean an overcoming of evil.

57 Alfred North Whitehead, *Process and Reality. An Essay in Cosmology* (New York: Macmillan, 1929, repr. 1967), 532.
58 See Whitehead, *Process and Reality*, 27–39, 163–6, 373–5, 519–33; Lewis S. Ford, *The Lure of God: A Biblical Background for Process Theism* (Philadelphia: Fortress Press, 1978), 82–5; Charles Hartshorne, *The Divine Relativity: A Social Conception of God* (New Haven, CT: Yale University Press, 1948), 134–8.
59 See Southgate, *Groaning of Creation*, 61–4.
60 See Fiddes, *Seeing the World and Knowing God. Hebrew Wisdom and Christian Doctrine in a Late-Modern Context* (Oxford: Oxford University Press, 2013), 161–6.

Poets such as Gerard Manley Hopkins bear witness to the conviction that the crucified and risen Christ is to be found in the natural world:

> I walk, I lift up, I lift up heart, eyes,
> Down all that glory in the heavens to glean our Saviour.[61]

Sensitivity of humans towards their natural environment and a partnership with the natural world will thus lead to a convergence of response and a greater resistance to evil. Ivan's question remains – 'Is it worth it?' – so that there can be no complete theodicy. But a theology of atonement can take us to the point at which we might say, in faith, that it all has indeed been worthwhile.

FURTHER READING

Aulen, Gustav. *Christus Victor. An Historical Study of the Three Main Types of the Idea of Atonement.* Trans. A. G. Herbert. London: SPCK, 1970.

Barth, Karl. *Church Dogmatics.* Trans. and ed. G. W. Bromiley and T. F. Torrance. Volume IV, Part One, *The Doctrine of Reconciliation.* Edinburgh: T. & T. Clark, 1974.

Brümmer, Vincent. *Atonement, Christology and the Trinity.* Aldershot: Ashgate, 2005.

Davis, Stephen T., Daniel Kendall and Gerald O'Collins (eds.). *The Redemption. An Interdisciplinary Symposium on Christ as Redeemer.* Oxford: Oxford University Press, 2004.

Fiddes, Paul S. *Past Event and Present Salvation. The Christian Idea of Atonement.* London: Darton, Longman and Todd, 1989.

Ford, Lewis S. *The Lure of God: A Biblical Background for Process Theism.* Philadelphia: Fortress Press, 1978.

Gunton, Colin E. *The Actuality of Atonement. A Study of Metaphor, Rationality and the Christian Tradition.* Edinburgh: T. & T. Clark, 1988.

Hick, John. *Evil and the God of Love.* New Edition. Basingstoke: Palgrave Macmillan, 2010.

Moltmann, Jürgen. *The Crucified God. The Cross of Christ as the Foundation and Criticism of Christian Theology.* Trans. R. A. Wilson and J. Bowden. London: SCM Press, 1974.

O'Collins, Gerald. *Jesus Our Redeemer. A Christian Approach to Salvation.* Oxford: Oxford University Press, 2007.

Tillich, Paul. *Systematic Theology. Volume 2. Existence and the Christ* (London: SCM Press, 1978).

Wink, Walter. *Naming the Powers. The Language of Power in the New Testament.* Philadelphia: Fortress Press, 1984.

---

[61] Gerard Manley Hopkins, 'Hurrahing in Harvest'.

12 Islam and the Problem of Evil

TIMOTHY WINTER

Islam's theological, ethical and mystical traditions have adopted a range of approaches to the question of evil. They share, however, a rootedness in the Qur'ān, a text which repeatedly attends to the fact of human suffering, having emerged in a society which it proclaimed to be miserably deluded by false belief and custom and in which the physical environment was harsh and human comforts were few and basic. The travails of its first adherents, who underwent severe persecution at the hands of the pagan Meccan aristocracy, ensured that the Qur'ānic vocabulary was replete with categories of grief (ḥuzn), misery (shaqāwa), pain (alam) and injustice (ẓulm), constants which defined a form of Arabian life held to be so insupportable that it triggered the birth of a new religion which sought to challenge Arab suffering and bring about a 'healing and a mercy' (17:82).

Especially significant as a catalyst in defining the new religion's treatment of God's action in the world and Islam's response to humanity's 'creation in suffering' (90:4) was the founder's own experience. Orphaned in childhood and living in straitened circumstances, watching all but one of his seven children die and experiencing recurrent ostracism and abuse at the hands of his own kinsmen, the Prophet, according to a report attributed to his widow 'Ā'isha, 'suffered more than any man ever did'.[1] In later times a belief developed that prophets necessarily endure excruciating physical and mental traumata as part of the sacrifice they make in proclaiming God's word. They may be beheaded, like John, fall sick, like Abraham (26:80), experience acute bereavement like Jacob (12:16–7) or be poisoned, like Muḥammad, and their lives are unusually beset by personal loss and setbacks which for them are believed to be especially hard to bear because of the softness of their hearts.

Human misery was the context for the emergence of the Prophet's religion. What, then, is its right interpretation? The Qur'ān suggests a

---

[1] For the hadith, see Tirmidhī, Zuhd, 57.

variety of approaches. Its *Heilsgeschichte* offers a cyclical narration of God's reparative activity worked through prophets and saints, habitually defied by a human recidivism which engenders mass suffering, which in turn is overcome by a new Prophetic correction. This cyclic alternation of misery and vindication generally implies that in the nature of things virtuous endurance will tend to receive its due reward: Moses finally prevails over Pharaoh (20:9–79), Joseph over his brothers (12:67–100) and Abraham over Nimrod (21:69). Job is washed clean by a holy spring, and his family are restored to him (38:42–4). Often the nomadic Arabian backdrop provides a key trope: Mary, Hagar and Job are all saved by miraculous desert springs which appear as the reward for patience and endurance, water being the tradition's most common symbol for divine mercy and succour. Life in the desert is precarious, and the wisest response to suffering is fortitude, maintained in the hope of a seemingly miraculous deliverance.

Often the Qur'ān proclaims suffering to be the wages of sin and warns that entire cities have been destroyed by earthquakes, deluges or gales because their inhabitants defied God. Thus had been the fate of those who rejected Noah, Moses, Lot and others whose cautionary tales are frequently rehearsed in the scripture.[2] This interpretation resonates in later Islamic historiography and preaching, which often sees natural disasters following human unruliness as the sobering tokens of God's punitive ways. In this fashion the depredations of Mongols and Crusaders were treated as the just consequence of Muslim religious sloth.[3] On occasion, certain illnesses were understood to be specific divine retaliations for sin.[4]

What of the apparently unrequited suffering of the innocent? Given its *sitz im leben* this also needed to be a significant theme of the scripture. The Qur'ān makes it evident that not all virtue finds a happy

[2]   David Marshall, *God, Muhammad and the Unbelievers: A Qur'ānic Study* (Richmond: Curzon, 1999); Thomas Michel, "God's Justice in Relation to Natural Disasters." In *Theodicy and Justice in Modern Islamic Thought*. Ed. Ibrahim M. Abu Rabi' (Farnham: Ashgate, 2010), 219–26, 220.

[3]   Ala-ad-Din Ata-Malik Juvaini, tr. John Boyle, *The History of the World-Conqueror* (Manchester: Manchester University Press, 1958), I, 16–19; Carole Hillenbrand, *The Crusades: Islamic Perspectives* (Edinburgh: Edinburgh University Press, 1999), 72.

[4]   Justin K. Stearns, *Infectious Ideas: Contagion in Premodern Islamic and Christian Thought in the Western Mediterranean* (Baltimore, MD: Johns Hopkins University Press, 2011), 198–9. Thanks to Galenic influence, this type of moralising seems to have been less common than in medieval Christendom, as witnessed by the relative toleration and social integration of lepers in Muslim lands; see Michael W. Dols, *Medieval Islamic Medicine: Ibn Riḍwān's Treatise "On the Prevention of Bodily Ills in Egypt"* (Berkeley: University of California Press, 1984), 23–4.

repayment in this world, and not every struggle will end in a mysterious but splendid vindication. Christian martyrs in Najrān are tormented in a fiery trench by a Jewish tyrant in a scene narrated by a sequence of mournful verses unwilling to foretell a positive outcome apart from the infernal chastisement which is the assured post-mortem fate of oppressors (85:4–9). In such cases justice will ultimately be done, but no relief or compensation appears to be on offer before the eschaton.

One clue to the Qur'ān's perspective seems to be supplied in its narrative of the Virgin Mary, who serves as one of its most deliberate paradigms of guiltless suffering. During the birth of Christ her labour pains become so excruciating that she cries out the nearly suicidal words: 'Would that I had died before this, forgetting and forgotten!' (19:23). After giving birth alone in the desert, this sinless paragon returns with the child to confront probable scandal and execution in Jerusalem. Her extreme physical and psychological misery are ended, however, by an unexpected miracle, as the baby in her arms speaks in her defence, proclaiming her innocence and startling the scribes and Pharisees with a brief explanation of his own Christology (cf. 19:30–32). The reader is expected to conclude that Mary's submission at the Annunciation and her patient trust during severe tribulation were in some way rewarded with the gift of Christ and the appearance of the 'good news'. Following this precedent, the idea of suffering as 'birth pangs' furnished a not uncommon metaphor in Muslim religious poetry.[5]

Such scriptural narratives were constructed as examples of what it means to be *muslim*, literally 'resigned', surrendered heart and body to God in a state of perfect trust. The Prophet's hearers in Mecca are heartened by the news that although suffering may seem entirely unmerited, it can be the enigmatic, perhaps entirely incomprehensible anticipation of God's miraculous work of deliverance. Perhaps this led to the frequent idea that distress is a sign of divine favour, an ascetical view which became widespread in some Sufi mysticism, which often identified the highest degrees of spiritual accomplishment with the virtue of *riḍā*, satisfaction with the divine decree: the saint openheartedly and without hesitation accepts tribulations simply because they are from the God whom he or she loves. This disinterested and dysteleological faith position, which sometimes reduces the significance of otherworldly redress, is regularly encountered in the Sufi literature: life with all its hardships is a divine gift in itself.[6]

[5]   A. J. Arberry, *Discourses of Rūmī* (London: John Murray, 1961), 33.

[6]   Abū Ḥāmid al-Ghazālī, tr. Eric Ormsby, *Love, Longing, Intimacy and Contentment* (Cambridge: Islamic Texts Society, 2011), 154–65.

Characteristic, then, of the Qur'ān's soteriology is its construction of episodes of suffering which, when bravely borne, lead to a wholly unexpected and miraculous outcome: like Mary's parturitive agonies they invite an attitude of resignation and are to be read as unmerited and mysterious foretellings and therefore acts of grace. The importance of this idea is evident even in the founding myth of Islam's salvation history, which may be located in its distinctive recasting of the harrowing Genesis episode of the abandonment of the matriarch Hagar in the wilderness along with her son, in which both refuse to condemn God's command to Abraham. When thirst threatens their lives the boy scuffs his foot in the dust, and the well of Zamzam miraculously appears.[7] In the further future, the Ishmaelites, although disdained by the sons of Isaac, then unexpectedly bring forth the 'gentile Prophet' of Mecca, thus illustrating the idea that God nurtures a preference, albeit often delayed in its accomplishment, for the suffering outcast (in this case the ethnically 'impure' African refugee woman and slave). The arduous and enigmatic rites enacted annually in the Meccan sanctuary are thought to remind pilgrims that God's providence may appear in the weakest vessels through forms of tribulation whose outcome was unimaginable at the time.[8] Hence Abraham can tell his son that God has ordained the cutting of his throat, and his son replies: 'Father, do as you are commanded; God willing, you shall find me to be steadfast' (37:102). The commentators admiringly add the detail that even though the son's suffering was to be greater than the father's, he declined to be bound with cords for the event, not wishing to show the slightest rebellion against God's instruction. They then quote a stanza of love poetry:

> Were the hand of the beloved to give me poison,
> So great is my love that poison itself would taste sweet.[9]

With such narratives the Qur'ān considerably simplifies and to some extent harmonises the Bible's moral worlds. One indicative shift is the lack of a teaching of transgenerational punishment, or (its ultimate expression) an original sin which requires human beings to suffer on account of an ancestor's choice. Further, the Qur'ān's heroes are

---

7 Ibn Isḥāq, tr. A. Guillaume, *The Life of Muhammad* (Oxford: Oxford University Press, 1955), 45.

8 Cf. Charles-André Gilis, *La Doctrine initiatique du pèlerinage à la Maison d'Allâh* (Paris: L'Oeuvre, 1982), 75–91; Ali Shariati, tr. Ali Behzadnia and Najla Denny, *Hajj* (Houston, TX: Free Islamic Literature, 1977).

9 Abu'l-Qāsim al-Qushayrī, ed. Ibrāhīm Basyūnī, *Laṭā'if al-ishārāt* (Cairo: Dār al-Kitāb al-ʿArabī, n.d.), III, 239.

constructed as ethically exemplary harbingers of God's desire to save sinners from evil and evildoing so that the Biblical 'texts of terror' which impute malfeasance to God's messengers all disappear. David does not now seduce Uriah's wife; Lot does not sleep with his daughters; there is no sacred extermination (*herem*) of civil populations at the hands of Moses or Joshua. The new scripture's ideal types never instigate random or unwarranted suffering, although they may justly and transparently punish the guilty or warn of God's condign yet fitting chastisement (Noah, Lot, Moses). The outcome is a thoroughly consistent theo-drama in which God's prophets endure but do not mete out undeserved suffering and are locked in ceaseless combat against agents of human wilfulness, the most extreme expression of which is idolatry, construed as humanity's perennial and most fatal temptation. In this prophetology the political and the spiritual struggle are understood to be inseparable, generating a type of liberation theology on behalf of the 'oppressed of the earth' (4:97). Religion becomes authentic in the battle against suffering and injustice: 'what ails you, that you do not struggle for the feeble among men, and the women and children who are crying: "Our Lord! Deliver us from this town where the people are oppressors!"?' (4:75). Suffering, while endured by the saints, is acknowledged as an evil to be resisted wherever possible, and the duty to reduce it is emphasised, for instance, by the imposition of a mandatory tithe, levied annually at the rate of one-fortieth of one's wealth, which is directed specifically for the relief of poverty and other forms of social distress.

A further Qur'ānic explanation of innocent suffering identifies it as a trial. God tests individuals, including the innocent, by giving them prosperous or evil times (5:48, 21:35), and in places the text indicates that the purpose of creation itself is to test souls (11:7, 18:7, 67:2, 76:2), so that misfortunes like hunger and poverty may be instruments for the discernment of spirits (2:155). These trials may also double as an earthly atonement for misdeeds which otherwise would attract punishment in the next world.[10] Often a soul-making theodicy emerges: adversity guides the faithful along the road to salvation. Abstention from pleasure sharpens the believer's piety, as in the case of fasting, which the Qur'ān suggests has been instituted for this purpose (2:183). Suffering may be a practice of divine pedagogy or therapy which enhances an ascetic, penitential outlook that enables or accelerates the soul's ascent to God. Why has God not created mountains of gold and silver? The answer is a privative one: so that man may strive and hence learn the virtues in the hard

---

[10]   Qur'ān 17:18; Bukhārī, Marḍā, 1.

school of a world of scarcity and competition.[11] The means are held to be justified by such ends.

For one Sufi, 'sadness prevents the heart from grazing in the valley of distraction', whereas 'a heart devoid of grief falls into ruin, like the house which has no inhabitant'.[12] Suffering may inculcate humility, protect believers from hubris and impel them to pray and repent;[13] after all, had not Pharaoh himself, the ultimate paradigm of hard-heartedness, repented to God when he felt himself being engulfed by the Red Sea (10:91)? The poet Rūmī (d.1273) writes of a chickpea boiling in the housewife's pot, which, from its limited perspective, feels outraged by her cruelty:

> Look at a chickpea in the pot, how it leaps up when it is subjected to the fire.
>
> At the time of its being boiled, the chickpea comes up continually to the top of the pot and raises a hundred cries,
>
> Saying, 'Why are you setting the fire on me? Since you bought (and approved) me, how are you turning me upside down?'
>
> The housewife goes on hitting it with the ladle. 'No!' says she: 'boil nicely and don't jump away from the one who makes the fire.
>
> I do not boil you because you are hateful to me: nay, 'tis that you may get taste and savour,
>
> So that you may become nutriment and mingle with the (vital) spirit: this affliction of yours is not on account of (your being) despised'.[14]

Soul-making theodicies are intrinsic to the *via purgativa* normatively commended by virtually all religion, and the Muslim literature is on familiar ground here. Tears serve to water the spirit and bespeak a fair-minded and objective view of the world and of life's brevity; they build a deeper relationship with God, Who is to be loved for His own sake and not because of a future favour He might have promised; they are 'the tithe of intelligence'.[15] Whether experienced or witnessed, suffering

---

[11] Eric Ormsby, *Theodicy in Islamic Thought: The Dispute over al-Ghazālī's "Best of All Possible Worlds"* (Princeton, NJ: Princeton University Press, 1984), 201.

[12] Abu'l-Qāsim al-Qushayrī, ed. ʿAbd al-Ḥalīm Maḥmūd and Maḥmūd ibn al-Sharīf, *al-Risāla* (Cairo: Dar al-Kutub al-Ḥadītha, 1974), 368, 369.

[13] Sherman A. Jackson, *Islam and the Problem of Black Suffering* (New York: Oxford University Press, 2014), 112.

[14] Jalāl al-Dīn Rūmī, *The Mathnawi Edited from the Oldest Manuscripts Available* (London: E.J.W. Gibb Memorial Series, 1925–40), III, ll.4159–63.

[15] Qushayrī, *Risāla*, 371.

is often edifying, as in the case of the transformation of the Christian servant 'Addās, who was so moved by the Prophet's patience during an episode of rejection and physical injury that he converted to Islam;[16] and in later times a whole literature developed consecrated to the theme of the Prophet's agonies, meditation on which was deemed to have a spiritually purgative effect.[17] Some even held that the problem of private suffering which appears to have no evidentiary benefit may be resolved by assuming a salutary and hortatory effect not on any human observer but on angels and other supernatural beings who must be assumed to be present.[18]

However, the straightforward accounts of suffering as a punishment, test or miraculous sign of future vindication, still struggle in the case of several key categories. We have already seen that the Prophets suffer although they are assumed to be effectively sinless. They are tested, but as they are already perfect messengers of God the value of this is at best evidentiary, as a demonstration of their steadfastness and sincerity to others. However, there are further categories in which suffering seems arbitrary and undeserved by its subject: animals and children, together with other innocents whose pain seems devoid of any possible utility. We shall deal with some Muslim responses to these categories in turn.

ANIMAL SUFFERING

If suffering can be understood as a tribulation or a judgment upon morally accountable human beings, what can be the verdict of Ishmaelite scripture and theology on the existence of ubiquitous and often extreme suffering in the animal kingdom? Muslims have not attributed this to 'Adam's sin' (a view which would in any case seem hardly tenable in the light of modern palaeontology) and do not regard creation as having been damaged by a primordial human choice. The issue of animal suffering thus seems acute and is made still more so by the founding documents' explicit claim that animals are sentient beings possessed of moral rights. A large number of hadiths report incidents in which the Prophet was miraculously able to communicate with animals so that, in one instance, a mistreated camel complained to him of 'too much work

---

[16]   Ibn Isḥāq, 193.

[17]   See, e.g., Ḥusayn Baḥrānī, *Iltihāb nīrān al-aḥzān wa-muthīr al-ikti'āb wa'l-ashjān* (Qum: al-Sharīf al-Raḍī, 1418AH); Muḥammad ibn Nāṣir al-Dīn, *Salwat al-ka'īb bi-wafāt al-Ḥabīb* (Dubai: Dār al-Buḥūth, 1998).

[18]   Cüneyt M. Şimşek, "The Problem of Animal Pain: An Introduction to Nursi's Approach." In Abu Rabi, 111–34, 116.

and too little fodder'. The Prophet reproached the animal's owner and ordered that its situation be improved. The story goes on to record that other beasts then 'called out' to it, saying, 'You belong to Muhammad', and that when the Prophet died, 'it would neither eat nor drink until it also died'.[19]

Texts such as these forced the exegetic community to take the problem of animal suffering very seriously. Generally the tradition found that the only solution was to resort to the prediction of eschatological recompense. So sentient are animals that the Qur'ān seems to promise that they will be resurrected: 'there is not an animal in the earth, nor a bird flying on two wings, but that they are nations like yourselves [...] Then unto their Lord will they be gathered' (6:38). Confirming the inference of eschatological evaluation and repair, a hadith predicted that

> on the Day of Arising, all of creation will be gathered together: the cattle, the riding-beasts, the birds, and every other thing, and it shall be by God's justice that He takes the hornless sheep's case against the horned one. Then He shall say, 'Be dust'.[20]

And again, it is said that on an occasion when the Prophet observed two sheep fighting each other he remarked, 'God knows why they fight, and He shall judge between them on the Day of Judgement'.[21] Prompted by such texts, the great majority of theologians had no difficulty concluding that some form of post-mortem indemnity will be awarded to animals. The Mu'tazilite school, widespread in medieval times, held that God was in effect subject to an ethical obligation to recompense them. This doctrine, known as 'Restitution' ('iwaḍ), was rejected by mainstream Sunni thinkers, who, as we will see, held that it was incoherent to speak of God as subject to any obligations whatsoever. God is expected to recompense animals for their innocent suffering but will do so out of His generosity and wisdom, not because universal moral axioms compel Him to do so. Still, all major schools tried to resolve or mitigate the question of animal suffering by predicting some form of otherworldly redress.[22]

[19] Al-Qāḍī ʿIyāḍ al-Yaḥṣubī, *al-Shifāʿ bi-taʿrīf ḥuqūq al-Muṣṭafā* (Damascus: Dār al-Wafāʾ, n.d.), I, 601.
[20] Cited in Abū Ḥāmid al-Ghazālī (tr. T. J. Winter), *The Remembrance of Death and the Afterlife* (Cambridge: Islamic Texts Society, 1989), 200–1; cf. Aḥmad ibn Ḥanbal, *al-Musnad* (Cairo: al-Maymaniyya, 1313AH), I, 72.
[21] Ghazālī, *Remembrance*, 200, narrated by al-Bazzār and al-Ṭabarānī.
[22] For more on animal suffering, see Sarra Tlili, *Animals in the Qurʾān* (Cambridge: Cambridge University Press, 2012); Şimşek, in Abu Rabi, 111–34.

THE SUFFERING OF CHILDREN

The case of children in some respects recalls that of animals. Since the prepubescent young (and also the insane) are considered exempt from the yoke of the Law and any binding moral performance while remaining unquestionably sentient, their suffering cannot be a punishment. Neither can it easily be seen as a trial, since trials entail reward, a category which, again, cannot properly apply to morally immature beings. In this very difficult case Mu'tazilites sought to preserve the principle of God's justice by evolving complex theories of anticipatory chastisement under which children suffer to atone for sins which they will commit in adulthood. If they die when still children, this is because God knew that as adults they would lead sinful or miserable lives. Alternatively, children's suffering may be evidentiary, imposed in order to diminish adults' distraction by worldly comforts; sceptics did not hesitate to point out that this solution was not an ideal defence of the predicate of divine justice.

Children who die before maturity go to Heaven, through God's generosity rather than through any merit they might have shown, and this may also comprise an indemnity for their suffering in this world.[23]

INNOCENT ADULT SUFFERING

It is not only in the cases of animals and children that eschatological reparation comprises a vital theme for the major theological schools. The entire Qur'ān is an apocalyptic homily which ceaselessly points to the brevity of human life and the eternity of the world to come, and its emphasis on divine justice in the context of the larger cosmic schema reflects its premise of the divine mercy and appropriate agency *sub specie aeternitatis*.[24] Against this background, much comfort was found in the idea that in the fullness of time, human forgetfulness and the intensity of the paradisal delights will help expunge the memory of any earthly misery. A hadith has the Prophet say,

> The man who had suffered most in the world is brought, and it is said: 'Dip him into Heaven for one instant!' Then he is asked: 'Have you ever experienced any suffering?' and he replies, 'No'.[25]

---

[23] Jackson Jane Idleman Smith and Yvonne Yazbeck Haddad, *The Islamic Understanding of Death and Resurrection* (Albany: State University of New York Press, 1981), 168–82.

[24] Hence its insistence on the survival of the individuated human after death: suffering can only receive its due compensation if the human subject is authentically itself in the afterlife.

[25] Muslim, Ṣifat al-Qiyāma, 42, cited in Ghazālī, *Remembrance*, 224.

And according to a modern devotional writer,

> one will wake up from a bad dream, full of fear and torment, to find oneself at home beside one's beloved, sunlight streaming through the window, a prospect of golden days before us and all our deepest longings satisfied, for how long would we remember the pain of our dream?[26]

Paradise, expected to be a more real and clearly perceived habitat than the world which humanity currently occupies,[27] and which will allow believers a better insight into the adversity they had encountered on earth, will not only be experienced as a compensation for worldly travails but as their radical erasure, vindicating the Prophet's belief that in the afterlife God will be more compassionate 'than is a loving mother to her child'.[28] The Prophet's heavenly 'pool' visited before entry into Heaven will wash away all the believers' sorrows, and he or she may then hope for the beatific vision, a doctrine of enormous importance to Sunnism. Just as the garden of Paradise makes the blessed oblivious to their previous sufferings, the seeing of God will be so exceptional as to make them forget not only their miseries on earth but Paradise itself.[29]

The recourse to eschatology was a frequent move. However, theologians often sought interpretations which allowed God's ways to be justified in this-worldly terms also. Many who reflected on the divine wisdom in creating instrumental, purgative or therapeutic suffering were driven by a strong determination to identify the divine purpose wherever they could. Just as God's law exists for human benefit and its individual enactments are consequently open to ratiocination (*ta'līl*) to determine God's merciful purpose therein, so also His agency in creation should be open to human analysis. This assurance was particularly habitual among Mu'tazilites. Regarding the principle of justice as the most determinative aspect of divine agency, they came to the view that God has created the best of all possible worlds, because had He not, He would have flatly contravened His own nature. God is, after all, 'the wisest of the wise' (95:8) who 'does not wrong anyone by so much as an atom's weight' (4:40).

---

[26] Charles le Gai Eaton, *Islam and the Destiny of Man* (Albany: State University of New York Press, 1985), 239.

[27] 'Your sight is sharp this day' (50:22).

[28] Ḥākim, *Mustadrak*, cited in Ghazālī, *Remembrance*, 255.

[29] Ghazālī, *Remembrance*, 251. For more on theodicy and eschatology, see Nursi's twelve arguments in Thomas Michel, "The Resurrection of the Dead and Final Judgment in the Thought of Said Nursi." In Abu Rabi, 29–40, 30.

In this theology God is bound to create *al-aṣlaḥ*, whatever serves His creatures best, for failing this He would not be God. If the world is imperfect, so that He has not instantiated a better world than the actual one, this must either be attributable to divine incapacity, negating His omnipotence, or to 'miserliness', in which case He would not be entirely just and compassionate.[30] In keeping with a wider Muʿtazilite admission this view conceded that God's agency was hedged around with a swarm of *impossibilia*: just as God cannot create His like or decree His own nonexistence, He cannot decree what is unjust. For the same reason God is not at liberty to determine human decisions, which are free, and therefore moral evil must be imputed to autonomous human volition rather than to the divine will. From this premise they spun a range of theodical moves, mostly returning to the hope of eschatological recompense for apparently unmerited worldly suffering; indeed, the whole doctrine of Restitution was driven by a conviction that God was morally bound to ensure a discernable and true justice in His cosmos.

Such conclusions about a limited divine freedom and capacity were heavily contested by the dominant school of Sunni theology known as Ashʿarism, whose founder had renounced his earlier Muʿtazilite commitment following a disillusionment with its theodicy. For Ashʿarism it is empirically demonstrable that ours is not the best of all possible worlds, since it is clear that a God operating under the constraints which the Muʿtazilites wished upon Him would not be able to create suffering paupers who die in disbelief and hence are destined for hellfire; and yet such people may reasonably be said to exist.[31] Even more gravely, Muʿtazilism effectively abolishes divine freedom by forcing only a single possible action on God in each situation, thus betraying an alien Hellenistic influence leading back, ultimately, to the *Timaeus*, proposing a First Cause stripped of the freedom and analogy to personal life upon which Abrahamic monotheism rested. The Muʿtazilites had bought man's freedom at the price of God's.

Ashʿarism's dissatisfaction with the choiceless Muʿtazilite deity threw up a very different set of solutions to the 'problem of evil', which amounted, in effect, to a thoroughgoing anti-theodicy. Where the Muʿtazilites had taken their cue from the principle of divine justice, the Ashʿarīs began with the axioms of God's omnipotence and freedom. Reducing the predicate of justice to an agency of correct creative

---

[30]   Ormsby, 62.

[31]   Ibrāhīm ibn Muḥammad al-Bayjūrī, *Tuḥfat al-Murīd sharḥ Jawharat al-Tawḥīd* (Beirut: Dār al-Kutub al-ʿIlmiyya, 1403/1983), 109–10.

disposition, Ash'arism boldly denied the existence of objective moral facts. Good and evil or, in the more usual aestheticising language of Muslim moral philosophy, 'the beautiful' (*al-ḥasan*) and 'the ugly' (*al-qabīḥ*), are not Platonic realities possessed of an autonomous existence, the grounds of an ontologically rooted axiology against which all actions, including God's, must be assessed, and neither can they be independently and reliably located by the human subject in the way that sensory phenomena are perceived. For Ash'arism, a school often linked to a Sufi devotional tradition nervous about the shaping of theory choice by hubris, it was arrogant as well as philosophically difficult to claim that one's mind could authoritatively identify natural facts of a moral nature and still more arrogant to claim that the Creator must be observed or considered to be constrained by those natural facts. God is not subject to moral necessity, for He is its ground. Hence for Ghazālī (d. 1111):

> Good and bad, for all mankind, are descriptions of two relational qualities that vary with that to which they relate, and not of qualities of essences, which do not vary with relations. It is surely possible that a thing is good for Zayd and bad for 'Amr, but it is not possible that a thing is black for Zayd and white for 'Amr, since colors are not relational qualities.[32]

For Ash'arism there is a valid sense in which one might hold that 'evil is from God', and yet this bald statement was thought to be an oversimplification as well as a sin of discourtesy. Instead, one ought to say that 'all that is created is from God', and this seemed faithful to the Prophet's own phrasing evinced in his prayer 'The good is all in Thy hands, and evil cannot be ascribed to Thee'. So for many Ash'arīs, 'evil' is a locution which carries negative evaluative content insofar as it is experienced by our human subjectivity, but it is fallacious to state that it is evil *per se* in the divine enactment.[33] This validation of human experience is said to be necessary to avoid any suggestion that evil is simply legitimate and to vindicate the rationality of acting to challenge it.

Against Mu'tazilite objectivism Ash'arism proposed a view variously described as a voluntarism, a divine command theory or a 'theistic subjectivism'. God transcends the framework of rights and duties which connect frail human subjects and so has no obligations towards us. Even

[32] Abū Ḥāmid al-Ghazālī, *al-Iqtiṣād fi'l-i'tiqād*, tr. Aladdin M. Yaqub, as *Al-Ghazali's "Moderation in Belief"* (Chicago: University of Chicago Press, 2012), 161.

[33] Muhammad Salih Farfur, *The Beneficial Message and the Definitive Proof in the Study of Theology* (London: Azhar Academy, 2010), 151. The hadith appears in the anthology of Muslim.

His greatest grace, the 'sending-down' of revelation for our guidance, was not the discharge of anything resembling a moral duty but was merely a free expression of His wisdom and gentleness (*luṭf*): 'His acts are not subject to reasons and objects; He is not asked about what He does; one seeks no "Why" of him: He sends Prophets simply because it is His will, not because the interests of His servants are served thereby'.[34] God is thus not 'morally good' in any human sense but habitually and validly acts according to wisdom. He is just, but according to a definition which is applicable to His nature, whereby justice is 'the proper placement of things by God'. He may act in ways that to all human moral intuitions are arbitrary, but this is in no way foolish. Divine acts are unlike human acts, not least because they are not axiologically shaped by the values of obedience or disobedience.[35] On this conclusion, divine omnipotence includes the capacity to impose suffering that by human measuring is certainly unjust or unbearable, but this cannot compromise the principle of divine wisdom.

To the extent that His 'most beautiful names' are disclosed to the mind in scripture and in the order of nature, values may be heuristically recognised, but it is revelation alone that supplies the normative framework. Yet even the moral code enunciated by revelation is not binding upon Ash'arism's entirely free and sovereign deity: 'thou shalt not kill' is an instruction known to be incumbent upon humanity because of divine command, and yet God cannot meaningfully be said to be bound by it, for that would restrict His freedom and power and force Him to bow to a higher and external code. Even the Qur'ānic principle that hints that God accepts to be constrained by values He has determined to be normative of His nature ('He has prescribed mercy upon Himself', 6:12) cannot overthrow His right to define those values. In this system, then, no theodicy is meaningful, since God is just and merciful according to a canon of wisdom which need not coincide at all with humanly detected aesthetic or revealed conceptions. Indeed, for Ash'arism, every attempt at a theodicy is likely to be hubristic, demanding divine submission to prior natural facts and compliance with humanly fallible intuitions.

Human minds cannot, then, adequately evaluate God's actions or even His legislation. True, the habits of Divine wisdom in practice tend to converge with mentally graspable patterns of appropriateness, allowing the cautious practice of *taʿlīl*, but the immensity of the divine-human

---

34   Muṣṭafā ibn Muḥammad Kestelli, *Ḥāshiya ʿalā Sharḥ al-ʿAqāʿid* (Istanbul: Shirket-i Ṣaḥḥāfīye-i ʿUthmānīye, 1326AH), 165.
35   Kestelli, 75.

gulf ensures that this cannot be guaranteed. Hence the argument that demonstrates the nonexistence of God on the grounds that He has failed various tests finds no purchase in an Ash'arite context. The Qur'ān itself seems to allude to this: 'He is not asked about what He does; it is they [humans] who are asked' (21:23). God is free to administer suffering that is neither a punishment nor a trial, to give pain to children and animals and to torment His prophets, and still His justice, His 'appropriate placement of things', is not compromised. The 'semitic' conception of a sovereign personal God here trumps the Mu'tazilite notion of God as a 'cosmic justice machine,'[36] a deity bound to deliver moral outcomes and a just world whose principles are, at least in theory, fully knowable via human cognition.

Whether Ash'arism thus made God's agency in the world essentially capricious was generally contested. The 'most beautiful names' which God gives Himself in scripture were normally held to have some content accessible to humanity: although a simple analogy between, say, human and divine love will quickly break down, a more complex and allusive relationship rooted in a matrix of equivocal predication was widely believed to exist. In the theology of the Māturīdī school (also Sunni opponents of Mu'tazilism, but distinct from Ash'arīs), the divine predicate of wisdom was understood as a quality which invariably led to a beautiful outcome, one which might in some circumstances be truly humanly knowable, at least in part. They agreed with the Ash'arīs that God's wisdom does not obstruct the occurrence of unmerited suffering but claimed that this would still serve a higher purpose which might be known only to God, in contrast to Ash'arism, which insisted that wisdom was in effect simply a synonym for divine agency.[37]

One counter-intuitive outcome of this Māturīdī mode of argument was the conclusion that humanly perceived imperfections in the created order are in fact signs of God's existence. Whereas Avicenna, following the Greeks, had held that only perfection may be originated by the perfect, the more reflective observer knows that in the cosmic plenitude every possible form or event is real if it is in keeping with God's truly autonomous wisdom. The world's apparent flaws are a proof that it is the artefact of a volitional being and refute any necessitarian system; in fact, the world's imperfections, including the presence of inexplicable

---

[36]   Khalid Blankinship, "The Early Creed." In *The Cambridge Companion to Classical Islamic Theology*. Ed. Tim Winter (Cambridge: Cambridge University Press, 2008), 33–54, 50.

[37]   'Alā' al-Din al-Usmandī, *Lubāb al-Kalām* (ed. M. Sait Özervarlı) (Istanbul: Islam Araştırmaları Merkezi, 2005), 101; Jackson 110–20.

suffering, are an argument for God. And the fact that God is truly free
and unconstrained is demonstrated by His ability to create a world in
which human utility is not in fact maximised. Our world is the most
beautiful and authentic expression of a perfect God's will and nature,
whether or not it gratifies our personal needs, and this beauty incorporates a host of apparent imperfections and sources of discomfort which
point to the radical autonomy of its maker.[38]

Somewhat distinct from both mainstream Ash'arī and Māturīdī conceptions was the position of Ghazālī (d.1111), whose conviction that
'nothing possible is more splendid than the actual' (*laysa fi'l-imkāni
abda'u mimmā kāna*), rooted in a quiet doubt about Ash'arite nomi-
nalism's ability to proclaim a meaningfully wise deity, generated a
centuries-long dispute. Ghazālī's is distinguished from the Mu'tazilite
position by his rejection of necessitarianism and from Māturīdism by
his belief in the possibility of seeing everything in creation as perfect.
It is conceived in part as a support to his devotional and mystagogic
programme of reliance on providence and the value of meditating on the
beauty and the rational order of the natural world. The devout must look
on God's works as showcases of His perfect wisdom, building on the
Qur'ān's cosmological arguments. A careful scrutiny of every organism,
and particularly the human animal, yields an amazement and humility
at the divine creative art. Scripture has insisted that 'thou shalt behold
no flaw in the All-Merciful's creation' (67:3) and that 'for Him all things
are according to a measure well-defined' (15:21), which means that the
world comprises a divinely willed web of finely tuned structures and
habitual norms of seeming causalities which in the 'most splendid'
way express the operation of God's 'beautiful names'.[39] Because some
of these are experienced by human subjectivity as strongly ethical,
these require objects among the *differentia* which permit contrast and
a reparative divine agency. As the twentieth-century Turkish thinker
Said Nursi put it, 'Just as the Name of Healer makes it necessary that
illness should exist, so too the Name of Provider requires that hunger should exist.[40] These seeming imperfections also form part of the
'splendour' of creation.

This perspective was further elaborated by the Sufi author Ibn 'Arabī
(d.1240). For him, 'evil', which is only *prima facie* and not authentic, is
a consequence not of Adam's 'sin' but of an earlier act which took place
in divinis; it is a corollary of the fact of creation itself. The Divine *fiat*

---

[38]   Jackson, 111–2.
[39]   Abū Ḥāmid al-Ghazālī, *al-Ḥikma fī makhlūqāt Allāh* (Cairo: al-Qabbānī, 1321/1903).
[40]   Şimşek, 124.

which enacted the world, which is composed of a vast field of interactions among the 'beautiful names', brings a distance from the primordial unity of the divine essence, which is perfect compassion. Providence brings the saint out of the idolatries of selfhood and the perception of alterities into authentic cognition of the One, in a journey from the shadows into the Light' (2:257), and the shadows which he or she leaves behind are the necessary consequence of the divine command 'Be!' which is differentiation itself, the 'stain of multiplicity'.[41] Imperfection is what is not God. So without manifestation there would be no entification of the divine names and hence no divinely desired human journey back to God: shadows, or what humans perceive as imperfections, are just a sign that the One God's fullness is being actualised.[42]

GOD'S OTHERNESS AND THE HELPLESSNESS OF THEODICY

Sunni theologians and mystics alike disputed the Muʿtazilite conviction that God and man inhabit the same moral community. For Sunnis, the Creator is not a component of the cosmos or a member of a class, whose existence is comparable to that of other entities. He is not subject to time, and therefore His 'decisions', not being preceded by states of indecision, are not analogous to our own. His will and power are not simply unrestricted versions of ours, since our own will and power are defined with reference to what restricts them.[43] His knowledge must be total, since if He knew only some things, He would be subject to some external factor which had determined which things He knows and which He does not; and therefore His knowledge is not simply a perfect version of human knowledge. It is hence likely to possess modalities which by their nature cannot be accessed or grasped by human cognition. Moreover, existing outside time exempts Him from ignorance of the future: where the Muʿtazilites had proposed a God unable to know actions before their occurrence, Sunni theology insisted on a full foreknowledge. The 'future' is a subjective human perception inapplicable to the divine totality.[44] All these conclusions strengthened the characteristic Sunni resistance to viewing the deity as a sort of humanoid.

---

[41] John Crook, "The Theocentric Pluralism of Rusmir Mahmutcehajic and Inter-religious Dialogue in Bosnia," *Forum Bosnae* 51 (2010): 138.

[42] William C. Chittick, *The Sufi Path of Knowledge: Ibn al-ʿArabi's Metaphysics of Imagination* (Albany: State University of New York Press, 1989), 290–303.

[43] Kestelli, 72.

[44] Kestelli, 72–4.

While theodicies of various kinds may helpfully serve pedagogic ends, Ghazālī is clear that they exist only for the majority of the faithful, who need a God made accessible by some straightforwardly anthropopathic descriptions. True metaphysicians find them unnecessary[45] and shift the focus away from the God of 'resemblance' (*tashbīh*) proclaimed in those scriptural passages which so profusely name Him, to the God of 'otherness' (*tanzīh*) announced in other texts such as 'Nothing resembles Him' (42:11). This immaterial God does not possess anything like the human physiological systems and organs which support our processing of the world and our emotions,[46] and He cannot be 'incarnated' (still less become a corpse[47]). He is properly non-affective and impassible (although this is not the same as apathy); and the seemingly humanising lexis of scripture and mysticism exists not to indicate an actual 'personhood' in God but to provide a context for a set of salvifically effective and needful human responses to divine initiatives and commands. This apophasis secures the final victory over the animism of ancient Arab idol-worship; a right understanding of the Second Commandment, famously dear to Islam, obviates any theodicy, and indeed makes it nearly blasphemous.

Any certainty about God's motivations not only reduces Him to a human level but undermines the struggle against evil. Complaint is indispensable to piety and to humanity itself; an indifferent and undignified *ataraxia* is inhuman and perhaps unattainable. Mary's cries are intrinsic to her dignity, and so is the famous and revealing prayer of the prophet of Islam, uttered after he was driven out with stones from the city of Ṭā'if:

> O God, to Thee I complain of my weakness, little resource, and low-liness before men. O Most Merciful, Thou art the Lord of the weak, and Thou art my Lord. To whom wilt Thou confide me? To one afar who will misuse me? Or to an enemy to whom Thou hast given power over me? If Thou art not angry with me I care not. Thy favour is more wide for me. I take refuge in the light of Thy countenance by which the darkness is illumined, and the things of this world and the next are rightly ordered, lest Thy anger descend upon me or Thy

---

[45]   Abū Ḥāmid al-Ghazālī, *al-Maqṣad al-Asnā*, tr. David Burrell and Nazih Daher, as *Al-Ghazālī on the Ninety-Nine Beautiful Names of God* (Cambridge: Islamic Texts Society, 1992), 57.

[46]   Jackson, 138.

[47]   The most vulnerable point in Peter Geach's Thomist antitheodicy, otherwise convergent in some ways with Ash'arite apophaticism. P. T. Geach, "Omnipotence," *Philosophy* 48 (1973): 7–20, see 19.

wrath light upon me. It is for Thee to be satisfied until Thou art well pleased. There is no power and no might save in Thee.[48]

It is in prayers such as this, finally, that Ishmaelite faith has most plausibly sought to engage with the pervasive presence of suffering in God's world while frankly acknowledging the implications of His power. Prayer does not deny apophasis but works with a different and more intuitive theology in a turn from the He to the Thou animated by a lived and experiential faith rooted in trust (*īmān*). This turn is validated by the rhetorical axis of the first and most liturgically indispensable chapter of the scripture, which begins with words of praise for an absent Lord and closes with an appeal to His personally experienced presence before the worshipper. The 'He', which Arabic grammar calls the 'pronoun of absence', typically denotes the transcendent God of *tanzīh*, who is misrepresented by the rationalising Mu'tazilites, who use their syllogistic apparatus to reason out God's reasons with a finite and unfit lexis and a precarious *via negativa* and thereby risk the invention of a static idol-God circumscribed by human subjectivity and culture (and gender). Such a project is apt to frustrate its own ends by contradicting the 'nothing is like Him'; for the 'He', ostensively a 'personal pronoun', is paradoxically a marker for what is radically unlike ourselves; nothing, indeed, is like 'Him'; and His 'beautiful names' recur in the Qur'ān in such a prodigious variety of contexts that they signal the provisionality and dynamic flux of all divine predication. The scriptural stories suggest that Compassion, Clemency, Justice and the other qualities never appear twice in exactly the same modality, indicating that analogising to God is an allusive, unstable enterprise more rewarding to the praying 'heart', with its fluctuating susceptibilities and insights alert to the uniqueness of the moment, then to the mind. This turn to the Thou, which somewhat resembles, in Kantian terms, the move from speculative to practical reason, cataphatically 'affirms' (*ithbāt*) the divine predicates as these present themselves to the worshipper via divine grace in each instant while recognising the futility of defining their modality (*bilā kayf*). And it is this God, as Job and Muhammad saw, who is worth believing in and complaining to.

FURTHER READING

Hoover, Jon. *Ibn Taymiyya's Theodicy of Perpetual Optimism.* Leiden: Brill, 2007.
Jackson, Sherman A. *Islam and the Problem of Black Suffering.* New York: Oxford University Press, 2014.

---

[48] Ibn Isḥāq, 193.

Kermani, Navid. *The Terror of God: Attar, Job and the Metaphysical Revolt.* Cambridge: Polity Press, 2011.

Michel, Thomas. "God's Justice in Relation to Natural Disasters." In *Theodicy and Justice in Modern Islamic Thought.* Ed. Ibrahim M. Abu Rabi' Farnham: Ashgate, 2010, 219–26.

Ormsby, Eric. *Theodicy in Islamic thought: The Dispute over al-Ghazālī's "Best of All Possible Worlds."* Princeton, NJ: Princeton University Press, 1984.

Schuon, Frithjof. "The Question of Theodicies." *Studies in Comparative Religion* 8/i (Winter 1974).

13 Naturalism, Evil, and God

MICHAEL RUSE

WHAT IS "NATURALISM"?

Let's start in by talking about "naturalism," for this is a word with many meanings. When I was a child, it meant nudism, going around without your clothes on. With some regret, this is not the topic of this essay, for it is rather with notions of naturalism that have to do with nature, that is to say with the physical world. How broadly conceived is part of the discussion. It is usual and convenient to distinguish two senses of naturalism in the way I am using it here.

On the one hand, there is "metaphysical naturalism," meaning that nature is all there is and that there is no God or gods. In this sense, metaphysical naturalism is opposed to metaphysical *super*naturalism. Related terms are "philosophical naturalism," which I take to be more or less the same thing, and "ontological naturalism" which is similar but not quite the same. The opposite to ontological naturalism is ontological *non*naturalism, which I take to include not just the divine but also nonnatural facts like G. E. Moore's nonnatural ethical facts and, if you are a Platonist, the facts of mathematics. I take it that in the old days, we might have spoken of "materialism" rather than naturalism but that in an age of electrons and so forth, materialism seems a bit old-fashioned. Also, the naturalist might be a mathematical Platonist – I edge a bit that way – but I doubt a materialist could be.

On the other hand, there is "methodological naturalism." This is a fairly new term, but the historians have shown that it is an old idea with roots back before the Scientific Revolution. This is the idea that within science, one can and must explain the physical world as if there were no God. In other words, given that scientific explanation means understanding in terms of unbroken regularities (including statistical regularities over groups) – natural laws – this is the only approach permitted. Today, I think we would often connect this with mechanism – understanding must be in terms of the world as if it were a machine. But

I don't see any *a priori* reason why an Aristotelian approach, invoking final causes, should not be naturalistic. I think Aristotle would think of himself as a naturalist. Again, I don't think naturalism is quite the same as materialism. As before, electrons seem to be natural but not material, and the same is true of mathematics if you are a Platonist. I am very glad to say that I don't have to get into the question of consciousness here, but I take it that it is something open to methodologically natural approaches – even if you deny that it is material. I think most naturalists would say that consciousness doesn't threaten metaphysical naturalism either, although whether it should is perhaps another matter.

Now what is the connection between methodological naturalism and metaphysical naturalism? Some, the Intelligent Design Theorist Phillip Johnson[1] for instance, say that if you are a methodological naturalist then you are a metaphysical naturalist and presumably conversely. This would be a considerable surprise to many scientists. Two of the most important evolutionists of the twentieth century, the Englishman Ronald Fisher and the Russian-American Theodosius Dobzhansky, were both deeply committed Christians. We can certainly say that if someone is not a methodological naturalist then he or she is not going to be a metaphysical naturalist. If, like the Intelligent Designers, you allow massive great interventions by the Almighty into your science, then obviously you are not a metaphysical naturalist. Assuming that Johnson's fiat is at least open to discussion, the interesting question on which we shall have things to say is whether being a methodological naturalist tips you toward or forces you into being a metaphysical naturalist. Without prejudice, we can certainly say that this often seems to be the case. People do science and it succeeds, so much that in the words of one of the great historians of the Scientific Revolution, the non–God-invoking machine metaphor at the heart of modern science led people to think of God as a "retired engineer."[2] It is but one more step to think of God as a nonexistent engineer. But things are rarely quite that simple. Charles Darwin was one who insisted on methodological naturalism in his science. He quarreled with his American friend, the Presbyterian, Harvard-based botanist Asa Gray, on this. But as he moved to agnosticism in later life, the main motivating reasons were theological. Darwin hated the idea of eternal damnation for nonbelievers, like his father and his brother. He felt, rightly or wrongly, that such a revengeful god as this

[1] Phillip E. Johnson, *Reason in the Balance: The Case Against Naturalism in Science, Law and Education* (Downers Grove, IL: InterVarsity Press), 1995.
[2] E. J. Dijksterhuis, *The Mechanization of the World Picture* (Oxford: Oxford University Press, 1961), 491.

supposes simply had to be the fabrication of a group of people (priests) determined to invoke fear in the rest of us and thus to control our lives. He wanted no part of such a system.[3]

METAPHYSICAL NATURALISM AND EVIL

This mention of Darwin starts to move us toward the central topic of this chapter, naturalism and the problem of evil. What Darwin shows is that whatever the relationship between methodological naturalism and metaphysical naturalism, there are often nonscientific reasons pushing people toward metaphysical naturalism – reasons that are philosophical or theological. I am one with Darwin on this. I cannot accept the existence of a god – for convenience, let us stick with the Christian God, although the argument can be generalized – for several reasons that have little or nothing directly to do with science. For a start, I think the Christian God is an irreconcilable confusion of two traditions, Greek and Jewish. The Greek God – the God of Augustine, Anselm, and Aquinas – is not a person.[4] He is a necessary being outside time and space. Of course, the Christianized Greek God reveals intentions as do people, but to use the vernacular, He is simply not "one of the chaps." Jesus certainly was, but then was he so very Greek? The Jewish God – the God of the Protestants, today of people like Richard Swinburne[5] and Alvin Plantinga[6] – is a person. He is beside me, comforting me, as I walk through the valley of the shadow of death. We have here two different notions, and I just don't think you can bring them together harmoniously. For the second, with David Hume, I have a lot of trouble with the notion of a necessary being. $2 + 2 = 4$ is necessary, but that is not a being. I won't go into full details here – I and others have done so at great length elsewhere – but you can see the point I am making.[7]

And so to the problem of evil. I take this in the pretty standard form: If God is all powerful, He could prevent evil. If God is all loving, He would prevent evil. Evil exists. Therefore God – the Christian God – does not exist. I realize that there are counterarguments to avoid this

[3] R. J. Richards and M. Ruse, *Debating Darwin: Mechanist or Romantic?* (Chicago: University of Chicago Press, 2015).

[4] Brian Davies, *An Introduction to the Philosophy of Religion: Third Edition* (Oxford: Oxford University Press, 2004).

[5] Richard Swinburne, *The Coherence of Theism* (Oxford: Clarendon Press, 1977).

[6] Alvin Plantinga, *Does God Have a Nature?* (Milwaukee, WI: Marquette University Press, 1980).

[7] I take up the question of necessary existence in Ruse, *Science and Spirituality: Making Room for Faith in the Age of Science* (Cambridge: Cambridge University Press, 2010).

conclusion, and we shall be looking at some of them soon. Let me say that overall I do not find them convincing and that some of the counterarguments I find downright appalling. Alvin Plantinga, for instance, thinks that our sins made necessary the death on the cross of Jesus of Nazareth and that this is such a good thing that the sins are a cost worth paying: "no matter how much evil, no matter how much sin and suffering such a world contains, the aggregated badness would be outweighed by the goodness of incarnation and atonement, outweighed in such a way that the world in question is very good."[8] This is a Calvinist position known as "supralapsarianism," and frankly it strikes me as being a very good reason for not being a Calvinist.

My position is absolutely clear. I am a metaphysical naturalist primarily because of the problem of evil, and not only do I not think there is an effective counterresponse, I don't want to be argued out of my position. I know I speak for many in making these responses. Let me highlight the deaths of two young women in the Second World War. Anne Frank, the brilliant, full-of-life, so-lovable diarist, ended her days dying of typhoid in Bergen-Belsen. Sophie Scholl was one of the White Rose group in Munich who handed out pamphlets criticizing the Third Reich. Her life ended under the guillotine. In the light of these two deaths, nothing can ever convince me (or the many who think like me) that the Christian God exists. Even to try to think otherwise would be immoral. On the subject of metaphysical naturalism, the problem of evil is definitive. And if you say that God's ways are mysterious and hidden from us, then you are asking me to go against what I presume you think is my God-given nature and to condone acts that by any reasonable standard are pure evil. That I think is unfair of both you and God.

FROM METHODOLOGICAL NATURALISM TO METAPHYSICAL NATURALISM?

This said, there is considerable philosophical interest in seeing if methodological naturalism really does contribute to metaphysical naturalism. In America particularly, there is also much social and political interest in seeing if methodological naturalism really does contribute to metaphysical naturalism. Many right-wing, evangelical Christians are deeply suspicious of science, particularly any science to do with origins, and are forever tampering with school curricula and trying to enforce

---

8   Alvin Plantinga, "Supralapsarianism, or 'O Felix Culpa.' In *Christian Faith and the Problem of Evil*. Ed. P. Van Inwagen (Grand Rapids, MI: Eerdmans, 2004), 10, 1–25.

their views on teachers and children, often by promoting and passing laws favorable to their agenda. Recognizing that for people like these the problem of evil is clearly not a definitive refutation of their God, here (apart from philosophy) we have another reason for digging into the relationship between methodological and metaphysical naturalism.

In the context of this collection, we are focusing on issues connected to the problem of evil; but, as it so happens, this is no strain, because one of the chief – if not the chief – arguments that is trotted out about the significance of methodological naturalism for metaphysical naturalism is based precisely on the problem of evil. Charles Darwin gave the classic exposition in a letter to Asa Gray just after the *Origin of Species* was published in 1859. "I cannot persuade myself that a beneficent & omnipotent God would have designedly created the Ichneumonidæ with the express intention of their feeding within the living bodies of caterpillars, or that a cat should play with mice."[9] Well, yes, you might say, but this is going to happen whether or not Darwin and Gray ever existed or wrote on the subject. What's it got to do with naturalism? The point is that Darwin's theory of evolution through natural selection – a methodologically naturalistic theory if ever there was one – focuses on these issues, stresses their widespread nature, and confirms their importance. All of which implies that if God did create through the evolutionary process, He did so in a particularly painful (for others) fashion, almost to the point of sadism.

The heart of Darwin's theory comes in two parts. First, he argues to a struggle for existence.

A struggle for existence inevitably follows from the high rate at which all organic beings tend to increase. Every being, which during its natural lifetime produces several eggs or seeds, must suffer destruction during some period of its life, and during some season or occasional year, otherwise, on the principle of geometrical increase, its numbers would quickly become so inordinately great that no country could support the product. Hence, as more individuals are produced than can possibly survive, there must in every case be a struggle for existence, either one individual with another of the same species, or with the individuals of distinct species, or with the physical conditions of life. It is the doctrine of Malthus applied with manifold force to the whole animal and vegetable kingdoms; for in

---

[9] Letter from Charles Darwin to Asa Gray, 22 May 1860, in Charles Darwin, *The Correspondence of Charles Darwin* (Cambridge: Cambridge University Press, 1985), 8, 224.

this case there can be no artificial increase of food, and no prudential restraint from marriage. Although some species may be now increasing, more or less rapidly, in numbers, all cannot do so, for the world would not hold them.[10]

Darwin then showed that given any natural population of organisms, there are going to be huge amounts of variation between the individual members – no two organisms are ever exactly alike. This led him to speculate that in the struggle, those that succeed – the fitter – will on average tend to do so because of the features they possess and that the losers – the less fit – will lose because they do not have such features. There will therefore be a process akin to the selective breeding in the domestic world that leads to fatter cows and shaggier sheep and bigger turnips. Given enough time, these successful types will spread through the group, and eventually there will be full-blooded change.

> Can the principle of selection, which we have seen is so potent in the hands of man, apply in nature? I think we shall see that it can act most effectually. Let it be borne in mind in what an endless number of strange peculiarities our domestic productions, and, in a lesser degree, those under nature, vary; and how strong the hereditary tendency is. Under domestication, it may be truly said that the whole organisation becomes in some degree plastic. Let it be borne in mind how infinitely complex and close-fitting are the mutual relations of all organic beings to each other and to their physical conditions of life. Can it, then, be thought improbable, seeing that variations useful to man have undoubtedly occurred, that other variations useful in some way to each being in the great and complex battle of life, should sometimes occur in the course of thousands of generations? If such do occur, can we doubt (remembering that many more individuals are born than can possibly survive) that individuals having any advantage, however slight, over others, would have the best chance of surviving and of procreating their kind? On the other hand, we may feel sure that any variation in the least degree injurious would be rigidly destroyed. This preservation of favourable variations and the rejection of injurious variations, I call Natural Selection.[11]

---

[10] Charles Darwin, *On the Origin of Species by Means of Natural Selection, or the Preservation of Favoured Races in the Struggle for Life* (London: John Murray, 1859), 63–4.

[11] Ibid., 80–1.

Pain and suffering are not just incidental. They are part of the very fabric of life. As it happens, Darwin was still hanging on, barely, to belief in a deity. But it was certainly one far from the God of Abraham and Isaac. "I cannot anyhow be contented to view this wonderful universe & especially the nature of man, & to conclude that everything is the result of brute force. I am inclined to look at everything as resulting from designed laws, with the details, whether good or bad, left to the working out of what we may call chance."

Richard Dawkins[12] feels no such qualifications or hesitations. He introduces the notion of "reverse engineering," meaning the process of picking backward to try to work out something's purpose, and the related notion of a "utility function," meaning the end purpose being intended. He then draws our attention to the cheetah/antelope interaction, asking, "What was God's utility function?" Cheetahs seem wonderfully designed to kill antelopes. "The teeth, claws, eyes, nose, leg muscles, backbone and brain of a cheetah are all precisely what we should expect if God's purpose in designing cheetahs was to maximize deaths among antelopes."[13] Conversely, "we find equally impressive evidence of design for precisely the opposite end: the survival of antelopes and starvation among cheetahs." One could almost imagine that we have two gods making the different animals and then competing. If there is indeed but one god who made both animals, then what is going on? What sort of god makes this sort of encounter? "Is He a sadist who enjoys spectator blood sports? Is He trying to avoid overpopulation in the mammals of Africa? Is He maneuvering to maximize David Attenborough's television ratings?" The answer is inevitable.

> In a universe of blind physical forces and genetic replication, some people are going to get hurt, other people are going to get lucky, and you won't find any rhyme or reason in it, nor any justice. The universe we observe has precisely the properties we should expect if there is, at bottom, no design, no purpose, no evil and no good, nothing but blind, pitiless indifference.[14] As that unhappy poet A. E. Houseman put it:

> For Nature, heartless, witless Nature
> Will neither know nor care.

[12] Richard Dawkins, *A River Out of Eden* (New York: Basic Books), 1995.
[13] Ibid., 105.
[14] A bold claim. Would you really expect humans to emerge in a world without purpose? Russell wouldn't. See "A Free Man's Worship." Well, Richard Dawkins has never pulled back from bold claims – but he thinks we can get humans without purpose.

DNA neither knows nor cares. DNA just is. And we dance to its music.[15]

There are others who feel likewise. Philosopher Philip Kitcher also dwells on the suffering brought on by the struggle for existence, writing,

[George John] Romanes and [William] James, like the evangelical Christians who rally behind intelligent design today, appreciate that Darwinism is subversive. They recognize that the Darwinian picture of life is at odds with a particular kind of religion, Providentialist religion, as I shall call it. A large number of Christians, not merely those who maintain that virtually all of the Bible must be read literally, are providentialists. For they believe that the universe has been created by a Being who has a great design, a Being who cares for his creatures, who observes the fall of every sparrow and who is especially concerned with humanity. Yet the story of a wise and loving Creator, who has planned life on earth, letting it unfold over four billion years by the processes envisaged in evolutionary theory, is hard to sustain when you think about the details.[16]

In our terms, Kitcher allows that he once thought methodological naturalism reconcilable with metaphysical supernaturalism but now steps back, insisting he alone should be held responsible for "the earlier errors that I recant here."[17]

IS NATURALISM INCOHERENT?

The issue is whether methodological naturalism, as exemplified by Charles Darwin's theory of evolution through natural selection, pushes us toward metaphysical naturalism because it underlines – stresses the inevitability of –pain and suffering in this world, something incompatible with the existence of the Christian God. Before we turn to this question, however, there is one preliminary matter we must clear out of the way. Does the very acceptance of Darwinian Theory negate the possibility of metaphysical naturalism? This is the position of Alvin Plantinga. He argues (in an argument that was started by the sometime British Prime Minister A. J. Balfour) that if you are a metaphysical naturalist, then you will be a methodological naturalist. If you are a methodological naturalist, then you will accept Darwin's theory as the essentially correct

15   Dawkins, *A River Out of Eden*, 133.
16   Kitcher, Philip, *Living with Darwin: Evolution, Design, and the Future of Faith* (New York: Oxford University Press, 2007), 122–3.
17   Ibid., 180.

explanation of all organisms, including humans, and you will agree that the way we think is a product of natural selection. But then you will agree that our beliefs are not necessarily a function of truth but rather of what will help us in the struggle for existence. Somewhat cheekily, Plantinga quotes Darwin: "With me the horrid doubt always arises whether the convictions of man's mind, which have been developed from the mind of the lower animals, are of any value or are at all trustworthy. Would anyone trust in the convictions of a monkey's mind, if there are any convictions in such a mind?"[18] As it happens, Darwin immediately excused himself as a reliable authority on such philosophical questions, but this somewhat awkward point goes unmentioned. Also unmentioned is the fact that Darwin was explaining why he saw purpose in life, something one might have thought Plantinga would have welcomed.

Plantinga's own example invites us to dinner at Oxford, where there are many courses and much conversation, including Richard Dawkins telling the philosopher A. J. Ayer the conditions under which one could be an atheist. (Coals to Newcastle, one would have thought.) It could be that our senses and reason deceive us so much that we could project being at this dinner to other, very different circumstances. We could be in the jungle fighting crocodiles, but the features that lead to croc fighting also lead to illusions about what we are doing – illusions that we are putting Freddie Ayer right on matters of religious commitment. "Under this possibility ... beliefs wouldn't have (or needn't have) any purpose or function; they would be more like unintended by-products, and the likelihood that they are mostly true would be low."[19]

Obviously this silly example does not do what Plantinga intends. No Darwinian would ever think that drunken discussions about God help fight crocodiles – one needs rather speed and cunning and strength. It is true, to bring about its ends of continued existence and reproductive success, evolution can and probably does deceive us sometimes. There is for instance a school of thought – "evolutionary debunking" – claiming that our belief in the objectivity of morality is an illusion, brought on to make us successful social beings. But the point about illusions, if such there be, is that we can tell they are illusory because we have other nonillusory beliefs that tell us what is so. It is like explaining a magician's tricks. That there are two girls in the box is truth. That one is sawn in half is not and is explained by the two-girl fact.

[18]   Alvin Plantinga, *Warrant and Proper Function* (New York: Oxford University Press, 1993), 219, quoting Darwin in Francis Darwin, *The Life and Letters of Charles Darwin, Including an Autobiographical Chapter* (London: Murray, 1887), 315–16.

[19]   Plantinga, Alvin, "An evolutionary argument against naturalism," *Logos* 12 (1991): 34.

Plantinga persists. Perhaps we are deceived all of the time. To take an analogy, suppose we are in a factory producing widgets, and all on the assembly line look red. We then discover that the redness is a function of our protective glasses, and once they are removed, we see the widgets in another, true color. Could we not be in a situation in which natural selection forces on us such glasses for our own good, and we can never take them off and know the truth? Even our basic statements – there are two girls in the box – could be mistaken. Perhaps selection-based evolution deceives us all of the time, and so all of our thoughts, including our thoughts about evolution and its causes, collapse into meaningless jumbles. The methodologically naturalistic pursuit about human nature has led to irresolvable paradox – a paradox that goes up the chain to metaphysical naturalism, which must now be rejected in favor of metaphysical supernaturalism. Then, with the good God guaranteeing the truth of our beliefs, we can happily adopt some form of evolutionary theory.[20]

There is an important philosophical point here, but it is not the one to which Plantinga points. It is that, in the spirit of Hume and Kant, we are always going to be looking at the world through our evolutionarily acquired natural abilities. Perhaps – almost certainly – these do give us an evolution-infected way of understanding reality. Absolute truth in the God's-eye sense that Plantinga desires is unobtainable. But we pretty much knew that even without evolution. We can be realists, in the sense of believing in a real world and in making judgments about good understanding of this world and bad understanding, but the realism that we have is the kind of neo-Kantianism or even Pragmatism.[21] Ultimately all understanding has to be processed through human nature. At the best – but it is a pretty good best – we can have a kind of coherence of our beliefs. It all hangs together, and at a pragmatic level, which is what really counts, it works. Within the system, we can have correspondence between our beliefs and the world about us. There is correspondence between our thinking that the plates of stegosaurus are for heat control and the nature of the plates themselves and the kind of functioning they seem capable of. There is no correspondence between the thinking you are at the dinner but really being in the jungle.[22]

[20] As it happens, perhaps expectedly, rather than Darwinism, Plantinga inclines more to Intelligent Design Theory, with its massive divine interventions. Since he is not a methodological naturalist, this causes him no tensions.
[21] Hilary Putnam endorsed a view like this in *Reason, Truth and History* (1981), although later he moved away from this.
[22] One could argue that this is a confusing combination of pragmatist, coherence, and correspondence approaches to the nature of truth. Why bother with the others if we

Let us bring this discussion to a quick end. Even if Plantinga were right, he too is open to skeptical worries. He has an absolute conviction that God is guaranteeing his beliefs about the physical world and the applicability of some kind of evolutionary theory. He is right open to that Demon that Descartes introduced in the first *Meditation* – the Demon that undermines even our most basic convictions about reality, about mathematics, about metaphysics, and indeed about anything we might believe to be true.

> I will suppose, then, not that Deity, who is sovereignly good and the fountain of truth, but that some malignant demon, who is at once exceedingly potent and deceitful, has employed all his artifice to deceive me; I will suppose that the sky, the air, the earth, colors, figures, sounds, and all external things, are nothing better than the illusions of dreams, by means of which this being has laid snares for my credulity; I will consider myself as without hands, eyes, flesh, blood, or any of the senses, and as falsely believing that I am possessed of these....[23]

We could be mistaken about everything – except perhaps that we exist. The metaphysical supernaturalist is in the same supposed jam as the metaphysical naturalist. Let us move on, taking Darwinian evolutionary theory with us.[24]

NATURAL EVIL

Does Darwinian Theory really make the problem of evil that much worse, meaning whatever the philosophical and theological issues, does Darwinian Theory in some sense intensify the problem of evil so that here we have a case in which methodological naturalism points towards metaphysical naturalism? To answer this sensibly, let us think a little more about the nature of evil. Without trying for anything new, what is the standard line on the topic? Traditionally one divides evil into two: natural evil and moral evil. Let us take these in turn.

can have correspondence truth? Well, that is the point, isn't it? In everyday life, we can have correspondence, but in the kind of metaphysical sense that Plantinga is demanding, we can never be absolutely sure. He thinks that God guarantees it through a kind of Cartesian clear and distinct idea. I am saying – or I will say in a moment – that Descartes' evil demon can never be put back in the bottle, and so ultimately it has to be pragmatic or coherence.

[23] René Descartes, Meditations. *Philosophical Essays* (Indianapolis: Bobbs-Merrill, 1964), Meditation 1, 59–143.

[24] It is true: Plantinga is completely undefended vs. skepticism, and he seems not to care about this. Strange.

Natural evil I take to be earthquakes and that sort of thing. The Lisbon earthquake of 1755, when about fifty thousand people lost their lives, is the paradigmatic example and certainly cured the French Enlightenment figure Voltaire of any illusions about the friendly nature of this world. The philosopher Gottfried von Leibniz is the author of the classic response. God could not do the impossible, and even the best world of law is going to have natural pain and suffering.[25] God could not make $2 + 2 = 5$. God could not make a cat the size of an elephant – the weight would be far too great for the legs of a cat. Thus, putting matters in modern terms, the planet had to have some kind of law-bound (methodologically naturalistic) geological system, and the one it has is continental drift brought on by plate tectonics. God could not stop this system having some dreadful effects in Lisbon – as it will surely have before too long in California. Of course, this all presumes that God had to create through law. I can think of some fairly obvious reasons why He would, starting with the fact that a world not subject to such law hardly seems coherent, with everything happening randomly. In fact, it would be hard to know what a world without any law would be like. I suppose God could keep intervening every time something bad is about to happen, but where would be the end to it? So if only to keep the argument going, let's cut God some slack here.

Of course, the assumption is that the physical laws are the best there are in the sense of getting the job done with the minimum amount of pain and suffering. I am not sure how one would prove this. Is there an alternative to plate tectonics that would cause more human suffering? It is well known that it was this kind of question that inspired Voltaire to write his brilliant satire *Candide*, arguing against Leibniz, and his claim that this world of ours is the best possible – thus natural evil is the unavoidable cost of getting anything to work at all. To make his point, Voltaire introduced one of the all-time classic figures of fiction, the Leibnizian philosopher Dr. Pangloss. It matters not how awful things may be or turn out to be, Pangloss had happy optimism that things had turned out for the best in this best of all possible worlds. A man of the people, with the desires of men of the people, Pangloss catches venereal disease, becoming "a beggar all covered with scabs, his eyes diseased, the end of his nose eaten away, his mouth distorted, his teeth black, choking in his throat, tormented with a violent cough, and spitting out a tooth at each effort." Is this not terrible? Oh no, responds the optimist, "it was

25 Bruce R. Reichenbach, *Evil and a Good God* (New York: Fordham University Press, 1982).

a thing unavoidable, a necessary ingredient in the best of worlds; for if Columbus had not in an island of America caught this disease, which contaminates the source of life, frequently even hinders generation, and which is evidently opposed to the great end of nature, we should have neither chocolate nor cochineal."[26]

Whether or not this is quite fair to Leibniz and his solution, we may be able to make a bit more progress on the matter when we turn to instances of natural evil in the living world, those predator–prey interactions for instance. One thinks of the untold suffering every day highlighted by Darwin, as one group of animals goes out to find food literally on the backs of another group of animals. Yet one can plausibly suggest that, even though it does mean ongoing suffering, here is a case in which we can talk of what is possible. God could not create organisms by law without the struggle for existence and natural selection. Richard Dawkins of all people makes this point.[27] He argues that in order to get organic adaption, the design-like nature of features like hands and eyes and mouths, no mechanism other than natural selection will do the job. Random large mutations do not lead to functioning organisms. The bigger the change, the more likely it is to be totally disastrous. The one other mechanism that does speak to functioning – Lamarckism, the inheritance of acquired characteristics – is false. It would be nice if the giraffe's neck got longer through stretching. It just isn't true. It is selection or nothing. If God wanted to produce functioning organisms through such natural laws, then the cost was going to be a lot of suffering.

MORAL EVIL: ORIGINAL SIN

The other side to the coin is moral evil. It is this that led to the deaths of Anne Frank and Sophie Scholl. One set of human beings, of their own free choice, deliberately caused great harm and suffering to another set of human beings. There are two ways in which methodological naturalism via Darwinian Theory impinges on the problem of evil – one perhaps brings more comfort to the metaphysical naturalist and one perhaps brings comfort to the metaphysical supernaturalist. Start first with the question of why we are sinful, why we commit moral evil. According to the Christian, we are made in the image of God. Since God is wholly good, why are we not wholly good? The traditional answer, at least for

[26] Voltaire, *Candide* (Harmondsworth, UK: Penguin, 1759 [1950]), 16–17.
[27] Richard Dawkins, Universal Darwinism. *Evolution from Molecules to Men.* Ed. D. S. Bendall (Cambridge: Cambridge University Press, 1983), 403–25.

Western Christians, goes back to St. Augustine.[28] Adam sinned, and humans from henceforth are tainted by this sin. Whether we are born sinners or with the predisposition to sin, either way we are sinful. "For that which I do I allow not: for what I would, that do I not; but what I hate, that do I" (Romans 7: 15). This tells us why Jesus had to die on the cross. We are incapable of lifting ourselves out of sin and can do so only by the saving grace of the blood of the lamb. He washes away our sins, and we are forgiven.

The trouble is that if Darwinian evolution through natural selection is right, there was no original Adam and Eve. There is debate about this, but no one thinks that the human population – including the prehuman populations leading to us – ever fell below at a minimum several thousand, and much of the time it was significantly bigger.[29] It is possible that going back in time, we humans today all share some individual as an ancestor. Much more likely is that we share a large number of individuals as ancestors. One or many, they would all have had parents and grandparents and more back through the ages. They would not have needed original sin to make truth of what St. Paul said. Evolution suggests that we are all going to be an ongoing combination of selfishness and altruism. That is how social beings work. In other words, whomever you pick out as Adam and Eve, they would have had parents, and those parents would basically have been just as good and bad as their children. Even if someone did sin and eat a forbidden apple, there would have been sin before that. There would have been apples, too, providing the opportunity!

Darwinian evolution totally undermines the Augustinian line on original sin. It cannot be saved. There is another line, more favored by Christians in the orthodox tradition.[30] Before Augustine, Irenaeus of Lyons argued that putting it all on the shoulders of one sinner seems an awfully stern thing to do. A rather naïve couple are seduced by the wiles of a duplicitous serpent, and death and pain ensue for evermore. Apart from anything, that seems a rather harsh reaction, overcompensating for the misdemeanor. More than this, it makes the whole Christian story of the Incarnation (Jesus's coming) and the Atonement (Jesus's death) very

[28]   It actually goes back to an ancient Jewish tradition, although it is Augustine who gets it in the neck on these occasions. But I don't think we need the digression here.

[29]   Michael Ruse, *The Philosophy of Human Evolution* (Cambridge: Cambridge University Press, 2012).

[30]   J. Schneider, "Recent Genetic Science and Christian Theology on Human Origins: An 'Aesthetic Supralapsarianism.'" *Perspectives on Science and Christian Faith* 62 (2010): 196–212.

much a matter of catch-up, Plan B as one might say. Adam sinned, and so God had to do something about it. Would it not be better to have the story of Jesus and his sacrifice intended from the beginning? Humans were created imperfect, and the Christian story is one of God helping us on our way until we are ready for eternal life. Adam and Eve are purely symbolic.

Although this tradition has much to commend it, there are still issues that need to be dealt with at a theological level. One still wants to know why God demanded the blood sacrifice of Jesus on the cross, especially now that we can hardly be blamed for our sinful nature. Let's leave the discussion here. The point is that the methodological level is reaching up to the metaphysical level. The answer by traditional Christian supernaturalism to one of the most puzzling questions about our nature, why we have this propensity to moral evil, is threatened if not destroyed by Darwinian Theory. Without a significant repair job, the balance tilts toward metaphysical naturalism.

MORAL EVIL: FREE WILL

The second matter of interest here asks why it is that we fell into evil in the first place. The traditional response is couched in terms of free will. Being made in the image of God, it is better that we have free will than that we be automata, even though great evils ensue. "God therefore neither wills evil to be done, nor wills it not to be done, but he wills to permit evil to be done, and this is good."[31] Philosophically, as you know, I do not think this an adequate answer. The free will of Adolf Hitler, Joseph Goebbels, and Heinrich Himmler does not outweigh the harm they did. But this is not the point at issue here. Ask rather about Darwinian Theory and what it has to say about free will. Does it strengthen the free-will defense in some sense?

What do we say about free will? There are two basic positions.[32] One, known as "libertarianism" (not to be confused with the political philosophy of that name), argues that free will is a matter of reasons that lie outside the usual causal nexus. Kant is the point person here.

Since the conception of causality involves that of laws, according to which, by something that we call cause, something else, namely the

---

[31]   St. Thomas Aquinas, *Summa Theologica, I* (London: Burns, Oates and Washbourne, 1952), 1a, 82, 1.

[32]   John Martin Fischer, Robert Kane, Derk Pereboom, and Manuel Vargas, *Four Views on Free Will* (Malden, MA: Blackwell, 2007).

effect, must be produced; hence, although freedom is not a property of the will depending on physical laws, yet it is not for that reason lawless; on the contrary it must be a causality acting according to immutable laws, but of a peculiar kind; otherwise a free will would be an absurdity.[33]

I will not stay to argue this position, simply to note that if it works, the whole matter is outside the domain of science and so says nothing about the sorts of issues at stake here.

The other position, much in the English empiricist tradition, is known as "compatibilism." Here the distinction is drawn between determinism and compulsion. Everything, including humans, may be part of the causal picture, so in this sense we are determined in all of our actions; but we can still draw a distinction between people being free, as I am now as I sit at my computer, and people being unfree or compelled, as the prisoner in chains or the subject of the hypnotist or the unfortunate individual in the grip of a dire mental illness. Now conversely, without judging whether this position works, do note that now science is very relevant. In particular, science is going to throw light on whether an actor is free or unfree. I take it that on the basis of science, we would judge that a snake striking a bird is dangerous but not immoral because it is not a free actor – it has no sense of right and wrong and does what it does by instinct without much choice. I take it on the basis of science, we would say that (whatever his childhood) Adolf Hitler was a free agent, and when he went to war in 1939, he bore responsibility.

I take it that several areas of science can potentially throw light on questions like these, and not just evolutionary biology. All of the sciences interested in matters of choice and decision – psychology particularly, but also areas like economics – have a role to play here. It is not a question of one science but not others but of all sciences being committed to the methodological naturalism program. Does science give us reason to think that the very distinction between being free and being unfree is significant? Does science give us a reason why Hitler might be judged free but the snake – or any of the other so-called lower organisms like the ants – be judged bound and fully determined in some sense? It does. Evolutionary theory today makes much of what it calls "altruism."[34] Organisms often do better if they help others, because then they might expect help in return. Think for instance – I write this piece while

33   Immanuel Kant, *Critique of Judgement* (New York: Haffner, 1951), section 3.
34   Michael Ruse, *Darwinism and Its Discontents* (Cambridge: Cambridge University Press, 2006).

in South Africa – of the meerkats and how one or two in the group will stand erect, functioning as sentries and warning against predators. In turn, the sentries expect others to do the same for them or their off-spring. The risk of sentry duty is balanced by the gains in being able to live normally in relative safety.

The question now is how Mother Nature gets organisms to function altruistically. There are two basic ways. It can all be a matter of instinct, if you like genetic preprogramming. Organisms have engrained on their genotypes (their genetic constitution) the ways in which they must behave whenever certain environmental circumstances obtain. Ants have gone this way. When a leaf falls in the neighborhood, the leaf cutters don't think about it. They act instinctively, as do their companions, following pheromone trails and the like. It is all very efficient because no education is needed. The drawback is that if something goes wrong, they are not really equipped to handle the change. A sudden rain shower washes away the pheromone trails and the ants are lost, literally as well as metaphorically. It matters little to the nest because there are millions more, and basically it matters little to the loser because the survivors are all close relatives and will carry on the genes.

Organisms like humans simply cannot function this way. As highly social mammals, we live in constantly changing circumstances, and we have only a few offspring that we cannot afford to lose in a rain shower. (I am sure that there was a feedback effect between our evolutionary path and its demands and opportunities and our fewness of offspring.) We must have the power to adjust and change in the face of difficulties or challenges. (This in the trade is known as being "directively organized.") As Daniel Dennett has pointed out, we humans have to be like the Mars Rover.[35] Note that it is entirely determined. It does nothing outside the world of unbroken law, but it has a dimension of freedom that a simpler machine would not have. When it encounters a rock in its path, it does not have to signal to base for instructions. Of its own accord, it can assess the situation and move around the rock. In short, in order for us to be altruistic – indeed, in order to function at all – humans have to have a dimension of freedom not possessed by the ants. This is something stressed by science, by evolutionary biology. It is, in short, a case in which science bolsters the Christian's free-will defense. It certainly does so inasmuch as it both affirms the compatibilist position but stresses the real and significant nature of our free choice.

---

[35] Daniel C. Dennett, *Elbow Room: The Varieties of Free Will Worth Wanting* (Cambridge: MIT Press, 1984).

ENVOI

The *problem* of evil is very much a problem for Western religions. Eastern religions recognize pain and suffering; indeed, pain and suffering are very much at the heart of Buddhism and Jainism and other such religions. But they are not a problem in the way they are for the Abrahamic faiths particularly. If you do not posit an all-powerful, all loving God, then you have no questions to answer about why He permits or cannot prevent evil. Science as we know it – an enterprise totally committed to methodological naturalism – is also very much a Western phenomenon, and this is particularly true for parts of science like Darwinian evolutionary theory. Any historian of science today will tell you that whatever the present relationships between science and religion, in major respects, the histories of science and religion are intertwined with moves in one being reflected by or causing reactions in the other. And this is particularly true of Darwinian evolutionary theory. It is no exaggeration to say that with its emphasis on things like adaptation, central to traditional natural theology, it is a bastard offspring of Christianity. It seems so different, but then in the half-light, you catch overwhelming similarity. It is therefore hardly a surprise that science has things of interest to say about the problem of evil. It is not the only thing that has things of interest to say about the problem of evil, and as we have seen, what it has to say is by no means one sided. But what it does have to say is both interesting and important. We should have expected this.

FURTHER READING

Dawkins, Richard. *The God Delusion*. New York: Houghton, Mifflin, Harcourt, 2006.

Haught, John. F. *God and the New Atheism: A Critical Response to Dawkins, Harris, and Hitchens*. Louisville, KY: Westminster John Knox Press, 2008.

McGrath, Alister and J. C. McGrath. *The Dawkins Delusion? Atheist Fundamentalism and the Denial of the Divine*. Downers Grove, IL: InterVarsity Press, 2007.

Plantinga, Alvin. *Where the Conflict Really Lies: Science, Religion, and Naturalism*. New York: Oxford University Press, 2011.

Ruse, Michael. *Can a Darwinian Be a Christian? The Relationship between Science and Religion*. Cambridge: Cambridge University Press, 2001.

Index

CPSIA information can be obtained
at www.ICGtesting.com
Printed in the USA
LVHW04s1933180918
590554LV00012B/270/P